MISSION FOR PEACE

William E. Warne
Country Director/Iran, 1952-1955

MISSION FOR PEACE

Point 4 in Iran

IBEX Publishers
Bethesda, Maryland

Mission for Peace, Point 4 in Iran
by William E. Warne, Country Director / Iran, 1952-1955

Copyright © 1999 Warne Estate

Originally published by the
Bobbs-Merrill Company, Inc. 1956

All rights reserved. No part of this book may be reproduced
or retransmitted in any manner whatsoever except in the
form of a review, without permission from the publisher.

Manufactured in the United States of America

The paper used in this book meets the minimum requirements
of the American National Standard for Information Services
- Permanence of Paper for Printed Library Materials, ANSI
Z39.48-1984

Ibex Publishers, Inc.
Post Office Box 30087
Bethesda, Maryland 20824
Telephone: (301) 718-8188
Facsimile: (301) 907-8707
www.ibexpub.com

Library of Congress Cataloging-in-Publication Information

Warne, William E.
Mission for peace : Point 4 in Iran / William E. Warne.
p. cm.
Includes index.
ISBN 0936347848
Originally published: Indianapolis : Bobbs-Merrill, 1956.
Includes index.
1. Technical assistance, American -- Iran.
2. Warne, William E.
HC475.W3   1999
338.91' 73055—dc21 98-042782
CIP

Foreword

Mission for Peace is the achievement of a public administrator, farmer, newsman and devoted public servant. In 1951 President Harry S. Truman asked William E. Warne to become the first Point 4 Director in Iran. Iran was in turmoil. The president wanted to test his Point 4 "bold new program" of placing U.S. scientific and industrial progress in developing countries. This experiment in international cooperation suited Warne. Point 4 called for the receiving government to define the services, there should be no foreign economic or political interference, and there should be no consideration of a political nature. Truman believed Warne to be uniquely qualified for the mission.

This foreword to the second printing of *Mission for Peace* focuses on William Warne's background, career and accomplishments from the perspective of his children — Jane, Robert and Margaret. The purpose of this foreword is to examine the themes of his entire career and the role that his assignment to Iran played in his career and in the future lives of his family. Clearly father Bill's decision to go to Iran in 1951 had a profound impact on each member of the sheltered family in the Alexandria, Virginia, suburb of Washington D.C.

Born in Seafield, Indiana on September 2, 1905, William was the fourth of five sons, He lived 90 years and died in Palo Alto, California. His life was permanently changed when he was nine and his father left his ice cream manufacturing business in Seafield to migrate to California's Imperial Valley to establish a dairy farm. All five sons worked as dairymen and attended the University of California. They all drew on their farming experience later in their careers. Bill attended grammar school at the one room Alamo School where at the age of thirteen he drove the school bus. He went on to Holtville Union High School and graduated from the University of California at Berkeley in 1923, majoring in English.

For the next seven years Bill worked as a journalist, first with *The Calexico Chronicle*, then with the Associated Press in Los Angeles and San Diego. In 1929 Bill married Edith M. Peterson in Pasadena, California. Edith, who graduated from the University of California at Los Angeles, was then a school teacher.

When the Associated Press decided to create a bureau in the nation's capital to cover Washington events in the context of the diverse regions of the country, they selected Bill as their first western regional representative. His experience with irrigated farming in the Imperial Valley won him the AP's assignment as the expert on reclamation, irrigation and water. When President Roosevelt expanded the Interior Department during the depression, Bill joined the Bureau of Reclamation. He assisted in the Missouri River Basin study and then conducted the Columbia Basin Joint Agencies Investigation and organized the Central Valley Investigation in California. Bill rose to Assistant Commissioner, where he led the Bureau's decentralization.

Truman then appointed him as Assistant Secretary of Interior for Water and Power. He was responsible for the Alaska development program and the Navajo Indian program among other activities.

Then came Truman's urgent call for Bill to lead the first Iranian technical assistance effort to help stabilize the Iranian economy. *Mission for Peace* is the story of those

Foreword

Warne and H.I.M. Mohammad Reza Pahlavi. In between is Ahmad-Hossein Adl, Minister of Agriculture. Hossein Ala is behind Shah.

years. During the four years Bill was in Iran, the aid mission set up agricultural extension programs which, similar to their counterparts in the United States, introduced new seeds, farming methods, hybrid cattle, and organized, with the Shah, land grants to peasants. Jackasses, much maligned by the Communist press, were brought in to increase the productivity of the Iranian farmer.

The mission's programs also included health programs which established immunization and rural health centers, water distribution systems in the urban areas and dams for water storage and irrigation. A literacy program promoted education throughout the country. Educational grants were provided to many Iranians to train in the United States. Through their training in new technologies they brought back to Iran, for example, hybrid cotton seed and improved cattle and sheep stocks. The public administration and technical schools were strengthened. A housing program was instituted. Village peasants were given incentives to increase production and acquire land. The story of these programs and the people is the reason Bill wrote this book in 1956.

The insurgent Communist Party attacked these efforts charging that the American assistance program was placing a "noose around Iranian necks" and that the technicians were spies and aimed to control Iran. The Point 4 Mission, however, carried out its agreements with Prime Minister Mohammed Mossadegh's government and the subsequent premier Fazlollah Zahedi under the Shah Mohammad Reza Pahlavi. Despite the turbulence of insurrection and coup d'etat, threats and forcible closure of regional offices, the aid mission stayed in operation. Dependents, though, were evacuated. Bill sent Edith and Margaret back to California. Jane and Robert had already left to pursue their education. As the politics in Iran settled Edith and Margaret returned home to Tehran to complete Bill's tour.

After nearly four years in Iran, Bill was assigned to Brazil to head up the aid mission, then called USOM (United States Operations Mission). In Brazil Bill continued to focus on water, irrigation, rural extension and agricultural development, among other technical assistance activities.

After fifteen months as mission chief, the U.S. government reassigned him, on loan, to the United Nations to help Korea rebuild after the 1953 armistice. There, Bill worked nearly four years to help stabilize the Korean economy. He directed the construction and reconstruction of more than 200 irrigation projects. Extensive educational, community development, industrialization, infrastructure, public health and commodity assistance programs were instituted. The mission set up a universal educational system which is now rated as the best in the world. The mission also fed and housed four million war refugees.

Foreword

During this period, over one billion dollars was invested in Korean development programs. Shortly after his election, California Governor Pat Brown sent a telegram to Bill asking him to return from Seoul to

From left to right: Norman Paul, U.S. Ambassador Loy W. Henderson, General Fazlollah Zahedi and Warne

take over one of "the toughest jobs I have." As a skilled public administrator, Bill first redirected the Fish and Game Department and then Department of Agriculture, where half of its top level people had retired in a single year. In 1961, Bill took over as the director of the Department of Water Resources where he planned and began the construction of the multi-billion dollar California Water Project. This project included eight major coffer dams to catch and store water to be transported through nearly 500 miles of canals through California's Central Valley for irrigation and to Los Angeles and points south for farmers and urban water users. Bill knew from his days in the

Imperial Valley, with the Department of Interior, and with the foreign aid program, that water would make arid California one of the nation's most productive agricultural areas.

In retirement, still a firm believer in the work ethic and values of the family farm, Bill developed a family walnut "wrancho" in the Sacramento Valley south of Arbuckle, California. Once his orchard was producing, he encouraged the children to join in a partnership to raise almonds nearby. The eldest, Jane with her daughter, Dr. Ann Beeder, now owns and manages these farms. The youngest child, Margaret, and her husband, John Monroe, and their family are developing an almond orchard near the "wrancho."

Edith Peterson Warne, who predeceased Bill in 1993, took an active role in all of the family's adventures. Before beginning her career abroad, she was President of the children's elementary school and Alexandria School District Parent Teacher Associations. She served as an officer of the Women's National Democratic Club in Washington, D.C.

The two led many civic organizations. Bill helped found the Group Health Organization in Washington D.C. and was one of its first presidents. Today Group Health has become a nationally recognized health maintenance organization. Bill also was instrumental in establishing a suburban cooperative grocery store in Alexandria. Edith helped organize and lead the International Women's Club in Tehran and took on similar roles in Brazil and Korea. An accomplished artist, Edith continued her studies and collection of art in each overseas country. In Korea she studied painting under a recognized master. Her scrolls and calligraphy were commended by a U.S. museum.

Foreword

Departing for Iran with the family in 1952, Jane Warne had just graduated from George Washington High School in Alexandria. The family sailed through the Mediterranean to Beirut. Bill met them there and arranged for Jane to

Warne with point four members. Among the Members (from left to right: Ardeshir Zahedi, M. Sarmad, General M.H. Jahanbani (retired Minister of State), Warne, Reza Djaffari,

attend the American University at Beirut. She went on to Northwestern University the following year after spending holidays in Iran. Jane married David C. Beeder, a newspaperman with the Associated Press, Reuters and the *Omaha World Herald*. Dave headed up the *Herald's* Washington bureau for nearly ten years. In Omaha and Washington, Jane served as an executive with the insurance industry before retiring in 1997. The Beeders have two children, John and Ann.

When the family departed for Iran, Rob Warne was a high school freshman; he attended the International School in Tehran for a year. Turbulence and concern for his safety caused him to depart for school in Honolulu in 1953. Rob rejoined the family in Brazil to graduate from Escola Americana. When he was attending Princeton University, he joined the family for the summer in Korea. Rob's international experience as a teenager caused him to focus on a career in the Foreign Service of the U.S. Department of State. He joined AID and then transferred to the Department of State. He served as a Foreign Service Officer starting as a rural development officer in the Mekong Delta in Vietnam in 1962. His Foreign Service career took him to Argentina, Belgium, France and Jamaica as both economic officer and Counsel. Rob currently heads

From left to right: General H. Jahanbani, Minister of State; Warne; and Jahanshah Saleh, Minister of Health.

Foreword

From left to right: Dr. Mahmoud Moghadam, Edith Warne, William Warne, Reza Ansari and Dr. Shadman.

up the Korea Economic Institute of America which works on East Asian economic issues. He is married to Susanna Ludwig Hassel; they have two children, Robin and Bill.

Margaret, only six when uprooted from a suburban public school in Virginia to go to Iran, batted between various overseas and California homes depending on security conditions. In response to various unexpected emergencies, She and her mother crisscrossed the globe three times. Margaret finally settled geographically, when she attended Vassar College in 1962. Following Vassar, Margaret earned a Masters Degree in Developmental Sociology from the College of Agriculture at Cornell University. She married John W. Monroe, an electrical engineer and executive with Hewlett-Packard. They have two children, John and Chuck. For the last fifteen years

Point 4 meeting. Included in photograph are Senator Parviz Kazemi, Warne and Dr. Mahmoud Moghadam.

Margaret has been the Planning Director for the City of Burlingame, California.

Bill's childhood experience of migrating to California and living with homesteading families scratching out an existence in the parched Imperial Valley shaped his commitment to public service, community development and water resource development. His career focused on agricultural, technical assistance, water development and community planning for the rest of his life.

He was among the nation's "great dam builders" contributing to the Hoover, Grand Coulee and Oroville dams and the water systems their reservoirs supplied, improving the productivity and the standard of living of many communities. As a professional administrator he became a Senior Fellow in the National Academy of Public Administration. He wrote numerous articles and a second book on the history of the Bureau of Reclamation. He

Foreword

received honorary doctorate degrees from Seoul National and Yonsei Universities in Korea, and numerous honors including the United Nations,' Department of Interior's and Agency of International Development's distinguished service awards. He was also awarded the Order of the Crown by the Shah of Iran.

Bill's exciting odyssey shaped the lives of his children, all of whom have followed aspects of his career in public service, farming, community planning, writing and journalism. Their children, Bill's grandchildren, are launched in similar directions. Yet another Warne gneration is being born, his great grandchildren. They are still very young but will no doubt feel his influence during their lives as his other siblings have. Villagers, farmers, public administration experts and government policy makers around the world have also benefited from and been influenced by his dedication, foresight and many contributions. His family testifies to his influence and impact on their lives.

— Jane Warne Beeder, William Robert
Warne and Margaret Warne Monroe,
October, 1998

Author's Note

THIS ACCOUNT has been written to illuminate a recent phase of history and to report to the people of the United States on the stewardship of a public charge. The enterprise described was the work of many men and women, American and Iranian alike. The people who appear are some who contributed to or influenced the work, but they do not make up a roster. Other incidents in our experience, projects in our general task could have been chosen with equal or perhaps more telling effect, and if they had been chosen other participants, with equal right to notice, would have been introduced.

This account is told as I saw and remember it. It is all true, within whatever limits are imposed by my abilities as a reporter. The direct quotations are all presented as though English alone were the language used, but this was not the case. In many instances the communication was through my interpreters, Messrs. Ardeshir Zahedi, Reza Ansari and Mohamoud Moghadam. Some of the public figures, such as Dr. Mossadegh, General Zahedi and Minister Djaffari, who figure here, used no English, and most of the countrymen knew only Farsee or another local tongue. I never learned the language of Iran but became familiar with words, expressions and phrases only.

The labor of setting this down on paper was done while I was a Philips Visitor at Haverford College in Pennsylvania during my home leave between assignments abroad. Without the unusual generosity of the donor of the fund and the invitation extended to me by President Gilbert F. White of the College it would not have been possible for me to perform the task. I acknowledge as well my debt of gratitude to the staff of the United States Operation Mission to Iran who when I left Iran bound and presented to me the reports and public papers. These have been used constantly as reference material. Without this kindness of the staff, which made quick and refreshing reviews possible, the writing could not have been completed in the time available. I am indebted to Mrs. Anne Ross for encouragement and suggestions and to Mrs. Dorothy G. Brownback and Miss Elsie A. Hartman for hours and hours of work on the transcriptions.

Spelling in English of Iranian places and proper names—and most other words—is a freehand matter. Iran would have been an ideal place for me as a schoolboy, for spelling then was the bane of my existence. It does not matter there whether an "A" or an "E" or an "O" or an "I" or "U" is used. In items in our official reports from Tehran, I find on review, a village that was wrecked by an earthquake was variously called "Tarud," "Toroud," "Torood," and "Taroud," among other spellings. It was always the same place, and no one on the staff was confused by such a variety of usages. This is exactly what I, as a boy, ineffectively tried to point out to my spelling teacher. So long as the reader can guess what is meant, what's the difference? There is no authoritative guide for the transliteration of Iranian words to English. At least four Farsee consonants have no equivalent English sound, and the Farsee writing omits the vowels, or mostly so. The purpose of this little disquisition is to warn readers that place names, surnames and other reference words may not appear in this book as they have elsewhere. The writer must, for instance, choose among Karadj, Keraj, Kerej, Keradj; Radji, Rajy, Ragi; Tadjrish—oh well, variations are almost infinite in almost any place name. Nevertheless I've tried to pick the spelling most likely to be familiar and—whatever my boyhood difficulty—to be consistent.

The opinions expressed are, of course, my own unless otherwise credited. They represent my point of view. Since I was a participant, these opinions may not have been arrived at in a

Author's Note

wholly objective way. They are, at least, the result of observation and earnest thought. A reader will not need, however, to be a detective to ferret out the fact that I am, and was from the start of this adventure, a strong believer in the program and was and am friendly toward Iran. I hope that I may have earned as well, as an employe of my government, the right to say that I have put service to the United States above other considerations here. My account may well reflect that value; I do not think it is distorted by it.

WILLIAM E. WARNE

CONTENTS

1/Point 4	13
2/Country Agreement in Iran	30
3/Jackasses	48
4/The Cabinet Committee Digs In	55
5/Clocks Turn Back	65
6/"35,000 Reds Fly to Iran"	75
7/The Thirtieth of Tir	87
8/Six Farsa to Shalamzar	100
9/Yankee Go Home	116
10/The Fight for Life	136
11/Pure Water to Drink	151
12/Opening the Windows of Heaven	170
13/A Project, Full Cycle	183
14/From Peasants to Freeholders	190
15/Sands Run Low	205
16/Doors to Progress	223
17/Twenty-eighth of Mordad	241
18/Rebuilding Iran	256
19/Khiaban Asle Chahar	277
20/Co-operation with Other Missions	293
21/A Country Director Goes Home	305
Index	315

MISSION FOR PEACE

The reader is asked to keep in mind that Point 4 is the term applied to the continuing technical co-operation program of the United States. This program is the central theme of this book. The term was never officially applied to the work. But it is understood everywhere. Even Americans fail to recognize the various formal designations. Point 4 is understood around the world. In the most remote places the words become a passport, a warranty of friendship, a whole language when no other words would have meaning.

Officially the agency that has administered the Point 4 program first was known as the Technical Cooperation Administration, and it was a bureau in the Department of State. In the summer of 1953 the Foreign Operations Administration was set up independently of the State Department and the Point 4 program was transferred to it. On June 30, 1955, the FOA died and on July 1 the Point 4 program was back in the State Department, this time in a new, semi-autonomous agency known as the International Cooperation Administration. The important thing is that the Point 4 *program* has been continuous despite these reorganizations. They affected the people and programs in the field less than might have been expected. As the Iranians would say, "It is the same donkey, but the saddle has been changed."

Mission/1

Point 4

THE ROAD through Khonsar climbs a narrow valley in the Bakhtiari Mountains among irrigated fields strung like emeralds on the thread of the river. Sometimes the fields are bunched in a little flat; sometimes, where ditches have been led off the plunging stream, they climb up the steep sides of the valley trench. Wherever the valley is broad enough the people have built mud villages. Khonsar is the largest of these.

Engineer Khalil Taleghani, Dr. Mahmoud Moghadam and I were bouncing over the rutted gravel road in my car, leading a procession into the valley. We were bound for the Khurang Tunnel then under construction far beyond Khonsar, up near Yellow Mountain at the crest of the Zagros range. It was my first trip into this beautiful, remote west-central part of Iran. Along the way we passed mud pigeon cotes as big as barns. These were designed to collect droppings to manure the fields. Tobacco leaves were spread on the clover fields to dry. Engineer Taleghani, who was then minister of agriculture, was telling me about the Golpayagan cattle, some of which we had just seen grazing at the roadside, small-boned, trim and colored like Jerseys.

"This cow," Khalil said, "is very efficient. The Golpayagan is a separate breed."

We entered a leafy tunnel. The mud walls of Khonsar pinched in against the track. Trees growing along the *jubes* (ditches) on either side arched across the road. So suddenly that there was no chance to avoid it, we ran into a massive road block of hundreds of men and boys. In a flash we were completely surrounded.

In the time it took Hossein, my driver, to stop the car, with the dust still billowing around us, Khalil turned to me and said, "They are friendly, I think. We had best get out of the car fast."

Until then it had not occurred to me that we could be ambushed, but 1952 was a year of great tribulation in Persia and violence was a tradition among the half-wild people living in pastoral isolation in these valleys.

I flung the door open and we piled out into the mud of the ditch.

A great cry arose.

"*Yea, yea, yea! Asle Chahar!*"

It was repeated.

"*Yea, yea, yea! Asle Chahar!*"

I knew enough Farsee to understand that cheer.

"Hurray, hurray, hurray for Point 4!"

Again, "Hurray, hurray, hurray for Point 4!"

The crowd pressed in on us, but the faces were smiling our welcome.

"I am Abolghassam Samii," one man, dressed as the rest in a western-type suit and a shirt without a tie, said as he stepped forward. "You are Mr. Warne, I believe, and this is Engineer Taleghani?"

I could only nod in speechless surprise.

"You are welcome to Khonsar. Will you follow me?"

The crowd divided to make a lane for us.

"How did they know we were coming?" I asked Khalil and Dr. Moghadam. "We didn't plan to stop here." They both shrugged.

"It is the giveh telegraph," Dr. Moghadam said. The giveh is a moccasinlike shoe woven of string, worn by all Iranian country people. The "giveh telegraph" is the Iranian version of the American Indian "moccasin telegraph." We'd say "grapevine."

Now an old ewe was sacrificed ceremoniously in our path and, to expiate the evil eye, the blood from the dripping head was spread before us in a pattern of red splashes in the dust. We were ushered to a long table set under a tree in the yard of a half-finished building. As others of our party arrived they too were captured and brought to the festive board.

While tea was being served in little glasses set in silver holders, Mr. Samii told us the story of the building. It was planned as a health clinic but for two years had been incomplete. There was no money to finish it.

"Will you tell the minister of health that we have no clinic, no hospital, no doctor for 100,000 people in this valley?" he asked.

After tea we were led, with a great comet's tail of men and boys following, through the winding *kuchehs* (paths or alleys) of Khonsar, while Mr. Samii explained the problems of the village. Now and then he saw a woman wrapped in her *chadora* going about some humble task, melting through a door in a mud wall on seeing us or, if there was no gate, turning and facing some niche until we had gone by. A few more watched us over the edges of the flat roofs.

Mr. Samii said that there was typhoid fever and that there had been some malaria. Many babies died of bowel sickness. The one school had no windows. It could care for only a few of the boys. Flies were a great nuisance.

At last we realized we were being led to the abattoir. Situated on the high side of the village, near the road, it was simply a grove of trees with hooks tied to the lower limbs. Here the slaughtering was done and the meat was cut up. The floor of packed earth drained directly into a flowing ditch which carried the water supply of Khonsar.

"Isn't it possible," Mr. Samii asked, "that this open-air slaughterhouse here on the ditch bank makes people sick in our village and causes the pestilence of flies?"

"Why, yes," I said. "The offal should be kept out of the water supply. The slaughterhouse should be moved to the low side of town."

Mr. Samii knew, as did some other *kadkhodas* (leaders) of the village, what should be done about this problem, but there was no institution through which to focus the energies of the people on a solution. He and the others were going to use my confirmation for its effect on public opinion. The slaughterhouse, I later learned, was moved the next day.

Then we were back on the road, climbing into the waiting cars.

We said our good-bys, and I waved out of the window as we pulled away.

"*Yea, yea, yea! Asle Chahar!*" I heard them shout once more behind us.

"Do you think," I asked Khalil and Dr. Moghadam, "that these country people know what Point 4 means?"

"They know Point 4," Khalil Taleghani said, "as you have just seen."

"I am not quite certain that I know what 'Point 4' means," Dr. Moghadam, my interpreter, assistant and friend, added dryly.

As we rode along I tried to explain about the name.

President Truman's inaugural address of January 20, 1949, described American foreign policy in the terms of four major courses of action. In making the fourth point he said:

> We must embark on a bold, new program for making the benefits of our scientific advancements and industrial progress available for improvement and growth to underdeveloped areas.... I believe that we should make available to peace-loving peoples the benefits of our store of technical knowledge in order to help them realize their aspirations for a better life. ...

Its position in the listing of the President's proposals, I explained to Dr. Moghadam, gave the Technical Cooperation Program the popular name "Point 4," since it was the fourth point that Mr. Truman made. For some reason the cryptic term "Point 4" has better conveyed the idea of American technical co-operation to the popular mind the world over than all efforts at more formal definition and nomenclature. But a definition of the term will be found in the words the President used, "a bold, new program" of the United States to share technical knowledge in order to help peace-loving peoples of underdeveloped countries to "realize their aspirations for a better life."

As we jounced along the bumpy road, the dust behind us engulfing the plodding donkeys and their drivers in refuge at the side of the track, my mind went back to the beginning of this business that had sent me and hundreds more to strange places around the world.

I remember thinking, as I waited on one of the huge fan of folding chairs arrayed before the Capitol in Washington on January 20, 1949, that most observers at such historic occasions as the inauguration of a President may remember little more than an uncomfortable chair too long sat on and the noise of a mechanical speaker too loud in the ear. Standing up while the band played "Hail to the Chief" helped somewhat. It restored circulation in my feet. It was so cold that one of the senators who had come out to the balustrade just before Mr. Truman appeared had drawn a blanket about his shoulders.

The ceremony got under way at high noon. As the inaugural address proceeded, many in the audience began to feel the lift of an important hour. For them as for me, it came with Mr. Truman's proposal of "a bold, new program" as the fourth point of his foreign policy. During the days that followed, news of Point 4 and comment about it raced around the world. America would share the technical advances that had made her great. America would help the peoples of underdeveloped areas to help themselves toward a better life. Soon this generous plan, like renewed hope, fired the hearts and minds of men almost everywhere.

In the sixth-floor corridors of the Interior Building, where I had my office, conferences were now being held. Our work in Interior had previously been as distinct as the name implies from that done by the State Department abroad. But now Interior was preparing to send some of its technicians to foreign fields to do the work they did expertly at home—planning irrigation projects, designing dams, directing geological surveys and teaching range management. These men were to apply techniques proved valuable in the Indian Service to encourage isolated peoples to adopt modern methods in their work, to devise ways to use native ores, to develop fisheries—in general, to utilize their resources to their own best possible advantage. Elsewhere in Washington other agencies were making similar preparations. Colleges and universities all across the United States were launching training for the same kinds of programs.

It takes time to start any vast undertaking. Congress ground away on the legislation. On June 5, 1950, the Act for International Development was passed. Then money had to be appropriated. Now an organization known as the Technical Cooperation Administration was set up in the State Department. For the first few weeks Capus Waynick, ambassador to Nicaragua, was detailed acting administrator. On December 1, 1950, Dr. Henry Garland Bennett, president of Oklahoma A & M, took office as administrator. In Interior we had our private jokes over the new work. Should, for instance, the office created to handle our participation be called "The Office of the Exterior?"

Now heavy official machinery necessarily moves slowly. Therefore I was surprised when one October morning the *Washington Post* told me that the first Point 4 agreement had been signed on October 19, 1950, at Abayaz Palace in Tehran by Ambassador Henry F. Grady and General Ali Razmara, prime minister of Iran. This agreement, creating an Iranian-United States Joint Commission for Rural Improvement, called for co-operation in a program under which American experts in agriculture, health and education would work with Persians to train the peasants and villagers of Iran. The plan was, most newspapers agreed, in the best American tradition of neighborliness. The choice of ancient Persia, many commented, was fitting. Through the strategic Persian deserts had been erected the "bridge of victory," over which American, British and Russian armies had sent material and guns to help turn back the Nazis before Stalingrad and drive them to final defeat. Some reporters recalled the promise made at the close of the Tehran conference of the Big Three in 1943 to help Iran once the war was over.

When E. Reeseman (Si) Fryer transferred from Interior to direct the work of TCA in the Near East and Africa region, I began to lose the detachment of a merely interested spectator. Si Fryer had been my friend and associate for a long time. He came to me with a problem.

"As you know, most of these areas are arid," he said. "Their physical problems will be much like the ones Interior wrestles with in our West. Their human problems, many of them, will be like those facing the Indian Service and the Office of Islands and Territories. In fact, TCA is already borrowing ideas from your Puerto Rico, Alaska and Indian operations. How about letting us have some experienced people, too?"

"Well now, Si," I bridled like any bureaucrat, "we have our own programs, you know."

"But we need help," he argued, "and, Bill Warne, you know that Interior can spare a few men."

"What have you got in mind?" I asked tentatively, not yielding.

"TCA will set up an office in each host country. We'll need a country director for each," he explained. "There will be special divisions in most country missions for engineering, agriculture and so forth. We need good men to head these divisions."

"What, specifically, would you like to have me do?" I asked, still sparring.

"Call a meeting of the bureau and office heads and let Dr. Bennett tell them what we plan to do and what we need."

Fair enough, I thought. I said, "I'll do it next week."

Fryer was particularly anxious at the moment to find men to

head programs in India, in Iran and in Egypt. We mentioned several common acquaintances in Interior as possible candidates. One whose name was discussed at that time, Clifford Willson, now has a long and successful record as country director in India.

Dr. Bennett preached the evangel of Point 4. He saw it as a worldwide extension service, a transmission belt to carry the results of research to farms, homes and factories, where technical knowledge could be put to use in practical ways. It was the land-grant-college idea grown up to world proportions.

Tough and blasé as were the Interior men I invited, Dr. Bennett's talk warmed them. I know I felt again at our luncheon the thrill that came with hearing the original Point 4 proposal. It was time, I felt, that the United States as a nation went earnestly to work to maintain peace.

During those months another series of events almost halfway around the world crowded into the headlines. The prime minister of Iran was assassinated—the same General Razmara who had signed the historic first Point 4 agreement. A new leader was pressing forward under a banner of fanatic nationalism. His platform was to force the British out of the area in which they had oil concessions in southern Iran and to "nationalize," or expropriate, the Anglo-Iranian Oil Company's Abadan refinery, the largest in the world. A bit of the personality of Dr. Mohammed Mossadegh began to creep into the newspaper columns.

When the British oilfield workers left Persia and the Abadan refinery was finally closed, the American public became faintly aware of the new problems. Newspaper reports reminded them that Iran contained the largest proved petroleum reserves in the world. Shutting off the spigot at the head of the Persian Gulf put new pressure on oil-producing areas all over. War in Korea had begun a month ago. Adjustments were both essential and difficult. This was an emergency.

Headline writers now struggling with the name "Mossadegh"

Point 4 21

began familiarly to use "Mossy" or "Old Mossy." The new prime minister spent most of his time in bed, and he wept and even fainted as he emotionally stated his case in public meetings. He stubbornly called the AIOC the "ex-oil company." His picture was on the cover of *Time*, and after his trip to the United States he became *Time's* Man of the Year 1951, who "oiled the wheels of chaos."

Perhaps in the Interior Department we were more than usually aware of the potential importance of Iranian oil in a war situation. One of our agencies was the emergency petroleum administration. So when Si Fryer came to see me again in October 1951, I was acutely conscious of Iran. I was preparing to make a flying trip to Billings, Montana, to attend the fifth anniversary meeting of the Missouri Basin Field Committee, which I had sponsored. I was packing my brief case when Si entered. He got to the point at once.

"Bill, we still have no one for country director in Iran."

"Why, Si," I said, "John Evans left Interior to go out there last month."

"Yes, John's there, but he didn't go to head the mission. He's helping to plan the program's expansion. It will be increased twenty times this year."

"And how about your man from Utah?" I asked. "Isn't his name Harris? I think you told me he was in Iran."

"Yes," answered Si, "he went over in the spring of 1950, just after he retired as president of Utah State Agricultural College. He set up the first project—Rural Improvement—and is technical director of the project now. But his two-year tour is almost over. Besides, we've got to expand Iran's program a great deal. The situation there is critical. You know something about our problems, so you know this is going to be our toughest job."

Catching me off guard he added quickly, "Why don't you go?"

I laughed and fled to the airport.

It was late October, and snow was flying over much of the Missouri Basin. We were snowed in when we made a trip to inspect a fish hatchery which was a part of the Missouri Basin development program. I had time to think about Si's question.

I had been in Washington eighteen years—two on the staff of the Associated Press, sixteen with the Department of the Interior, working constantly in the resource development fields. My first position with the Department was in the Bureau of Reclamation. As a Department representative, I had worked on the preparation of the reports of the Water Resources Committee of the National Resources Planning Board. I later became involved in directing the Columbia Basin Joint Investigations to plan the Grand Coulee Dam Irrigation Project. I had also helped to establish regional planning and development by the Federal agencies and had conducted a program of development in Alaska.

But during the past four years, as Assistant Secretary for Water and Power, I had felt at times a need for field experience. I knew, in any event, that one could not make a career of being an assistant secretary in any department of the United States Government. It is more or less an end-of-the-line job. But I was engrossed at the moment in the immediate problems connected with the great works under way.

As we sat before a roaring fire in the guest lodge at the fish hatchery, awaiting the snow plow that would open the road to Billings, I ran over in my mind a dozen times what Si Fryer had said—no director yet for the program in Iran. That a strange turn of events in a far-off country had presented us with an emergency emphasized to me that all the world is related. By a chain of cause and effect the needs of one country create problems that become urgent in countries continents and oceans away.

In the Interior Department our guiding philosophy had always been that each region of the United States should be helped and encouraged to make prudent use of its resources, for this would strengthen all.

Now, suddenly, a new concern gripped my mind. Could we

carry out throughout the world the types of programs on which we had been working in the United States? How could we help the underprivileged peoples in remote, difficult lands to use their own energies to improve their lives? How could we lead them through all the various steps to the point where they might undertake great works for themselves. By helping and encouraging these people to work out their own problems we could reduce the number of emergencies. The poverty, disease and ignorance that prepared the seedbed for trouble could be overcome as they had so successfully been in the United States. It came to me as a conviction that the Point 4 program could be made to lead directly to these ends. It could give a people inspiration and a start on small tasks which would lead them, in turn, to bigger things.

I wanted to be a part of any attempt to make the Point 4 program produce such a design. If hunger and disease were defeated, I felt, mankind should have less occasion for strife and war. Warm and sheltered from the snow, I reflected on the years since the end of the war.

Some think of peace as protected by war. Actually war represents a defeat in peace. For the first time in the life of our nation, through such programs as Point 4, we were actively waging peace. Some seem to doubt our ability to win a third world war, atomic or otherwise. I, on the other hand, would dread its coming but not fear its eventual outcome. But if such a war came, it would mean the loss of this peace, won with such difficulty and sacrifice in World War II. But now the United States had decided to work at the arts of peace—to prepare its defenses and to send out its soldiers in a campaign on fields where peace must be won or lost in the hearts of people. I was ready to enlist!

The night we returned to Billings I telephoned my wife. This, in itself, was surprising to Edith, since I seldom called when I was away on short field trips. Then I asked her what she thought of going to Iran.

"Would we be back before Christmas?" she asked.

"I mean how would you like to *move* to Iran?"

"And take the children out of school?"

I understood her hesitation. Jane would hate to leave in the middle of her senior year at high school. It would be hard for Robbie, then a freshman, to pull up roots. Second-grader Margaret was doing well and enjoying school. Would it be fair to ask her to adjust to a situation so radically different from the one she was used to?

"Well?" I asked.

"Yes, if you want to," Edith said, "but where is it?"

I asked the operator to get me Mr. Fryer in Washington.

"Bill!" Si almost shouted as soon as the connection was made. "When can you start for Iran?"

"I guess that's what I called to tell you. I'll go to Iran if we can get the necessary clearances from Oscar Chapman and the President."

The next morning I called Secretary Chapman at Interior. He talked to the President that day, and by the time I returned to Washington everything was settled but the formalities. Things moved very swiftly indeed, though, as the hundreds who have followed know, there were countless official forms, fingerprints, health examinations and inoculations. All sorts of arrangements had to be completed. We decided that my family would wait until summer and follow me after school closed, but I had to go at once. My resignation from Interior became effective on November 7, 1951, and I was sworn in the next morning in the office of Under Secretary James A. Webb of the State Department as Country Director of Technical Cooperation for Iran.

Late in 1951, while I was struggling to settle my own affairs, Dr. Mossadegh arrived in the United States hoping to obtain help for his country. Iran was going broke. The oil had stopped flowing. She had no way to market it.

The American public, by this time inured to visits of kings, prime ministers and presidents, nevertheless took note of Dr.

Point 4

Mossadegh's dramatics. A fainting spell in a crowd of reporters at Idlewild Airport was only the beginning. Inept though it was, people remembered the nickname "Old Mossy." For reporters it neatly dodged the problem, not yet satisfactorily resolved, of spelling the real name. The final consonant has no English equivalent and might be written "gh" or "q."

It developed that my first duty in my new post was to tell Dr. Mossadegh how much money was allocated for the Technical Cooperation program in Iran. The Congress acted very late in 1951 on the appropriations for foreign aid. Because of Dr. Mossadegh's presence, however, it was quickly decided after the bill was passed to make available to Iran a total of $23,450,000. This amount would serve Point 4 for the 1952 fiscal year, which would end June 30.

I was at this time introduced to a young American Army major who was to interpret for me when I called on Mossadegh. He was one of the retinue assigned to assist the Mossadegh party while it was in the United States.

En route from the office to the Shoreham Hotel in a State Department car, the major and I talked about the size of the allotment. Dr. Mossadegh had asked for much more.

"Don't be thrown by his first reactions," the major said. "The whole party has become greatly discouraged and he is apt to be glad to get something, almost anything, so he can go home."

An Iranian who was introduced to me in the lobby quickly ushered us into an elevator. A few moments later he, in turn, introduced me to half a dozen more Iranians who were standing around in Dr. Mossadegh's suite. Many times later Iranian friends in Tehran reminded me that we had first met at the Shoreham Hotel, but they couldn't prove it by me, for I was directed immediately into a bedroom to meet the prime minister. I had hardly the opportunity to nod to them, much less catch the strange names.

As I entered the bedroom I found Dr. Mossadegh lying against a pillow. Drawn about him he wore a dun-colored camel's hair bathrobe, and he had pulled the coverlet well up toward his chin. He sat up spryly as my interpreter found a seat on the side of the second of the twin beds. I was given the position of honor on a very straight-backed hotel bedroom chair.

Iranians are apt to be formal and to exchange many pleasantries before getting down to business. During a great deal of the early part of the conference we discussed Dr. Mossadegh's health. When I said that I hoped he was feeling better he assured me that nothing really serious was wrong—he simply was very tired. Next the major and Dr. Mossadegh exchanged comments regarding previous meetings. I was fascinated by the prime minister's expressive hands, his gentle voice and his sensitive face. He was an old man but in no way feeble. I had been told that he had a keen sense of humor and liked a quiet joke.

Finally I said that I presumed he knew that I had been chosen to go to his capital as director of the Point 4 mission. I had come to tell him that the United States was prepared to undertake what seemed to me to be a fairly sizable program in the immediate future. At that point I had intended to try a little joke. I didn't get the chance.

"That will be fine, Mr. Warne," Dr. Mossadegh said quickly. "How much?"

Though I did not need the reminder, I unfolded from my pocket a paper with a figure written on it. "$23,450,000."

There followed a rapid-fire conversation in Farsee between the prime minister and the major.

After a while the major said, "Dr. Mossadegh is seriously disappointed."

He didn't try to fill in all the blank spaces for me. "Dr. Mossadegh believes that $23,450,000 for technical co-operation isn't enough. He's of the opinion that there must be other means of aiding him, and he'd like to know whether you mean that this is the total amount of United States aid Iran will receive this year."

I replied that, according to my information, this was the amount to be extended to Iran in the 1952 fiscal year, which would end next June 30, seven months hence. Compared with sums for other countries in the region, it was a very large amount indeed.

The major relayed what I'd said to Dr. Mossadegh. We talked for some minutes longer about the level of aid. Our discussion related to Dr. Mossadegh's belief that the sum was inadequate, but I am not sure that he was genuinely disappointed. After a while he dropped back against the pillow—a unique conference mannerism which I came to know meant that Dr. Mossadegh was ready to change the subject—and we began to discuss seriously how the money might be used. He would sit up again if he became interested in the new subject.

I stressed to him that the Point 4 program should be a cooperative effort. I would work with whomever he appointed to represent his country. I emphasized that Point 4's aim was to develop projects that would help the people of Iran to better their own ways of living—rural sanitation, health measures, improvement of rural schools, better farming methods and some demonstrations in basic industries. There would be more projects, all with the single purpose of training the people to help themselves. Dr. Mossadegh seemed to me to be genuinely interested in the welfare of his people. Although he would rather see some big, spectacular project, like a dam, undertaken to provide the immediate action which Iran craved, he could see the point of the technical assistance approach. He was sitting up again.

"Oh, but, Mr. Warne," Dr. Mossadegh said near the end of this first meeting, "you must control every penny of this money. None of it must be let out of your hands."

I was surprised. Others had intimated to me that Dr. Mossadegh would try to gain control of the funds, despite his reputation, which I never had cause to question, for personal honesty. This was a completely different approach from what I had been led to expect. I again explained that it would be our purpose to work co-operatively with his people. We did not want to start American programs in Iran, but to assist Iran in the development of her own projects. I told him I thought the money ought to be spent according to a joint plan which should be agreed upon by me and the people representing his government.

"Oh, but, Mr. Warne," Dr. Mossadegh said again, "you must not let the crooks get this money."

I said that I should have to work with whomever he designated and stressed again that no program or project undertaken would be considered worthy of the name Point 4 if it were American and not Iranian. Iran would have to request any project and Iranians would have to participate actively in it. All the work would be carried on in co-operation with Iranians, with and through Iranian agencies and experts.

Dr. Mossadegh was nodding his head as the major translated this. I wanted to drive home the point at this moment, so as soon as the major stopped I went on with my explanation. I underlined the fact that unless the work was done by Iranians it could not be useful in training people and demonstrating techniques. Work done by others could not later be duplicated by Iran.

"I shall choose my people carefully," Dr. Mossadegh said. "We must not let the crooks get this money. But then I know them, every one."

We agreed that as soon as we were both in Iran a joint group would set up complete plans. A country agreement, as we already were calling the basic document of understanding underlying the Point 4 programs, was required by our law.

"I hope," Dr. Mossadegh said, "that the terms will not be too arduous."

"They will not be very demanding," I said. "Iran will have to agree to use our help and to help finance joint projects so far as she can. That's about all."

"The people of Iran are very sensitive right now," Dr. Mossadegh continued, making a very expressive gesture with his hands and long fingers. With this one motion he seemed to include in the conversation the reaction against the British oil concession and all of his country's newly felt nationalism. "I hope the language of the agreement will give no affront."

"I promise you," I said, anticipating little trouble, "that I will make every effort to make the agreement satisfactory to you before it is formally presented."

The major and I were ready to leave. When we rose, Dr. Mossadegh cheerily waved a farewell.

"When you bring me that paper," he called, "I will sign it."

Mission/2

Country Agreement in Iran

THE NEXT time I saw Dr. Mossadegh I was in Tehran. I arrived at Mehrabad Airport at 8:00 P.M. on November 28, 1951, and was met by a welcoming group of Americans and Iranians. In the crowd I saw one familiar face grinning at me. Si Fryer had rushed on ahead.

"Why are you late?" Si yelled from behind the fence as officials were checking my passport.

"Engine conked out at Damascus and we spent last night in Syria. Just got out ahead of a revolution there today."

My trip from Washington to Iran had been made on a tight nine-day schedule. I had stopped in New York to visit the United Nations Technical Assistance group, in Paris to confer with the UNESCO Technical Assistance directors, in Geneva to meet with officials of the International Labor Organization and the World Health Organization and in Rome to confer with Food and Agricultural Organization officials. All of these agencies also had programs in Iran.

We made two attempts to reach Tehran on November 27, but the plane finally had to turn back to Damascus, where mechanics frantically repaired an engine.

Several weeks elapsed before I fully appreciated what had been going on in Tehran while I was en route. It had not occurred to me that at Mehrabad there was no way to keep tab on approaching planes. I finally learned through comments dropped here and there in casual conversation that a reception

Country Agreement in Iran

had been arranged on the twenty-seventh at 9:30 A.M., the time my plane was scheduled to arrive. No plane, no Warne, no explanation. The committee had returned at 5:00 P.M., thinking that the plane would arrive then. It didn't. The group returned to the airport at 9:30 the morning of the twenty-eighth. Still no plane. Most of the committee didn't believe a report that the plane would arrive at 8:00 P.M. It was then and is today most unusual for an international carrier to schedule its arrival in Tehran after dark, since there are no night landing aids at the airport. But rising tension forced us to leave Damascus when we did, regardless of when we would reach Tehran. The faithful were present, however, for the fourth time, and they did welcome me. With my head buzzing from long hours of flying and with the dreary customs line still before me, I am afraid I did not fully appreciate their courtesy.

"I am leaving at six o'clock in the morning," Si said as we started to drive the ten miles to the Darband Hotel.

"But," I protested, "it gives us no time to talk!"

"I had hoped at least to have with you the day that your plane used up in Damascus. Dr. Bennett wants me to join him in Rome for a few days before I return to Washington. He's going to continue his trip through the Middle East and Asia. He'll be here in three weeks and hopes the country agreement can be signed while he's here. Perhaps I can come back with him."

Si and John Evans were in my room until the eleven o'clock curfew maintained under martial law drove John home. Si and I talked on. Gradually the whole picture emerged. About forty technicians had been assembled, mostly in agriculture and mostly from Utah. A plan had been laid out to decentralize operations by establishing a regional office in each of the ten major provincial capitals, Tehran, Tabriz, Resht, Babolsar, Meshed, Kermanshah, Isfahan, Shiraz, Ahwaz and Kerman. This plan would pull the Iranian Government programs, now hopelessly centralized, out into the field. The Rural Improvement Program would remain our mainspring, since nearly eighty-five of every hundred Iranians lived in villages. Some new programs were needed nevertheless—in industrial development, especially with regard to processing farm products, in agrarian reform and in public administration.

"By the way, Bill," Si said, "Dr. Mossadegh won't recognize the Razmara agreement. He won't renounce it, either. Some new shape will have to be given to the program, but that won't be hard because of the expansion."

"You're talking Greek to me," I complained. "I haven't got this straightened out yet."

"The agreement Ambassador Grady signed with General Razmara in October 1950," Si explained, "the one setting up the whole Rural Improvement Program, you know. It's as good as useless now, and until you get the new country agreement there won't be much foundation for the work here."

"Well, Dr. Mossadegh talked in Washington as though the country agreement wouldn't be too difficult."

"Perhaps not, but our law requires that the countries receiving aid give certain assurances of collaboration too, in advance of the country agreement. These assurances are causing some bickering."

"I'm still not sure I have this clearly in mind," I said uncertainly.

"Boy, will you have to learn fast!" With that we went to bed.

It was scarcely gray dawn when I said good-by to Si Fryer at the airport. "See you in a few days," I shouted into the cold wind as he started up the ramp.

"I'll try to come back," he promised. He didn't return with Dr. Bennett, however, but went on to Washington.

John Evans and I rode back to the city in a jeep. I was seeing Tehran for the first time by daylight. The early morning parade of donkeys was on the road near the airport. One train of four camels passed in the distance. Within the city limits the street was wide and paved. The buildings were low but, except for their shuttered fronts, did not appear strange to me. We passed the university grounds, surrounded by a high iron fence.

"It all looks quite modern," I observed.

"Don't be fooled," John cautioned. "Reza Shah imposed this grid of wide streets on the city. Simply razed the old buildings. There are a few of these modern streets north and south and a few east and west. This one is called Shah Reza. But between the broad streets the old *kuchehs* wind like alleys. And beyond the Bazaar, in the south, the city simply teems with them!"

"Somehow I expected Tehran to be more quaint."

"Oh, it has its color, but not along Shah Reza Avenue," John explained. "Some of the old palaces and houses are grand. And the people in the shops are interesting. They sit and make shoes or fashion trinkets in their laps, and they're crafty traders. But Tehran is only a few hundred years old. The old city of Rey that stood just there at the foot of that mountain was destroyed by the Mongols. Isfahan or Shiraz or Tabriz are more the quaint and storied cities of Persia. But Tehran is the capital and the principal manufacturing center, and it's much the biggest."

The early day had grown bright. A great ring of mountains made a partial semicircle around the city. The Elburz were magnificent, but only on one peak at some distance east could we see any snow.

"The big cone out there," I said, pointing toward that peak. "It must be very high. What's its name?"

"That is Demavand. Isn't it a beauty? It's 18,900 feet high."

"Whew!" I whistled. "It beats Rainier or Hood or Shasta. And that great escarpment to the north. What a tremendous wall!"

"That high point is Tchotchal—Icepit. It will be covered with snow soon. It still had some on it two months ago when I came."

My hotel, the Darband, stood high against the Elburz escarpment at the base of Tchotchal, above Tehran. Each morning I rode down the long, straight drive known as Pahlavi Avenue, fascinated by the changing views of the city spread out below. On the morning of December 6, 1951, a week and a day after my arrival, as we approached Takte Jamshid Avenue, the first cross street at the city's edge, I was amazed to see the way blocked by a rushing mob brandishing sticks and chasing another group.

Hossein, my driver, in whom I learned to put my faith on such occasions, calmly turned off into an alley. After some turning we re-entered the avenue further down. I looked back, but the mob was gone. Later in the day another group of rioters threatened damage and violence to the United States Information Office. Point 4 headquarters were temporarily located in a corner of one room of this building while an old house on Sepah Avenue was being made ready for use as permanent headquarters.

Though I knew martial law had been instituted and the curfew imposed after repeated trouble in the streets, I did not yet understand the issues that fomented these riots. Later in the day I saw milling crowds at other places in the city. Everyone not actually engaged in the disturbances went calmly about his business. Even when the shouting was loudest outside the Information Office it was calm inside. The few rocks thrown did not even hit a window. So when I heard next day that several people, including a few students from Tehran University, had been killed, I was deeply shocked at the violence and intensity of the disorder. Nearly twenty years earlier, as a reporter, I had covered an affair that had become a riot in a city park in San Diego. Perhaps because I had been afoot and around the edges of it, I remembered that affair as a few minutes of extreme violence. But I had learned when it was all over that there had been only one broken arm among several hundreds of participants to evidence the event.

I began now to reappraise my impressions of the day in Tehran and of the situation into which I had entered.

Ambassador Loy W. Henderson, who in September 1951 had

Country Agreement in Iran 35

succeeded Dr. Grady, took me to make my official call, a purely social one, on Prime Minister Mossadegh. As we drove up to the gate of Kakh Avenue a formidable armed guard opened it for us. The ambassador noted that there were more machine guns visible than there had been before the riot two days earlier. We soon found ourselves in a small courtyard entirely surrounded by high mud walls, gray under a thinning coat of whitewash. A house occupied one side of the garden. The ambassador explained as we crossed the narrow walk that this was Dr. Mossadegh's old family residence. The prime minister preferred to use a tiny bedroom on the second floor and never went to his office at all.

We entered an unimpressive hallway, neither spacious nor well furnished. Again an armed guard, this time a single soldier holding a bayoneted rifle at present arms, confronted us. One of Dr. Mossadegh's secretaries came forward. He was a big, heavy-set man with an easy smile. We were ushered by gestures (since our guide spoke no English) to the second floor, where we entered another unimposing hall. Through a door I saw a large sitting room, around which were arranged a number of heavy, old upholstered chairs. At one end stood an iron bed, at this moment unoccupied. This was the Cabinet Room, in which Dr. Mossadegh received his ministers. There were almost no formalities in this hallway-reception room. A few men sat waiting in chairs at one end, and another guard stood near the head of the stairs. We were joined by Dr. Ali Pasha Saleh, who for thirty years had been an employe of the American embassy. A neighbor and friend of Dr. Mossadegh, he served as our interpreter. Almost immediately Ambassador Henderson, Dr. Saleh and I were ushered into the bedroom, where the prime minister received us alone.

While Dr. Mossadegh and I exchanged pleasantries, reminding each other of little things that had occurred at our meeting in Washington, a servant fetched tea into the room. Always there would be tea. Soon I was serving it to visitors in my own office. The servant laid out tea-things on a low table at the bedside then passed lump sugar and an Iranian candy called *ghazd*. This sweet, made of a desert plant, has a unique flavor that much intrigued me. I tore a sheet from a tablet on the table and wrapped a square of the *ghazd* in it. As I placed it in my pocket I explained to Dr. Mossadegh that my eight-year-old daughter, Margaret, would be delighted with this candy when she arrived. Seven months later, on the day Margaret and her mother arrived in Tehran eight boxes of *ghazd*, one for each year of Margaret's age, arrived from the prime minister addressed to "Little Miss Margaret Warne."

The ambassador also took me to meet His Majesty Mohammed Reza Pahlavi, Shah-in-Shah of Persia, at his marble palace in Tehran. The palace of yellow-green marble stood in the center of a beautiful formal garden that occupied two city blocks. Its dome was covered with tile in lovely arabesque, the scroll-like pattern that dominates all Persian decoration. It was similar to the domes of the most imposing of the great mosques of Iran. The building itself was square and boxlike, though large. The interior was pleasant but rather formal, with heavily carved doors and mantels and extraordinarily high ceilings. The graceful staircase was elaborately decorated with painting resembling that used in Persian miniatures. Among the furnishings I found only the lovely carpets altogether arresting. Many were almost paper-thin, the pride of the Persian looms for generations back.

I had been told that certain formalities were expected at an audience with His Imperial Majesty. In addressing him, for example, I had been cautioned to say "Your Majesty." But on neither this nor any of the other occasions when I met and talked with him did I find His Imperial Majesty inclined to stand on formal ceremony.

The Shah was a grave young man dressed in a dark business suit. Then in his middle thirties, he was fully ten years younger than I. We had tea, seated on opposite sides of a low table.

Country Agreement in Iran

There is nothing opulent about the court of Persia today. The time of fabulous splendor is gone with other dynasties and is only now and then glimpsed in a museum or an old palace converted to an office building. The only "other-worldly" touch that I recall connected with entertainment at the court was a delightful hour after a ball at the summer palace in Shimron. The royal couple and most of their guests stayed late, many seated on cushions and rugs in an aquarium room. Some sang, some played on the quaint old three-cornered guitars of Persia, and one or two were even persuaded to dance. At this a few of the parakeets asleep in the foliage in the solarium window fluttered about in the soft light of the chandeliers, which were shaped like huge clusters of grapes on turning vines of delicate green and amethyst-colored glass.

The Shah, I found on my first call, was completely at home in English. He seemed intelligently interested in the program and hopeful that it would bear fruit in continued good relations between our countries and in improved living for the people of Iran.

In this first meeting, as at later times, the Shah showed deep compassion for his people. He discussed the need for land reform and for raising the living levels of the peasants. He saw these programs as protections of the western way of life.

His Majesty explained a program that he had worked out and recently set in motion through the agency that managed his estates. This agency, Amlock, was distributing the Crown Land villages among the peasants.

"The peasants will receive title to their fields," the Shah said, "and they will pay for their land in twenty-five years at rates about equal to the usual share taken by a landlord."

Ambassador Henderson, who had discussed these plans with the Shah on earlier occasions, explained that the Crown Lands contained nearly 3,000 villages.

"The people need a stake in their country," His Majesty continued. "I hope that Point 4 will take an interest in programs like this."

Pleasant as they were, these first meetings in Iran had little influence on the negotiations then in progress to obtain the assurances required by our law from the host country. We were little nearer, therefore, to signing a country agreement.

I was spending many hours with Franklin Harris, technical director of the Rural Improvement Program, John Evans and Robert M. Carr, economic counselor of the embassy. We four were drafting the agreement, reviewing the plan for establishing ten decentralized provincial offices and assigning staff. New personnel arrived on almost every plane.

Some field work had already begun. The health and agriculture teams had been growing in number since early summer. Visiting nurses were already working in Shariar. A plan for rehabilitating Isfahanek, a run-down village near Isfahan, was complete. Light rains on the winter wheat were creating an emergency in Azerbaijan, the northwestern province, and much land would need reseeding in the spring. Horace Byrne, later regional director in Tabriz, was sent north to work out a plan to provide seed wheat for these new plantings. A myriad of administrative details demanded attention. The problem of setting up to do business in an emergency abroad began to take on large proportions. And always in the background was the matter of negotiation with the Iranians.

As the days wore on pessimism turned to certainty that there could be no country agreement before Dr. Bennett's arrival. He and his party had been expected for several days, but there were the unexplained delays so common in Iran. We planned a Christmas party at the Darband Hotel, where all our people would be brought together to meet the director. Some of the Point 4 wives were making a neighborly project of decorating a tree. There was still a chance that Dr. and Mrs. Bennett might arrive before Christmas, but the time was growing short.

I went to the ambassador's office at five o'clock on December 22 to tell him I thought it unlikely that the plane would come that day. Through the large picture window which opened to a magnificent view of the Elburz Mountains, I watched an icy, foggy dusk settling down. The atmosphere congealed. Visibility would be entirely blotted out in a few minutes. At this moment someone handed me a note from the airport. Dr. Bennett's plane had taken off from Baghdad, Iraq, and would arrive at Mehrabad about seven o'clock. I started for the airport. Snow had begun to fall. Except for one antiquated radio beacon and a few rather pale lights around the airport and along the runway, there were then no night aerial navigation aids at Mehrabad.

I stopped at the Point 4 office on Sepah Avenue to pick up Ardeshir Zahedi, my principal Iranian assistant, and we hurried on. When we confirmed that the plane was en route I telephoned for the reception party.

At a few minutes after seven Ambassador Henderson, Ardeshir and I heard a plane high overhead in the cold darkness. The flares shot from the tower seemed only to emphasize the darkness. Wet snow blew in our faces. In the next thirty-five minutes we heard the plane four times. The last time it was so low that the roar of its motors shook the windows of the airport customs building at our backs.

None of us beside the runway could see the plane in the murk, but Ardeshir thought he had seen the glow of a wing blinker.

We heard the plane no more.

After a few minutes Ardeshir climbed the wood stairs to the control tower for news. "The pilot told the tower 'I see your lights' as he came over that last time," he reported when he returned. "No word at all since then."

The ambassador shook his head and blinked snow out of his eyes. "Let's invite the committee to have tea in the airport building."

But the people were restive. I suggested that some of our friends quietly persuade members of the committee to disperse. We did not want to alarm them.

Ardeshir and I remained at the airport until midnight. He had rustled me a curfew pass. No word came from Baghdad, Basra or Abadan, where alternate landings might have been made. Driving past the embassy on the way home, I was flagged down by a Marine guard. He had just learned from the airport that the plane had arrived safely at Baghdad. I went to bed relieved and happy. I had been sure we were waiting for news of disaster.

The morning of December 23, 1951, was startlingly, crystalline clear. A heavy mantle of snow covered the mountains, the hills and even the plain. At the Darband I heard a small plane circling over the foothills but paid no attention. At the office an hour later I learned that a search plane had located the wreckage of Dr. Bennett's airliner. My shock was even deeper because of my trust in the false information of the previous night. No satisfactory explanation of that telephone call was ever made.

Ardeshir, son of a prominent Iranian general who later became prime minister, somehow hurriedly obtained a jeep for the trip into the Elburz foothills. We drove through rutted snow as far as roads went, then broke trail. Soon the ground became too rough even for a jeep. At the steep edge of a canyon we began a slow trek toward the reported site of the wreck. On a hilltop we saw a shattered propeller standing like a cross. We rounded a shoulder. In the bottom of the canyon we saw the little that remained of the plane. All but the wings and tail had burned. The impact had thrown Dr. and Mrs. Bennett forward, clear of the wreckage. They had died instantly. They were still side by side, strapped in their seats. Between them lay a Bible which Mrs. Bennett must have been reading. Most of the twenty-one victims were in the burned wreckage. One of these was Benjamin Hill Hardy, chief of public affairs for the Technical Cooperation Administration, whom President Truman praised as "a convinced idealist" who made "important contributions" to the Point 4 idea. James Thomas Mitchell, a staff photographer, and Albert Cyril Crilley, a foreign service assistant to Dr. Bennett, had also been on the plane.

As we drove back to town Ardeshir and I took some comfort in the fact that I had not been able to persuade Si Fryer to return. It was impossible not to talk about Dr. Bennett. Ardeshir listened with a friend's indulgent silence.

"I went to say good-by to Dr. Bennett the day before I left Washington," I said. "It was only about five weeks ago. He said that we had a hard job ahead. An easy job, I told him, would not have attracted me any more than such a task would have drawn him. He said he had absolute confidence in the success of Point 4 because it was right for the great United States to help her neighbors as our pioneer forefathers had co-operated with each other on the frontiers. He added that talk of atom bombs did not frighten him. Then he said, 'I think you are like me in that we do not scare easily.' I am sure Dr. Bennett did not scare even at the end."

Ardeshir was one to understand. A tall, handsome young man, he is among the very few I have known whom I believe to be without any sense of fear. He was not reckless beyond reason, but he would and did risk his skin fearlessly when he thought it was important and right to do so. "Right," to him, meant "in the interests of Iran."

Dr. Harris had brought Ardeshir into Point 4. This was not their first contact. On an earlier advisory mission to Iran Dr. Harris had met his father, General Fazlollah Zahedi, and his family and had persuaded Ardeshir, then only a boy, to follow him to USAC to complete his education.

Persian to the very core, Ardeshir was a generous and considerate friend. One must know something of his country's history to understand how he has been molded. His father was a distinguished military commander. He had reached army field grade at an earlier age than any other in Iran's recent history. He had stopped invading rabble in a mountain valley in 1921 and had pacified rebellious tribes in the 1930s without open warfare. He had been interned by the British during the Second World War, and his son, then just a lad, had not known his father's fate for months. Rugged and independent, the general had continued to serve his country where and when he could, though his health had been undermined by some of his experiences. He carried several bullets in him. Ardeshir and his father were deeply attached.

"When you believe in a thing deeply, Bill," Ardeshir explained, "you just have to go ahead whether it's dangerous or not."

In the United States today not many are called on to live dangerously. But peril is not unusual in Iran. Dr. Bennett would have understood Ardeshir. He had died on a gravel bank by an Iranian mountain stream for something he believed in strongly.

Late on the afternoon of Christmas Day we finally completed the last identification of the victims. I returned to the hotel weary and sick at heart. The manager mentioned the forgotten Christmas tree.

"You may take it down," I told him.

"I am sorry, Mr. Warne," he said. "Our little orchestra had learned some of your Christmas carols. Everyone grieves."

During these bad days new technicians kept arriving. Recruiting in the United States was in full swing. Our growth in numbers alarmed some, who doubted our chances of signing a country agreement. A few, more experienced than I in international negotiations, repeatedly urged stopping recruitment. If, as seemed possible, no mission at all were needed in Iran, the cost of assembling one would be wasted. Dispirited one evening shortly after Christmas, I drafted a message that would have had the effect of suspending all further action until an agreement had

Country Agreement in Iran

been completed. I decided to hold over sending it until morning.

That night it occurred to me that my cable might completely dry up the pipeline that served us. It certainly would mean several months before recruits started coming again, even if we got an agreement within a few days. It might mean that I had headed the shortest mission to Iran in all history. Someone else would have to take such desperate measures, I concluded, because I wouldn't. Almost the very next day things began looking up.

Early in January 1952 Ambassador Henderson proposed to Washington a new formula for obtaining the required assurances and received tentative clearance. He presented his plan to Dr. Mossadegh. Within hours the crisis had passed. Satisfactory assurances were given by the prime minister. These he based on a citation of Iran's commitments to the United Nations. Thus he avoided affronting either his own supernationalists or the neighbor to the north. I have never ceased to congratulate myself that for once in my life I did not act immediately on reaching a decision but held unsent that potentially disastrous cable. Months later, in cleaning out the drawer, I found and read it again. With a shudder I burned it.

Once we had the assurances, Ambassador Henderson and I began immediately to negotiate with the prime minister for the country agreement. Dr. Mossadegh was not entirely satisfied. He was still complaining about the size of our assistance program. And in one meeting, only half jokingly, he said, "Point 4 resembles an Iranian tarantula. It jumps up and down and scares everybody, but it has never been known to bite."

Even the chuckle with which he accompanied this jibe did not dull its point. It seemed to me to be grossly unfair, since our slowness in starting was at least half his responsibility.

Finally one afternoon I took a Farsee translation of the latest and best draft of the agreement from my pocket and laid it on the coverlet at the prime minister's knee.

"You said, Mr. Prime Minister, when we had our first meeting in Washington that when I brought this agreement to you, you would sign it," I reminded him.

Dr. Mossadegh dropped the whole posture of bargaining and said seriously, "Please leave it with me until tomorrow. I will sign it."

The draft, with a note he scribbled on a pad, was added to a stack of papers on a small table in the corner behind the bed. I was curious about this pending file. It grew day by day, and it seemed to me that to sort it out and distribute it would be a prodigious task.

Later that evening I received a telephone call from Mr. Javaud Busheri, who was then minister of roads and spokesman for the Iranian government. He asked that I come immediately to his house. It was, I found, an old Persian town house completely overgrown by the city, as was our Sepah Avenue office. From the *kucheh* one would not suspect that behind the wall was a charming home. The old gate opened into a garden. My first impression was that the garden was completely filled with great Danes. When the beasts quieted a little I counted only four, but the sniffing of even this number much hurried my walk across the courtyard to a door.

I scarcely caught a glimpse of the servant who motioned me into a hallway. My impression was of a *chadora*-wrapped figure and a pale arm beckoning. The minister had apparently been detained somewhere. There was no one in this whole part of the house. I wandered about looking curiously over the magnificent memorabilia of generations of Busheris. The furniture in houses like this one is apt to be large, heavy and overstuffed. To some of our Western tastes it often seems overdone, but I found that this room hung together. I was especially attracted to a gold-plated piano, which had been given to the minister's grandfather by a Russian nobleman, and to an aquarium filled with papier-mâché fishes made by Mr. Busheri's father. On a low table set for tea were a variety of splendidly iced cakes and a dish of pistachio nuts done the Persian way in salt brine that cracked the hard shell open and crusted the kernel. I sampled the nuts and had to devise quickly a means of disposing of the shells when my host entered. Americans in Tehran are forever cleaning pistachio shells out of their pockets and pants' cuffs.

Mr. Busheri took from his pocket the copy of the proposed agreement I had left with Dr. Mossadegh. My first thought was that papers were, after all, not forever lost in the pile on the prime minister's bedside table. Waving a pencil at various paragraphs, Mr. Busheri said many changes would have to be made. Most of his proposals were for word substitutions. In English the words he suggested seemed synonymous with those he wanted stricken, though in Farsee they may have been different. Here and there he suggested an alteration in phrasing that likewise seemed to have no material effect on the English meaning. Now two substantial changes were left.

One of these points in dispute concerned exempting from customs duty goods imported to Iran by Point 4 for use in the cooperative program; the other, extending to our technicians the courtesies granted members of a diplomatic mission. These, I realized, the supernationalists might publicly construe as "concessions" and so draw fire on Dr. Mossadegh's government.

I said immediately that I thought negotiations from this point should proceed with Dr. Mossadegh himself. I left with the sobering thought that the country agreement, which had seemed so close, might yet be blocked.

Early the next day Dr. Mossadegh's office asked that I call on him. Once again I faced the unpredictable prime minister. His copy of the agreement was before him. I told him that I did not think we could agree to two of the suggestions made by Mr. Busheri and that I hoped he would not press me to do so. While I waited for him to speak I recalled that he had objected to similar provisions when the agreement establishing the Joint

Commission for Rural Improvement was being considered by General Razmara's government. The present prime minister had then been a leader of opposition to Razmara in the Majlis (Iranian parliament). It was unlikely he would take a different view now, when he would have to bear directly any censure about "concessions."

Dr. Mossadegh responded as I had thought he would. "This has been discussed," he said. "Can't we leave these provisions out of the new agreement?"

"Look at it from my point of view," I urged. "The United States is freely offering a co-operative development program to Iran. It would be impossible to explain to our Congress why we paid duty on such things as jeeps and DDT brought to Iran at our expense to help the Iranian people. And our technicians deserve and elsewhere are accorded the privileges of the diplomatic mission."

Then I added, "I had so much looked forward to the end of these negotiations and a start of work."

"Well," he said, "go ahead and sign the note. It is satisfactory to me."

And while I did just that, he scribbled on a pad on his knee his draft of a response agreeing to the proposal. This, dated January 20, 1952, reached me the following day.

In his reply, the prime minister named a group with whom I was to work. This Cabinet Committee consisted of Dr. Mahammed Ali Maleki, minister of health, who was designated chairman, Dr. Mahmoud Hessabi, minister of education, Engineer Khalil Taleghani, minister of agriculture, and Dr. Ahmad Zanganeh, managing director of the Seven-Year Plan Organization, an agency created in more auspicious times to carry out, using oil revenues, a comprehensive development plan. This group was the hopper into which requests for Point 4 technical co-operation projects were dropped. To this committee I looked for the designation of the appropriate person with whom to sign agreements for separate projects.

The Cabinet Committee asked me to meet with it. We decided to hold one formal meeting each week. The men with whom I sat were to help me direct and control expenditures. As our association lengthened I came to appreciate firmly the care with which Dr. Mossadegh had selected them.

With the agreement signed, the whole program moved swiftly forward. Come riot or havoc, civil strife or revolution, under Dr. Mossadegh and his successor we progressed month by month toward our goal of improving the level of living in Iran by cooperative planning, by instruction and eager response to it, by work shared by Iranians and Americans. But Dr. Mossadegh never permitted a mention of the Joint Commission for Rural Improvement to creep into any formal paper. He stubbornly ignored the existence of the agreements signed by Razmara. But the prime minister's Cabinet Committee, when it was necessary, quietly acted as members of the older commission as well. Thus we retained in its full extent the government consent and advice we needed.

Even the anomaly of the unrecognized agreement was straightened out eventually. First, Dr. Mossadegh had signed a *third* agreement in December 1952 creating a Joint Commission for Social and Economic Development. This effectively superseded both the Joint Commission for Rural Improvement and the Cabinet Committee. Then General Zahedi, when he became prime minister, revalidated, in September 1953, all previous agreements, including the one with General Razmara on October 19, 1950. This last, as has been pointed out, had the distinction of being the first agreement in the world under the Point 4 program and was really the beginning of our trial at making humane and neighborly arts serve the interests of international harmony.

Mission/3

Jackasses

"Jackasses," Dr. C. S. (Steve) Stephanides, head of the Point 4 Livestock Division, patiently explained to me one February day in 1952, "are considered not quite nice in any language. I don't know why, but it's true at home too."

Steve's remarks were inspired by the Communists' first campaign against Point 4 in Iran. The first fruits of the Point 4 program were just then beginning to show. In spite of the fact that it was a prodigious task merely to assemble a staff—more than eighty experts were working at that moment—there were still those who exploited a national desperation and impatience to persuade the Iranians that our help was ineffective. Work was actually under way in scores of places in crop improvement, public health and schools. But it was too early for much of it to be evident, and far too soon to look for good results.

At the request of the Livestock Bongah, an agency of the Ministry of Agriculture with which our Livestock Division co-operated, James R. Dawson had been sent to Nicosia, Island of Cyprus. There he selected ten jacks and ten jennies to be brought to Iran to improve the local breed and to sire stronger mules. The Livestock Bongah bought the animals but had no foreign exchange to pay for shipping them and no expert to select them. Mr. Dawson, a livestock expert, was in Nicosia when I arrived in Tehran. He had a regular Odyssey of trouble getting the jacks and jennies to Iran, but last month they had finally arrived.

"If you ask an Iranian farmer how much stock he has," Steve now went on, "he will say, perhaps, that he has ten head of sheep, two oxen and, 'excuse me please, a jackass.'"

Jackasses

Being clever propagandists, more clever than wise, I think, the Communists quickly distorted our interest in jackasses and took advantage of the Iranian attitude to ridicule Point 4.

The columns of many newspapers of Tudeh (the local Communist party) stripe said, "Ah, the great United States comes to help Iran and what does Iran get? A few jackasses! The people are hungry, but what do the promises of the wealthy Imperialists amount to? Jackasses!"

Even one friendly newspaper, only half in jest, published my picture alongside the drawing of a jackass. Radio Moscow tipped its hat to the story and its hand in the campaign by braying thousands of words about jackasses into Iran every night.

The ridicule campaign played acutely on Iranian impatience for immediate results. Our long-range program of development built on technical assistance seemed to many to lag, and delay inevitably chafes when needs are very great. The prime minister and other advocates of one big, spectacular project had feared a popular reaction of this sort. They argued that at least a big project, involving a lot of busy work around its site, would be evidence that *something* was being done. We knew, however, that we could make much greater contributions to Iran's general welfare by leading and educating its citizens. This training would multiply its effects by thousands and spread its results broadly among all of the people, even though the results might be slow in coming. At first they might be visible in only half a sack more wheat at harvest time for each of the poor farmers reached. The first tangible effects of the jackass project would be a few hundred sturdy, long-legged mule colts foaled after almost a year. In their pastures they might not be seen by anybody but their owners. But Point 4 *is* a long-range technical assistance program. And there is simply no escaping the difficulties that such a program presents at the start when challenges cannot yet be answered by demonstrations of concrete results.

Having been a farm boy myself, I naturally doubted that poking fun at rustic things was good politics or good propaganda. To city boys, breeding better animals may sound like material for dirty jokes and may call for sniggering. But to country boys it is sound and serious business. The WPA outlived the "Chick Sale" jokes that its privy-building campaign set off. The results of the jackass campaign would probably vindicate it. It would eventually draw attention to the real value of the Point 4 work. Among the masses of the people we would win more approval than censure. But that would come later.

Meanwhile I was shaken by the force and volume of the campaign. One writer advocated that Warne be set on his jackass and sent home. We received anonymous diatribes through the mails. Some Iranian officials became nervous about being seen with us. Still we felt that the reaction was sure to come.

The first break came when the Ghashghai tribesmen wired from Shiraz for four of the jacks. Iran is a vast parallelogram of deserts and mountains. Of her 18,000,000 people 4,000,000 are members of nomadic tribes that follow the season and the grass from winter pastures in the low, warm valleys to summer pastures in the high mountains. "We need to breed better pack animals for our migrations," the Ghashghai explained.

Then the Iranian Army asked for two dozen for its remount service. Soon from every side came the clamor for Cyprus jacks from breeders who knew the animals' worth. We couldn't supply a fraction of these demands. For generations the eastern Mediterranean Island of Cyprus has produced jacks sought for breeding throughout that part of the world. The breeding there has been closely controlled for quality.

Thus the propaganda against us became unwitting advertising. It actually gave the program in rural Iran a great lift. But the propagandists did not see this right away. They didn't foresee what happened and, of course, didn't know the tide of opinion had changed until it was running strongly against them. We knew by the number of requests for jacks. The propaganda campaign carried on beyond the end of its effectiveness.

In March some of the jacks were shown at the Hyderabad Livestock Station. I made a little speech, saying that Point 4 was proud to have been of assistance to the Livestock Bongah in its attempt to meet the needs of the Iranian farmers. I deliberately mentioned the jacks among the breeding stock supplied and had some pictures made with them.

A distinguished group was present and many newspapers were represented. There was a general air of surprise that jackasses were not hidden and left out. Madjid Adl, director of the Livestock Bongah, bravely stepped forward too and said that after all Point 4 had taken enough kidding about the jackasses. It was not commonly known, he added, that the Livestock Bongah had bought the jacks and had started the project on its own. Point 4 had contributed technical advice and transportation. Mr. Adl added that the jacks had been royally received in Iran. The Tehran newspaper coverage of the livestock show pretty well took the heart out of the entire ridicule campaign against Point 4.

The Communists abruptly changed their propaganda line to attempt to persuade the people that American assistance programs were tightening nooses of control about the Iranian neck and that our technicians were spies. Ridicule was used no more. Too much was being done. That tactic couldn't be profitable again, even for a short time.

With some relief I saw the jackass business die out of public print. Imagine my consternation, therefore, when I saw in *Newsweek* and some clippings from Associated Press dispatches that the old jacks story was being broadcast generally throughout the United States in the early summer. These reports, probably mailed from Iran, brought cables from the Washington office asking for an explanation. In June 1952 Washington was particularly sensitive to criticism of field activities in the host countries. I wired back, "There has not been a jackass story here for two or three months."

Newsweek and the Associated Press were apparently unaware that the story ridiculing the jacks was originally anti-Point 4 Communist propaganda. To understand this final chaper in the jackass story a little background is necessary.

Except when there were major crises or extraordinary news developments, there were few American reporters in Iran. Associated Press had a representative there all the time, the *New York Times* very frequently for periods of weeks, *Time* and *Life* part of the time and others only occasionally.

No one ever just stopped off to visit us in going through Iran. Many airlines served Mehrabad Airport, but every flight originated or terminated there. Since no flights went through, those who came either on official business or to observe the program had to make a long trip for that purpose alone. As a consequence there were not many visitors. A few senators and some representatives managed to spend a little time in Tehran during trips to study various field problems. Some members of the State Department and of the Foreign Operations Administration and, very rarely, representatives of other government departments managed to get that far. Vice President and Mrs. Nixon made good impressions on a brief trip in the fall of 1953.

On two occasions Wick tours of editors, publishers and a few radio-station executives, traveled by chartered plane to visit us briefly. Many of these continued their interest, among them Mrs. Jerene Appleby Harnish, who was in the first of these parties. Mrs. Harnish is publisher of the *Report* in my home town, Ontario, California.

After a succession of hit-and-run experiences I had a curious conversation with one editor who was present overnight.

We were at the ambassador's residence drinking cocktails.

Jackasses 53

The editor was explaining that he was sorry the plane had arrived a little late, since his party had hoped to arrive in Tehran at noon. Nevertheless they would take off on schedule, at nine o'clock the next morning. He enumerated a whole string of capitals in Europe and the Middle East, many of which he had similarly visited and some of which were still in prospect.

I asked whether he believed it possible on such a furious trip to learn anything about the people, the issues and the problems of the countries touched on.

"Well, no," he replied, "but I have certainly confirmed a lot of my opinions."

"We can't be hurt by allegations that we are doing something for the Iranians—even helping them to get some Cyprus jacks here," I replied to the Washington office cables. "I advocate this line of response: go on about our business."

This proved to be the correct response. Soon earnest advocates urged bringing more jacks.

"Jacklift" or "Mule Plane," as wags on our staff called it, was completed in mid-October 1953, when the Iranian Air Force flew thirty-five Cyprus jacks, hale and hearty, into Mehrabad airport.

By then the initial embarrassment of the propaganda attack had so far been forgotten that the second chapter of our adventure into Cypriote jackasses began in an almost carnival atmosphere.

Many officials lined the airstrip to meet the three Air Force C-47 carriers that flew the jacks from Beirut as a training problem in air transport. Major General Robert A. McClure, head of the United States Army Advisory Group in Iran and an old cavalry officer, had worked out with me the plan in which everyone joined with enthusiasm. The Livestock Bongah and the Remount Section of the Iranian Army wanted the additional jacks for breeding to extend a project undertaken in 1951. Dr. Charles

E. Pegg, Point 4 veterinarian, who was in charge of the jacks in flight, coined the puns we used to describe the project.

By that time young mules were on display. They were the major exhibit at Tehran's first national livestock exhibition. No such fine young animals had been seen in Iran in a long time.

The demand for the first shipment, advertised as it was by the propaganda attacks, had exceeded all expectations. I took some satisfaction in the fact that these requirements could be met only by importing a little later three times more jackasses than the original order.

Mission/4

The Cabinet Committee Digs In

THE CABINET COMMITTEE named by the prime minister in January was organized in February 1952 and went promptly to work. The various field activities started under the old Rural Improvement agreement were now written up as projects, or units of projects. This proved to be a big job. A technician's inclination is usually to get started on the actual job. Many a good one dislikes to set down on a piece of paper what he plans to do, and almost all find writing the hardest task.

This disinclination and inability makes serious administrative problems. American technical colleges have been failing us in one regard, good as they are in most others. They have not been teaching their students to write the English language. It is pathetic to see a man who can solve mathematical equations, make graphs and direct great construction projects chewing up pencils and sweating so that his nose drips, as he tries to complete a description of his project. An experience even more painful is trying to read what he has written after he has gone home to bed exhausted. In the end though, someone has to set the plan down so it can be reviewed and approved. Our program officers—Ralph Workinger, later Jerome Fried and still later Dr. Lucy Adams—had the job of pulling the stuff out of the technicians and putting it in readable shape. The programs had to be reviewed in Washington and justified to the Congress.

After the spring of 1952 the program work became more orderly. With all the piecemeal undertakings swept up, related to central programs and made parts of larger projects, our job was easier. Point 4 in Iran was at first no more than the sum of all its parts. The only way to describe it was to enumerate its activities. By early summer this weakness had been corrected. The Cabinet Committee agreed to basic statements that unified and clarified the program.

For example, on April 1 Khalil Taleghani, minister of agriculture, and I signed an agreement describing the entire Agriculture Program. The agreement provided that technical men from each of our staffs should "participate jointly in all phases of the planning and direction" of projects to help the "development of agriculture and related fields in Iran through co-operative action." Through the interchange of "knowledge, skills, and techniques," the program was to "further the overall economic development of Iran." As established in this agreement, the Agricultural Program was to last five years, until June 30, 1957. If either country wanted to stop it sooner this could be done on three months' written notice. This document was amended three times and then was rewritten on February 4, 1953, to establish a joint fund to finance the projects and to extend the program until June 30, 1958. After being amended four times the first extension was revised on September 12, 1953, to extend the program to June 30, 1959. This second extension was amended twice. On December 1, 1954, it also was revised to extend its effectiveness until June 30, 1960.

Thus year by year the program crept forward. We agreed each time that our work should cover a five-year period, which kept moving into the future.

The importance of continuity of effort in programs such as those Point 4 launched in Iran cannot be overemphasized. The agency supervising this work has had various names. It has been reorganized several times. At the outset it was the Technical Cooperation Administration, a bureau of the State Department. During the life of this agency our Point 4 field organization in

The Cabinet Committee Digs In

Iran was called the TCI—office of Technical Cooperation for Iran. In July 1953 the government agency became the Foreign Operations Administration. The FOA was independent of the State Department, and its administrator, Governor Harold E. Stassen, was accorded rank with cabinet members. The FOA was terminated on June 30, 1955. It was succeeded by the International Cooperation Administration, a semi-independent agency within the State Department. John Hollister headed this agency.

When the FOA was organized, the field office in Iran lost its identity as TCI and became USOM/I, or OM/I—United States Operations Mission in Iran. From the very first the people of Iran referred to our work and our office as *Asle Chahar,* or Point 4. Principle number four might be a more accurate translation. This informal name might have vanished, but no other name was retained long enough to replace it among the people. So Point 4 it remained and Point 4 it is, though formally Point 4 it never was. No matter the name, the program of technical cooperation did not change. The benefits of Point 4 grow, accumulate and multiply year after year, though the level of the program remains the same. The results of training spread as ripples expand in a pond.

In Point 4 language *program* designates a plan for accomplishment in a broad area; *project* describes specific work done to further the ends of a program. Thus the importing of jackasses was a *project* under the agricultural *program.*

An ideal project would follow a prescribed pattern. It would have a life of five years. The first year would be spent in preparation—training Iranian technicians, locating sites and importing the required tools and equipment. During the second year the newly trained Iranian technicians would launch the field work and demonstration projects, working through the agency sponsoring the project. Activity would reach its peak in the third year. The American technicians, the Iranian technicians and all co-operators would then be putting every ounce of energy into the operation of the project. In the fourth year the American technicians would turn their responsibilities over to their Iranian counterparts. And in the fifth year the Iranians would conduct project activities with little or no assistance, except for occasional consultation or advice, from the American technicians. If all projects followed this perfect pattern maximum requirements for technical personnel and supporting funds would be reached in the second and third years. Demand on Point 4 services would fall off rapidly in the fourth and almost disappear in the fifth.

In actual experience no project will fit this pattern perfectly. Some actually run through their cycle more quickly than anticipated. Some will require more than five years to reach the point where American technicians may withdraw.

The whole Technical Cooperation Program, however, was never designed for a five-year life. The program in Iran was conceived as a continuous rope pulling that country forward. The rope was to be made up of strands of projects, each five years long. These projects would be intertwined to make a single program for the improvement of the life of the people. New strands will be woven in as the ends of old ones are reached. It is long-range.

Agreements similar to one covering the Agriculture Program were made before June 30, 1952, for these fields: health and sanitation, education and training, student assistance, industry, sugar importation, transportation, community housing, natural resources development, and communications. Later that year one was added for land distribution. In 1953 similar agreements were signed for public administration and for agrarian development or land reform. One more, labor, was added in 1954. All but two of these programs were designed to move forward from year to year, always projecting five years ahead until either the United States or Iran should call a halt. The two exceptions were those agreements covering sugar importation and aid to Iranian students enrolled in American colleges. These were not designed

The Cabinet Committee Digs In

to run on. The sugar importation program has already stopped and started several times and may do so again. It depends on the needs of the season and the amount of ready cash to satisfy the needs. Assistance to students continued, but with a gradually diminishing United States participation. It ended, so far as Point 4 was concerned, on August 31, 1955. Except for these two, each program agreement has been amended and extended about as often as the agriculture agreement, and each has been kept current.

Every program agreement called for joint effort in planning and carrying out projects by our technicians and those of the ministries concerned with the particular field covered by the agreement.

I made a flying trip to Washington in April 1952 and stayed into May. I carried a pack of program agreements in my brief case. A few knotty problems had arisen in connection with the one in industry, and the only way to solve them was to talk them out with staff members at headquarters.

It was good to be home for a breather.

One evening during this hectic visit I showed some pictures to my family at our home in Alexandria, Virginia. They were getting ready to join me.

"Now," I asked, "do you know where Iran is?"

"It looks like Utah," said Margaret, "but it isn't in the West."

"No, silly," Rob, her older brother, said scornfully, "it's in the Middle East."

"But no one," observed Jane in her turn, "has defined the Middle East."

"It certainly is a long way from home," their mother remarked mildly. "If I had known it was the same as ancient Persia, I wouldn't have asked where it was when you phoned from Montana last fall."

"Well," I said, "I've found that few Americans know much about it. But it's a big and important country to mislay."

Iran *is* vast. Bigger than Alaska, twice as big as Texas, it lies deep in the Asian desert between the Caspian Sea and the Persian Gulf. Its location is strategic. Since the dawn of history—very probably even before history was recorded or handed down from generation to generation by stories and traditions—Iran has been the crossroads between East and West, between the Mediterranean and India and China.

Iran also has the longest common frontier with the Soviet Union—1,200 miles—of any nation not a satellite. This fact was never absent from the thoughts of Iranian leaders who wanted to keep their country economically and politically independent. Fundamentally Point 4 was designed to help strengthen Iran's economy and to help underwrite her political integrity.

Iranians will tell you that their country has been invaded thirteen times. The occupation of their land by Alexander the Great of Macedonia effectively ended the Achaemenian era of Persian domination over much of the world from Egypt to India. And, they point out, the occupation of northern Iran by Soviet Russia and southern by Great Britain during World War II brought to an end the reign of Reza Shah, founder of the present Pahlavi dynasty.

But much as I wanted to answer all my friends' questions about the country, I could not take much time from the business that had brought me home. A new complication had arisen.

"It begins to look as if you'll have to get agreements covering each project too, Bill," Si Fryer told me one morning after I had been in Washington about ten days. "You know how lawyers are. This program is new and they keep laying down more legal requirements."

We had just settled the last point at issue in the Industry Program. I was appalled at this new turn. We had expected to refine the program into project statements at leisure as the year progressed.

I quickly protested to Si that only a few weeks remained

The Cabinet Committee Digs In 61

before the beginning of the 1953 fiscal year. I was thinking ahead to my return to Tehran. Nightmarish visions rose before me. I foresaw the labor of drafting legally tight language to describe multiferous project activities in detail. This would be only the beginning. Our staff would then have to translate the English into exact Farsee by scores, even hundreds, of pages. Making sure that the agreements would operate would require countless hours of staff time. And there would still be the problem of commanding enough attention from the Cabinet Committee and other Iranian officials to review and act on the project agreements. But all the sputtering comment I could muster had no effect.

The feeling prevailed that the program agreements that had been negotiated would not be legally binding unless they were backed up by the project agreements drafted in greater detail.

I hurried back to Iran and called the staff together. At that time they numbered 114, mostly technicians. Almost without exception each had a part in the intense campaign at hand. The technicians had to discuss in minute detail with their Iranian co-workers exactly how they, together, were to get their proposed jobs done. Then they had to write down what they discussed and explain it to their superiors both in the appropriate Iranian ministry and on our staff. These explanations had to justify any plan to buy equipment and had to state where any additional staff required could be found or how new recruits could be trained. In short, the technicians had to draw up project plans.

If a project involved an installation such as a livestock station, a seed-multiplication field, a health center, a demonstration school, a cement mill or a waterworks, the plan not only had to say where it would be placed but also why it would be placed there and not somewhere else. How much native stock was within the effective radius of the proposed livestock station? Did the seed plot have a secure irrigation water supply? How many people could be served from the health center, and what were the major illnesses in the vicinity? Could the demonstration school be easily reached by the numbers of teachers who would observe it? Were there children near by who could be enrolled? How about the raw materials for the cement mill? What was the power supply? Who owned the water to be used in the waterworks, and how could people be persuaded to tap the mains?

After the technicians got the answers to these questions and many more, the accountants had to check the available funds against the estimated needs. Then the personnel officer appraised the staff requirements, the lawyer, the form and language and the program committee, the appropriateness of the whole project under the program agreements already drawn. Did each project fall within the basic plan to help Iran to help herself to improve the lot of her people?

When it had been approved by these various members of our staff the agreement had to be presented in two languages to the Cabinet Committee and stand its scrutiny. If the Cabinet Committee consented it must then command the approval of the head of whatever Iranian ministry would be involved in carrying out the agreement. He, if all went well, would sign the dotted line at the end of a document that was, by that time, really formidable.

And just forty-nine days until June 30. All of our projects must be covered by formal agreement by July 1, the start of the new fiscal year. Measured against the time remaining, the details of our job looked overwhelming.

We made it. In June the Cabinet Committee met ten times, usually for at least three hours each time. Twenty-nine project agreements were completed that month alone, and when the fiscal year ended we could say that the whole program was safely documented. Three of the four regular members of the Cabinet Committee, all of ministerial rank, attended these meet-

The Cabinet Committee Digs In

ings regularly. In addition, the minister of interior, Mr. Mostafa Gholi Ram, attended four meetings; the minister of roads, Mr. Busheri, three; the minister of post, telegraph and telephone, Mr. G. H. Sadighi, two. Also, as required when matters of particular interest to them were under consideration, other officials attended. Some of these were Dean M. Attai of Karaj Agricultural College, Cholam Ali Maykadeh, director general of the Tehran Water Supply Organization, G. H. Ghavami, mayor of Shiraz, Major General Vosough, chief of the Imperial Gendarmerie, as well as technicians of the missions of United Nations specialized agencies.

I never had the heart to tell the Iranian committee members who had worked so untiringly that the lawyers in Washington later decided that it would not have been necessary to complete the project agreements by June 30, 1952. The exercise of pulling these projects together and firmly defining them was what really made us an organization. By the time it was completed everyone concerned, Iranians and Americans alike, from the ministers down to the one-project technicians, knew what we were trying to do. This sense of objective and unity of purpose carried through.

And the pressures of work and time were increased by another development.

As the end of June approached it became obvious that the Mossadegh government was on its last legs. Disorders in the streets were more and more frequent. Controversies sprang up at every hand. Dr. Mossadegh quarreled with the Shah over the prime minister's demands for power over the Army, traditionally responsible only to the Crown. There were schisms within the cabinet. Some of these involved us and called for a new kind of expertness and adroitness.

For example, Dr. Hessabi, minister of education and a member of the Cabinet Committee, fell out with Dr. Mossadegh. It was freely reported that the prime minister had asked for his resignation and that Dr. Hessabi had refused to give it. Dr. Hessabi contended that the constitution provided a means by which he could be dismissed—namely, by the prime minister's resigning and bringing down the whole government. The government since 1905 has been a constitutional monarchy, with an elected Majlis and a Senate, half of the members of which are elected and half appointed by the Shah. The Cabinet, though not chosen from the Majlis, is nevertheless responsible to it. As in parlimentary systems, a vote of no confidence in the Majlis or the resignation of the prime minister dismisses the whole government.

It was not considered entirely safe to engage in controversies with the prime minister, at least not in controversies of the scale of that stirred up by Dr. Hessabi. The minister of education began to stay away from his office. At times he carefully avoided going home as well. We had a project agreement ready for his signature. We could not find him, even with the help of his fellow ministers and some of his friends. Finally Clark S. Gregory, my legal counsel, and Reza Ansari, my Iranian assistant, a retriever who never quit once put on a scent, found Dr. Hessabi in a back room of the public library. There he signed the agreement.

Early in July 1952 the Mossadegh government fell. It was not until late August that we again had an organized Iranian group with which to work. Fortunately many weeks had been saved by our June rush. We were able to keep field work in progress all through the desperate and hectic weeks that led in Iran's capital to the Thirtieth of Tir, 1331—July 21, 1952, by our calendar—when hundreds were killed in the streets.

The meaning of the street riots that had so puzzled me a few days after my arrival in Tehran became clear in the upheaval that solidified Dr. Mossadegh's control. Political and religious fanatics ruled the city and won over the moderates a victory that set all of Iran's clocks turning backward during the next thirteen months.

Mission/5

Clocks Turn Back

ONE OF the best-known figures in Iran was Seyed Abdol Ayatollah Kashani, a leader among the Shi'ite sect of Moslems. He rose to great heights under the regime of Dr. Mossadegh and later fell completely from view. He acquired a temporary notoriety on the fanatical anti-foreign—xenophobic is the scholar's term—phase of the supernationalism that carried Iran so close to the brink of destruction.

A leader in Iran may be, as was Ayatollah Kashani, self-proclaimed. The size of his following and degree of loyalty it showed may remain undetermined. It is certain that at the height of his power Ayatollah Kashani could and did influence large numbers of young hoodlums. They appeared at his call in the streets of Tehran as if produced by magic.

In 1952 the people of Iran were peculiarly responsive to a revival of "old-time" religion. It was a concomitant of the retreat in politics to old-style ideals. From morning to night the radio chanted or sang the austere, deep-rhythmed Mullah prayers or quotations from the Koran. Agitators stimulated the revivals and derived political profit from them.

Responsible Moslem elders of the Shi'a sect, to which most Iranians belong, held aloof and seemed to take little interest in the movement. The religio-political reversal was reflected in the hinterlands and in the cities as well by the return of the women to the *chadora,* the veillike cloth worn as a cover from head-to-toe. They ignored the order of Reza Shah that had ended its use twenty-five years earlier.

The drive for an "oilless" economy was part of the general

backward movement. Perhaps that drive really motivated the larger movement, since the loss of revenues and foreign exchange after the nationalization of the petroleum industry set the stage for what followed. Iran was being told to seek refuge in her past and to reject all foreign influences.

Ayatollah Kashani was an influential figure even before the election of the Seventeenth Majlis early in 1952. (Iranians number the convocations of their legislative groups as we do. Hence the Seventeenth Majlis is equivalent to our Eighty-fourth Congress.) Kashani and a small group of his hard-core supporters were elected to the Majlis. His position was thus greatly enhanced. Hastily organizing their forces, Kashani's followers succeeded in making him president of the Majlis. This was done in his absence, for he resolutely maintained that a leader of the faith should not be expected to concern himself with mundane duties of government. He therefore never attended a session of the Majlis throughout his term, president or not. His resolution did not keep him from political activity or the exercise of the prestige of his important political office. Holding meetings at his house and at the houses of his friends, Kashani exerted his influence on the Majlis and the prime minister, who, like him, lived in a kind of isolation.

The paradox of the two most influential political leaders of the country remaining aloof in their homes amused nobody in Iran. Their insulation only added to the unrealism of the times.

The fanatics who responded to Kashani had a record of violence and terrorism. Youths of thirteen and fourteen years had on occasion been selected to act in political assassination plots.

A feeling of great power surrounded Ayatollah Kashani. In mid-August 1952 I received a summons to wait upon him at a garden in Tedjrish. With Ardeshir Zahedi I drove to the meeting-place on a very hot morning. The garden was rather small and the house, while typically Persian, was not elaborate. A number of young men, some in Mullah robes and some in ordinary dress, scurried about as we entered the hall. One or two, I learned later, were sons of the Ayatollah.

Almost immediately we found ourselves in a smallish living room that bulged with heavy, uncomfortable furniture and was distinguished only by a beautiful Persian carpet. Kashani did not rise to receive us but motioned for me to sit beside him on a sofa. Some tea-things were arrayed on a low table. Ardeshir pulled up an ottoman to sit near us. It is not uncommon at such interviews for strangers to at least some of those present to wander in and out, sometimes to stay. A stream of people, including some Mullahs, flowed through the room during our talk. The residue of this stream filtered out and found chairs, joining the circle.

The formalities on this occasion were longer than usual. Sipping our tea likewise took more time. I studied the Ayatollah. He seemed curious about me too. He was a small man, distinctly elderly, with wispy white hair and a full gray beard. He wore the white turban of a Mullah. Over a business suit and white shirt he had drawn a priest's robe of dark-brown, coarse mohair.

The compound in which the house stood was well up the mountain, and the room in which we sat was high ceilinged. It was nevertheless uncomfortably warm on the sofa, especially for one dressed as fully as Kashani. From time to time, for relief, he removed the turban from his sweaty head.

I had always thought that the turban was wrapped around the head anew at each wearing. I had seen Indian friends re-wrap theirs. But the Ayatollah's turban simply lifted off. The cloth was sewed or so permanently entwined that the turban was much like a bulky hat. I thought of a ready-tied bow tie.

Kashani let me know that he appreciated the interest the United States showed in Iran's welfare, but he displayed no understanding of our program. He thought the plan to assist rural people to help themselves to better living standards was impractical. He hoped, he told me, that the United States, through Point 4, would do "something substantial" for the people of Iran. He said he believed the plight of the people was inclining them toward Communism, which, he added, he abhorred.

"In our country," Ardeshir offered, supplementing what Ayatollah Kashani had said, "we have an old proverb: 'An empty stomach has neither faith nor loyalty.'"

Ardeshir quickly repeated this in Farsee to Kashani. The old man beamed and nodded. Given food, he said, the faith of the people would protect them. The friendship between the United States and Iran might be strengthened, he thought, if we built one or two large, spectacular dams. He thought one on the Ziandehrud River near Isfahan and another one on the Karun in Khuzistan Province would just about do the trick.

I pointed out that we had only a little more than $23,000,000 for the new fiscal year, an amount almost the same as we had for the 1952 program. He seemed to think that sum was astronomical. I protested that a dam on the Karun River would be extremely costly. Furthermore, I explained, expenditures for such large projects would be not technical assistance, but large-scale economic aid. Kashani finally asked me what I thought the Karun River dam might cost. To understand the answer to this question requires some knowledge of the geography of Iran.

The country has only one important river system. This drains the western slope of the Zagros mountains, which run north and south from one end of the country to the other, on the west side of the central plateau. The chief rivers are the Karun and the Ab-e-Diz. The system collects in the Khuzistan Plain, a vast delta. In this dry flat the rivers of Iran join the Tigris and Euphrates to form the Shat-al-Arab, the single channel through which all empty into the head of the Persian Gulf. Abadan, the refinery and city where the oil controversy centered, is on Abadan island in the Shat-al-Arab. More precisely, it lies between the

Clocks Turn Back 69

main channel and a meandering side channel. The Shat-al-Arab, freighted with the erosion silt of most of Asia Minor, year by year reclaims land from the shallow, brackish waters of the gulf. At the time of Alexander the Great several of these rivers had separate mouths. The invader is reputed to have sailed his fleet to points that now, 2,000 years later, are more than fifty miles inland.

In earlier times such streams as the Karun, Ab-e-Diz and Karkeh were used for irrigation, but the old canals have vanished. These waters represent a great source of potential wealth. The Karun resembles our Colorado River. Its flow is about the same, and it too carries a heavy load of silt. The Karun drains distant, snow-covered mountains and has cut a series of magnificent canyons. It flows sluggishly through its flat delta which forms a hot, dry but potentially fertile plain. The river keeps building its delta out into a narrow gulf. Unlike the Colorado, however, the Karun is not dammed or controlled. Its power is unused. Bringing it under control for use would be comparable to harnessing the Colorado, a task that, though incomplete, has cost hundreds of millions of dollars.

I had visited the Gotwan site, where the Karun emerges into the Khuzistan Plain. A dam there would have to compare with the very largest in the United States. A dam of this size, with project canals to use the river's waters, would, in my estimation, cost about $350,000,000. I gave Kashani the figure. He thought at least scores of such dams could be built for that. The sum I had quoted was, I believe, a low estimate of the cost of the Khuzistan Plain development. The Ayatollah was completely unrealistic when confronting technical questions.

Iran is literally full of monuments to this kind of inexperience. Too many projects have been begun but not completed because the money ran out. The need for planning is one of the hardest lessons for those unfamiliar with resource development to learn. Even after two hours of talk Kashani still had a sneaking suspicion that I was overestimating the cost of the dam to cover up other, unstated reasons for refusing his proposed "useful projects."

I described to the Ayatollah some of Point 4's many undertakings in Iran, starting with the jack project. Our deep-water well program, I told him, was providing pure drinking water for villages and small towns. I discussed our peoples' working, through the ministry of education, to improve teacher training and teaching methods. I outlined the aims of the malaria-control project and the seed-improvement program. I mentioned our participation in developing the treatment plant for the Tehran water supply, the Fars Cement Plant and an exhaustive list of our other efforts. Still the Ayatollah held stubbornly to his position that we should do "something substantial." He wondered, he said, whether the United States was really expressing an interest in Iran and her welfare. Perhaps, he went on, all this program should be discontinued.

I had made several efforts to break off our conference. I sensed that the old man was tiring and guessed from the increasing numbers popping in and out of the room that some other appointments were probably being delayed. But each time I made an effort to go, Kashani would motion me back to my seat. At almost one o'clock I heard a considerable commotion. Several men entered.

Someone announced that luncheon was served. I again tried to excuse myself, but Kashani and his friends swept us along to a lower floor of the house. There a table was lavishly set with Iranian foods. I was seated ceremoniously at the Ayatollah's right. The others grouped about. As is usual in Iran, there was a high pile of plates in the center of the table. Before us were stews and barbequed chicken, several pilau and other Persian delicacies. It was one of my very few times at table with Iranians when most of them did not use silverware.

After lunch Ardeshir and I were taken down still another

flight of stairs to a room opening on the lower garden. Here we bade our host adieu. Though it was time for his siesta he said he hated to see us go. There were so many more things he wished to discuss.

The fact that I had called on Kashani, though privately as he had requested, was nevertheless reported in the papers.

The Ayatollah's influence can be understood only in terms of the Iranian devotion to religion. Nothing about Iran stirs a visitor more deeply than the response of the people to religious ceremony. The muezzin call over the rooftops at early dawn is as moving as the pealing of bells over a country churchyard. The faithful practice their devotions wherever they happen to be—on a city street or along a donkey track. They bow their heads completely to the ground, facing Mecca and repeating their prayers. They do not disturb and are not disturbed. Beside a *jube* or a mountain stream I have frequently seen a man wash ceremoniously before prayer, then rise, spread a rug and bow on it to the earth. High and low alike faithfully keep their religious traditions. While much of Iran's great poetry extols fine wine, the Koran's injunction against alcohol is rather strictly observed. At official functions Iranians drink their toasts in pomegranate juice. Rarely is an intoxicated person seen in the streets. The mosques are the finest buildings in Persia. Some, like the great Blue Mosque in Isfahan, are among the most beautiful in the world.

The ceremonies on the day the Shi'as commemorate the martyrdom of Hossein, son of Ali, the Prophet's son-in-law and fourth Caliph of Islam, to whom the Shi'as trace their branch of the faith, are deeply moving experiences for the whole people. Perhaps there must always be a thin edge of fanaticism in any mass response of such magnitude. In 1952 there was a revival of the old practice of marchers beating their own backs with chains. Yet one could feel encouragement in the resentment of the return to the past. The general pleasure in the day was not diminished. The passing in the night of chanting men stirred everyone deeply.

About eighty-five per cent of the Iranians are Moslem. The Armenian Christians make up most of the rest, but there are Jews in the cities. Some Zoroastrians, descendants of the fire worshippers, live near Yazd. There is also a sprinkling of Bahais. The Shi'ites of Persia are of the Imami sect, who believe in the divine inspiration of the twelve Imams. The Shi'a heterodoxy is the official religion of Iran, and some assume that its history was founded there. Only the Eighth Imam lived and died on Persian soil. His tomb at Meshed is the outstanding religious shrine of the country. Pilgrims trek there by the tens of thousands to earn the right, as Meshedis, to wear green turbans.

I found the Moslems inclined to accept Americans without thinking of religious differences. Christians, likewise, were apt to accept the Iranians without being conscious of religion. Devotion is to God, and the use of the name Allah makes Him no different.

In the months following my visit to Kashani it seemed that he was determined to pull Iran down about his ears. He quarreled with almost every public figure. His followers raised new waves of fanatic hate for all that was not Iranian—as they understood the term. While tension was still building Kashani summoned me again.

Since I didn't know his motives, I declined the invitation. It was repeated through a third party but even more anxiously and forcefully. My curiosity was aroused. I agreed to visit him.

On a cold spring morning I again set out to meet Kashani. The address he had given was on the far east side of Tehran. I could not remember ever having been on the street, and we had some trouble finding the house, which opened directly off the street with neither compound nor garden. We were admitted into a cold hallway to wait while servants scampered in a swirl of *chadoras* to find someone to receive us. A young man finally appeared. He was most surprised to see me. After I had explained he said that the Ayatollah was his father-in-law. He had not been told that we were coming.

Well, I thought, Kashani really does want secrecy this time!

The house was unheated. I sat bundled in my overcoat, still chilled, waiting for the Ayatollah. I remembered noting that this room was as crowded with heavy, uncomfortable furniture as the one where we had first met.

A great clattering on the stairs announced Kashani's arrival —at the head of a train of followers. He did not bother to introduce most of them, but one or two I knew.

Before tea was over a second group clattered up the stairs. This one was composed of newspaper photographers and reporters. They were royally welcomed by Kashani, who grabbed my hand, clutched my thumb in his fist and extended his thumb in a gesture strictly for the cameras. The next day all the papers carried pictures. Mr. Warne, director of Point 4 (bundled up in his overcoat, looking very cold), met with Ayatollah Kashani (very chipper in his robe and turban) to discuss common problems. Kashani was evidently on good terms with his guest. The peculiar handclasp made that obvious. Private meeting indeed!

The meeting was short. Getting the pictures taken had apparently been the major objective. Kashani brought up his proposed Khuzistan Plain development. He was not at all in sympathy with my compromise suggestion for a series of planning studies to determine how best to place the lands in the hands of the peasantry.

The dam should be built. There was no more time, he thought, for planning. In any event, the Ayatollah said that he thought Iran's future would be better served if the landlord system were extended to the new lands watered by the Karun. He considered the peasants very poor material on which to build a community.

I mentioned to Kashani the new law for an increase in the farmer's share, which granted the peasants twenty per cent more from the landlord. Under the law they were also to be organized into councils within the villages so that they could do some things for themselves. This law, Kashani said, might be good politics, but it wasn't good policy.

After this conference I did not see Kashani again. He seems to have been a political phenomenon of those hectic days. When General Zahedi became prime minister in August 1953, his administration began preparations for electing the Eighteenth Majlis, since the old one no longer had a quorum. Kashani had no part in these elections. If he gave his mobsters—whom he had intimated to me he did not direct, but who seemed to answer spontaneously his slightest wish—any further directions, they did not obey them. The Ayatollah went abroad to religious places in Iraq and elsewhere. When he returned, he seemed no longer to be a political factor. The supernationalism that had prepared his way was losing force under Zahedi.

Mission/6

"35,000 Reds Fly to Iran"

WHY NOT bring eggs and perhaps even baby chicks from the United States to Iran to improve the scrawny poultry? The men in the Agriculture Division asked this question as the spring of 1952 approached. The peasants own their chickens. Improving the poultry would benefit the poor people directly. We could make a wide impact quickly. Chicks soon become roosters and hens. Their eggs could then be used to carry the program forward in the second year.

The Iranian chicken is a small, wiry, tough little bird. Its eggs are only slightly bigger than a pigeon's, and it doesn't lay many. Nevertheless chickens represent a major source of meat for the country people's austere diet. And four out of five Iranians are country people.

The plan worked out with the Livestock Bongah called for trading a blooded chick for a native chick, a good cockerel for a poor one. Not only would new blood be introduced but the old breeding stock would be diminished at the same time. Dr. E. J. Halbrook, our poultry expert, believed that a simple cross of blood lines, the first cross, would improve the Iranian chicken materially. Repeated crosses, he thought, would probably change Iran's poultry population completely in five years.

No one had had any experience with flying hatching eggs or baby chicks halfway around the world. The distance from San Francisco to Tehran is about the same going either east or west.

A baby chick can remain strong and healthy without being

fed or watered for a little over seventy-two hours after it leaves the egg. Hatching eggs, some experts thought, would remain hatchable for much longer periods before they were set. In theory, therefore, we would have a better chance of success if we imported eggs, since it seemed doubtful chicks could be flown from incubators in Ohio or New Jersey to feeding pens in Tehran within the three-day time limit. Imported eggs could be set in Tehran so the baby chicks would hatch next door to the feeding pens. We decided to bring in 75,000 eggs and to try some experimental flights of baby chicks. Just as well have two strings to our bow.

For several weeks a thousand chicks a week were flown from the east coast. These came through surprisingly well. There were no hitches in plane schedules. Some of the little fellows were several hours over the danger line, but there was no high percentage of loss.

Meanwhile, the Agriculture Division prepared to gather enough incubators for a full trial of the second method. Thirty-five thousand eggs were flow to Tehran and were rushed to incubators all around and about the city. We filled virtually every incubator we could light. After a few days our men candled a sampling of the eggs. To our consternation few of them seemed to be fertile. When the three-week incubation period ended, only about fifteen per cent of the eggs hatched. Sadly we noted that many chicks were weak and some were deformed. Another batch of eggs was on the way. To our horror we had about the same results with it. Somehow the eggs were being damaged en route, either by the change of air pressure at high altitudes or by the cold.

We ordered two large shipments of chicks. The first, of 30,000, was delayed when a chartered plane had motor trouble. The chicks, when they finally arrived, were beyond the seventy-two-hour survival limit. Although the pilot and crew had tried to feed and water them in a hangar at the Cairo, Egypt, airport, many were dead and others seriously weakened. We were understandably depressed when the second chartered plane took off from New York carrying 35,000 New Hampshire Reds just out of the egg.

By this time people at home were aware that something unusual was happening. One New York newspaper facetiously headlined a story about this shipment "35,000 Reds Fly to Iran."

The anxiety with which we awaited that plane at the Mehrabad runway can well be imagined. It appeared on schedule, circled once, landed and trundled up. The motors stopped and the door flung open. Never before had I heard such a concert of chirping and cheeping! Nothing was wrong with the lot. We took the chicks out of the boxes to feed, water and warm them and counted the losses at less than one in a hundred. We had solved the problem, but it was too late in the season to bring any more chicks in 1952. To do the job we planned we would have to repeat the project in 1953. We could make some exchanges with the poultry already flown in. Some brood flocks were started that first year, but not enough.

We sent four hundred chicks from the second batch to Alan McAnlis, a missionary at the Faraman Orphanage at Kermanshah. In offering to help distribute them he had showed a gratifying awareness of our purpose. His family was sitting down to Sunday dinner when they heard an unfamiliar horn at their compound gate. They hurried to greet a Point 4 truck loaded with hungry, thirsty, travel-weary chicks. Mr. McAnlis and his wife unloaded the chicks into a fenced area, counting them as they went. The count reached 397. The trip had been hard on the chicks. Quite a few were unable to stand. Every suitable pan in the kitchen was borrowed to water and feed them.

"I couldn't help figuring the amount of feed those birds would consume in a week," Mr. McAnlis explained later. "And so far as I knew, I was going to have them several weeks. Once earlier we had raised a small batch of chicks with the help of a Point 4 brooder. They were about ten days old when we got them. After seven weeks nobody had come to take any of them away, though I had told everyone about the chicks and offered to trade them any time. Finally our foreman's wife brought up seven scrawny, half-grown chicks in exchange. That started the ball rolling. A couple of weeks later the chicks were gone. But they had eaten my budget out of balance."

McAnlis' first batch of American chicks had been watched carefully, not only by their proud owners but by the owners' neighbors as well. So word traveled quickly when the new chicks arrived.

"Before breakfast Monday one of the workmen told me that several people had come to get chicks," Mr. McAnlis said when he told me about it. "By the time I had taken care of them, there were more folks waiting. Finally I had to ask them to wait until I grabbed a quick bite of breakfast. By the time I got out to the chicken yard again more than twenty villagers were waiting for me. Some of them had hens or roosters under their arms. Others carried baskets of chicks of various sizes. It was a hectic day. I no sooner got one group off my hands than more people arrived. Men and women, boys and girls, from villages near by and several miles away. They came for the American chicks that got so big. Toward evening I tallied up the number of chicks traded off and found we got rid of 354!

"Our own chicken yard is built for about forty birds. We were forced to crowd in there the hundreds of chickens we took in trade. Twenty died from suffocation in that overcrowded pen before morning. The orphan children had a good chicken dinner that day. They ate the trade-in chickens that were big enough that day and many times later. That's one way to cut down overcrowding in the chicken yard!"

Before sunrise the second morning two men from the village across the river were waiting for their chicks. Soon eighteen people had arrived to trade. To the disappointment of those who had brought several chickens Mr. McAnlis had, in order to be fair, to fix a limit of two chicks per person. Before ten o'clock Tuesday every one of the 397 chicks had been distributed to more than ninety different families from seven villages.

In 1953, impressed with the success of the first year's program, we brought 75,000 more chicks to Iran. Many of them were contributed to Point 4 by the heifer project. Some were paid for by the pennies of school children in Ohio. We set up brood flocks at livestock stations in twenty-one different areas, and used the chicks hatched at these stations for trading. It will never again be necessary to bring chicks so far. Good chicks are now being produced all over Iran.

The chicken project gave me an opportunity to become better acquainted with the country people of Iran. I welcomed every chance to learn more about this land to which I had been a complete stranger only a few months before. My already great respect for the history of the country and its people deepened as my knowledge grew.

Archaeologists have said that it may have been in Iran that man first ventured out of the mountains to found settlements based on cultivated agriculture. Mounds of great antiquity dot the plains at the foothills of the Elburz and Zagros mountains. Many isolated communities remain in remote valleys cut off from the rest of the world. There is no proper road, for example, into the Taleghan Valley. Here an estimated 30,000 people live in villages scattered among the fertile flats that separate the dashing streams and rugged peaks. The Taleghan may be the largest of the valleys cut off from civilization except by donkey trails. It has no wheeled vehicles. Traffic moves at a walk, as it must have even before the first settlement of the world was founded. Commerce, of course, is elemental, and life is close to the self-contained subsistence level. The livestock is herded on the surrounding hills, and every tiny plot to which water can be led is farmed by irrigation. The women and the children gather and use in many ways all sorts of wild plants in the valley. The men and boys harvest the vegetation on slopes so steep that the uninitiated would guess that only goats could scale them. They bundle this brush and weed harvest and carry it laboriously to the villages to save against the incredible cold of the high mountain winters. In winter wolves—some residents contend even tigers—driven desperate by the snows at higher levels, invade the villages, kill the great sheep dogs and carry off anything they can. Civilization may have moved down from the valley to encircle the earth, but it has sent few of its trappings back home. Even today the principal export of the Taleghan Valley is promising young men. It is legend that an unusually large number of Mullahs come from the valley. The reason is supposed to be that during the long, idle winters the religious leaders gather the boys and instruct them.

Iran's mountain fastnesses are historically as well as archaeologically significant. In the next valley was the stronghold of Ali Hassan, known to the crusaders as "the old man of the mountain." Ali Hassan held his followers by hashish. He lifted political murder to such a height that the word "assassin" was derived from his methods and time. In this valley too the last fortress held out against the Tartars for 200 years after they had overrun the rest of Iran. Here in 1921 General Zahedi, then the youngest brigadier in the Iranian Army, defeated a Bolshevik army and turned back a modern invasion threat. The general told me the story with great animation when he learned that I planned to visit the Taleghan Valley.

Many a surname in Iran has been adopted from a place name. It was from the Taleghan Valley that Khalil Taleghani got his. The valley was the home of his forefathers. Modern Busheris, Kashanis or Isfahanis may have no knowledge of when their families lived in Bushir, Kashan, or Isfahan. But as a boy Khalil visited his grandfather at the ancestral home in Avonek, one of the little villages in the Taleghan Valley.

Khalil and I had talked for many months about visiting the valley. He had raved about it so much, he said, that his wife longed to see the old places. We decided to get up a small party and go when the snows were off the passes. We assembled a party of eleven. Khalil sent a messenger ahead to round up horses and bring them to the nearest point our jeep could reach. Tents and bedrolls we would take along. We planned to try the fishing in the Taleghan. Khalil thought it might be good.

The valley is not far from Tehran. A rough road leads into the mountains from Abeyek, a hundred kilometers west of the city. It passes through a few villages as it climbs but deteriorates into a donkey path before it reaches the summit of the ridge. From this ridge, to the north, falls the valley of the Teleghan River. The pass must be nearly 8,000 feet high. The Taleghan rises in the high mountains northwest of Tehran and flows west for about thirty-five miles. Finally, cutting breath-taking canyons through the ridges to the north, it joins the Saffidrud and flows into the Caspian Sea, below sea level.

The people of the valley are not literally landlocked. The sturdier and more venturesome make their way back and forth across either the northern or southern ridges, but the excursion is a daring adventure. The great majority of the people born in the Taleghan Valley never leave it. The principal route leading to the outside world is the one we used to enter the valley, up over the southern ridge and down on donkeyback.

As we approached the first village a large crowd of men and boys came up the mountain to meet us. Village elders and Kadkhodas were drawn up at the head of the line. Kadkhodas generally are overseers of the land, and may be group leaders of the peasants or representatives of landlords. A heifer was sacrificed. The villagers welcomed and cheered us. I was pleased to hear one great shout, *"Zendeh-bad Dowlat Americaei"*— "Long live the government of the United States." Point 4 was known even here.

We entered the village through an arch erected over the *kucheh*. Made of poles, it was covered in traditional fashion with the villagers' most colorful rugs. An advance guard of one or two men ran ahead of us, trying to shoo the women and children from their vantage places on the roofs. While we observed few women in the streets, we noticed that those on the rooftops paid little attention to the pickets. Their modesty didn't seem to require them to give up their grandstand seats.

As we walked along, a rude door beside the *kucheh* opened. A hand reached out. Over our path it waved a brazier of charcoal into which *esfand,* an incense, had been sprinkled. The door pulled shut. Someone else was welcoming us and wishing us well. Children tossed roses in our path from doorways and roofs. The valley is famous for its roses. Its people make a good quality rose water. Iranians believe that the rose was first cultivated in their country.

Down a side *kucheh,* now and then, we glimpsed quiet tableaux—young women beating clothes in the *jubes,* a boy prodding along a donkey so laden with hay that he looked like a moving rick. At one door we saw a child playing, and beside him stood—yes—a pair of big, beautiful Point 4 chickens!

Every village along the trail following the Taleghan River was in holiday dress. Each had its similar arch of poles covered with the finest rugs that could be found in the town. In the centers of many of the arches hung mirrors to reflect the evil eye and cause it to frighten itself away. If anyone in the town had such a prized possession, a portrait of the Shah was displayed at the very top of the arch. Sometimes a Koran was suspended as a blessing on the visitors who passed under the arch.

In each village the men and the boys would form two long lines facing each other at the approach to the arch. We visitors dismounted a few hundred feet before we reached the welcoming committee. Grooms would lead our horses around the crowd to the far side of the village. We walked down to meet the committee and stopped, if we could, the sacrifice of a heifer or a sheep.

At every town we listened to a speech or a poem of welcome and received the petitions of the town. "The roads should be improved.... Our bridge was carried away by the spring flood. ... There is no school here.... The roads should be improved. ... The people are sick... We need a bridge to reach our fields. ... The roads should be improved." We appointed one member of our party secretary to carry all of these messages.

And there were thank-yous for the chickens and the visits of the DDT sprayers, who had been through in their fight against malaria.

Ofttimes we found the arch and the reception committee just outside the village gate. Whenever this was true we saw the women standing at some vantage point not far away.

Only at Avonek, where the villagers apparently felt that Mrs. Taleghani, coming to see her husband's old home for the first time, had equal rights with the men, did the women and girls make themselves a part of the reception committee. Here one side of the lane was given over to them. They were dressed in their very best. A short ballet-type skirt was fitted over the upper part of the jeans they normally wore.

These skirts are colorful, useless and very decorative. I saw them in many parts of Iran at such high occasions as weddings. I asked one of my Iranian friends once how they came to be worn in the remote villages. The story he told me is that a Persian king visited Vienna more than a century ago. Of all the new things he saw, he was most impressed by the ballet. He decreed on his return to his capital that the ladies of his court on certain state occasions should wear the ballet skirt. The style was replaced in the court after a few years but, as so often happens, the example was taken up by the higher strata of society.

It gradually spread until it reached the peasant people in the outlands where, as nowhere else in Iran, the ballet skirt remains high fashion today.

At each village, after the formal reception and our walk through the streets, we were invited to have tea with the elders. Usually we sat on a few rugs spread in some grassy spot under the trees. Several men busily attended the samovars. Tea-things and little cakes were laid out. Some fruit was served, usually apples, pears or cucumbers.

Frequently during these teas our hosts, who never participated in them with us, would sit stiffly in rows of straight-backed chairs brought into the fields for the occasion. The hosts were the older men of the village. Here, as elsewhere in Iran, I was struck by the strength and character in the faces of these old peasants. They were endowed with a natural dignity. The tether of their lives may not have permitted them to wander much beyond the confines of their fields, but they had been plunged deeply into living. Their minds were unlettered, but not encompassed. They wore with self-respect the best clothes they had. If one's best clothing were a topcoat this rule dictated that one should wear that topcoat, hot though the day might be. The men of rural Iran generally wear Western clothes for dress—mostly dark-colored suits, patched but clean. For work they wear pajamas in hot weather, but not pajamas for tea.

Along the noisy river now and again we saw an old mill wheel grinding flour. There are no other industries. The people have hand looms in their homes, and they make a few things, some of which they sell around the mountains. Their principal product is a gaily decorated woolen socklike foot covering for winter wear. The valley people make an excellent mast, yogurt, for local use. They also export some cheeses—by donkeyback up the steep trail leading to Samakabad, on the other side of the mountain, and thence by bus to Tehran. Samakabad is five hard hours from the center of the valley, but it is the nearest point buses can reach.

The *kuchehs* of Avonek were squeezed narrow by the mud walls of the houses or compounds on either side. They seemed to be laid out on cowpaths. Some of them were flanked by ditches and shaded by trees. I learned that some curious holes about head high in the well on one side of a *kucheh* were the openings of beehives fastened to the inside of the wall. The air was full of bees, all purposefully going about their business. I wondered how many village boys had been bucked abruptly from their donkeys.

In Avonek a few of the houses of leading citizens were built with balconies opening through the second floor. This was to me the most remarkable thing about the village. I had not seen anything like it before in Iran. The balconies were quite attractive and provided a place for the family to sit in the warm summer evenings.

"My great-grandfather built a house like that," Khalil Taleghani explained. "Now there are several of them in the town."

"Do you know what the name Avonek means?" someone asked me.

"No, I must confess, I do not."

"Literally translated, it means something like 'The town of the houses with balconies.'"

Even here where one felt that our busy Western civilization had never reached, there were unmistakable signs that it had. The doorways were painted with the DDT sign left by our antimalaria sprayers.

And, there were the chickens. Already these big red chickens were becoming common sights everywhere.

Many stories are told in Iran about the attitude of the villagers toward the Point 4 chickens, which usually are called *Asle Chahar* or *Americai*. One of these concerns Warren Silver of our embassy. While on a hike deep in the mountains, he stopped at a mud hut in a hidden valley, hoping for a cup of tea. The householder invited Warren in. He sat cross-legged on the rug while his host's wife got tea glasses out of a corner and poured tea from the pot steaming at a charcoal grate. With his smattering of Farsee Warren made the man understand that he was an American who had just come from Tehran. Voluble with excitement, his host hurried him through his tea, motioning Warren to follow, went to a doorway covered by sacking. The man dramatically drew aside the curtain. In the next room Warren saw two chicks happily scampering about a nest that had been prepared for them.

"*Asle Chahar*," the man kept repeating until he saw that Warren understood.

Then there were the two peasants who appeared at the Hyderabad Station one day, each with four chicks to trade. They explained in Turkee, the language of the North, that they had come by bus from Azerbaijan, a fifteen-hour trip.

When Dr. Halbrook left Iran to go back to the Montana State College at Bozeman in the early summer of 1955, he had the satisfaction of knowing that his poultry project had been successful. By that time there were literally millions of improved cross-bred chickens in Iran. And the breed was being improved by the constant introduction of purebred cockerels, locally raised.

Mission/7

The Thirtieth of Tir

THOSE VIOLENT weeks in July 1952 were a poor time for me to introduce my family to Iran. Edith and the children docked at Beirut, Lebanon, after a nineteen-day trip. The Mossadegh government had fallen several days earlier. It was generally assumed that Dr. Mossadegh would form a new government, but he had not yet selected a cabinet when I left by plane to meet the family at the Mediterranean shore. On July 13, when we arrived in Tehran, there was still no cabinet. Dr. Mossadegh contended that without him no new government could be organized. His price was control of the Army and a delegation by the Majlis of full power. The Shah, unwilling to meet Mossadegh's demands, issued a *firman*, a royal decree, designating Ahmad Ghavam-Es-Sultaneh prime minister. So decisive a move had not been expected.

The designation of a new prime minister, even one as distinguished as Ghavam-Es-Sultaneh, came as a shock to the country. Ghavam was more than eighty years old. He had several times previously been prime minister. When he headed the government under the last of the Khadjar kings, both Dr. Mossadegh and Reza Pahlavi, who later became Shah-in-Shah and founded the present dynasty, served in his cabinet—Mossadegh as minister of finance, the latter as minister of war. He had been prime minister in 1946 when the Russians were finally forced out of the northern province of Azerbaijan after Iran's historic appeal to the United Nations. Immediately after taking office Ghavam made a strong speech declaring that he intended to restore law and order at once.

Unrest became disorder and disorder became riot when the new prime minister failed to obtain Army support for his efforts to combat the mobs. Leaders of the Iran Party, supernationalists and supporters of Dr. Mossadegh, were inciting to violence crowds called out by Kashani. The National Front, which Dr. Mossadegh headed, was never a political party in the American sense. The National Front as an organization did not oppose Ghavam. But some of the elements that sometimes helped to make up the organization did. Except for the Tudeh Party, which had been outlawed as Communistic and foreign-led but which nevertheless was active, there were no disciplined political parties in Iran in that period. There was a multitude of splinter groups, mostly the personal tools of individual politicians. Of these the Iran Party was then the most active. Poor Ghavam, however, had no organization with any form or substance to support him.

To my family, so recently come from the quiet suburbs of Washington, everything in Iran was so new that the rapid build-up of political tension held no great significance. Many of us had become used to fighting in the streets. Now riotous displays disconcerted us because they emphasized that no effective government existed.

On July 21, 1952, the Thirtieth of Tir, 1331, by the Iranian calendar, Dr. Mossadegh's supporters made an all-out push to reinstate him. He continued to contend loudly that without him the government could not function. By nightfall the Shah had formally called the doctor back to power. And he called him on Mossadegh's own terms—full and absolute power for the prime minister.

It was a bloody day. Inflamed mobs fought one another. Some gruesome events transpired. One hospital caring for wounded and dying from an earlier affray was raided. The dead were carried off, hoisted by many hands. Grim leaders headed a marching column bound in furious zeal on further depredations.

Rioters burned newspaper plants. Other mobs set other establishments afire in retaliation. Shops were looted.

In the days that followed the family got used to my setting up an emergency office in the garden of our compound. We put card tables on the porch, placed "out" and "in" baskets on them and tried to maintain at least rudimentary office routines. At four o'clock each afternoon the principal staff officers assembled to report and make plans and to try to decide whether to move the office back downtown the next morning. Edith always served tea at these extraordinary staff meetings. Since Margaret and her dog Cookie were locked in the yard they were often underfoot, but we got a surprising amount of work done despite the informalities.

This was a period of great trial to foreigners in Tehran and other Iranian cities. Antiforeign propaganda was on the lips of most factions. It was largely directed against the British, who were blamed for most of Iran's troubles, but for the first time America and Point 4 were specifically mentioned too. Outside the cities, though, life went on much as though nothing unusual were occurring anywhere in Iran. The villages are not greatly affected by Tehran's convolutions. Here our people and their Iranian co-workers were calmly going about their work. For six weeks, during which riot, confusion and change left government ineffective, Point 4 continued to operate with little loss of efficiency. One reason, of course, was the completion in June of the Cabinet work. The other, equally important, was the nature of the Iranian village.

The Iranian village is without a counterpart in the United States. It is so different from place to place, from rich to poor, from big to small, that it is hard to classify even in Iran. The village is made up of the people who till the soil around it. As the land may be owned, so may a village belong to a landlord. Probably more than forty per cent of Iranian villages are so owned. Thirty per cent more are the property of the Shah or a government agency or a shrine such as that which administers the burial place of the Eighth Imam in Meshed. Ownership of a village does not necessarily carry with it all power over the population—the people are not cattle—but it does vest the right to say who may till the soil. And tillage provides the main source of livelihood to most villagers.

Until quite recently villagers had little to say about the affairs of the village. The Kadkhodah was usually appointed by the landlord. The gendarmes represented some distant, awesome authority—the government. The Mullah was in charge of the mosque, if the village had one, the holy places and the burial ground. He was also the judge.

Iranians say there are 40,000 villages in their country. The figure is a guess; there has never been a census. In Fars Province, where a trial rural census was made with Point 4 help, only a little more than three quarters as many villages were actually found as had been estimated. A village made of mud has little permanence. One need not drive very far along most roads in order to see the husk of one abandoned to ruin. The weather soon melts these down into the earth, though for a decade or more enough walls remain to show that here was once a village.

The peasants prize the adobe of old walls as a sort of fertilizer. Something about baking in the sun, rest of the earth from growing crops, decay of straw in the bricks and, perhaps, the general habit of facing walls to urinate enriches this chosen mud. It is often broken from its clods and scattered over the land. For the most part people leave their villages as a swarm of bees leave a hive—only to establish another colony. The old village site has some fault. A new one seems better. Since it is hard for a villager to re-establish himself in another village where all of the land is already being used, there is not much shifting about by single families. In recent years peasants have been drifting from the villages into the cities.

Tehran has grown from about 700,000 to a present estimate

of 1,200,000 in the years since World War II began. Villagers have dislodged themselves from their villages and have found nooks and crannies in the city. Here they put down tender roots. Since there has been no equal growth of industrial employment in Tehran, grave problems have arisen. From among these dislodged countrymen are recruited the mobs that occasionally sweep through the streets. Whether Tudeh, Kashani or other agitation pulls the trigger the same mass of men at loose ends provides the gun cotton for the explosion that is set off.

But in the villages life is relatively well ordered. It may be short and difficult, and of a gray monotony, but things are done as they have been done and people live together as they have learned to live together for 6,000 years.

Justice William O. Douglas, who has passed on his observations of Iranian rural life in *Strange Lands and Friendly People,* said, "I have not seen a village between the Mediterranean and the Pacific that was not stirring uneasily." I have not traveled so extensively as he. But in Iran I have visited many, many villages. I have deliberately tested the justice's observation there.

If I understand an "uneasy stirring," Justice Douglas is correct. The villages of Iran are not individual powder kegs with lighted fuses. They are not so explosive as the cities. No revolutionary fervor stalks the countryside. These people are not waiting breathlessly for a Moses to lead them out of bondage nor for a Jefferson to crystallize their thinking. They are stirred, however, by an aspiration seemingly now common to all men—the hope of a better future. Ill defined, inarticulated, humbly held, this hope is nevertheless stirring everywhere in Iran.

Point 4 was fortunately offered to the people of Iran at the right time. Only just now, it would seem, after sixty centuries, would this stirring have been found present. Only now are the village people co-operative and ready. Later, if not enough is attempted now to meet the needs so deeply felt, who can guess the results? A sinking back into hopelessness and sloth, no more to be stirred? Or a rising wrath in an awakening giant made unreasoning by denial?

Less than a year from the day on which we opened our headquarters office at Sepah Avenue in Tehran it became clear that rural Iran had accepted Point 4 as its hope. But just as what happened in Tehran in the summer of 1952 had little effect in the villages, so what was happening in the villages went unnoticed in the cities.

The Thirtieth of Tir, in midsummer, came during the time of the most intensive activity in rural Iran. Teacher-training schools were in session. Vital work was being carried on in health and sanitation. Veterinarian teams worked in the mountains with the tribal people. Experimental plantings were being harvested. Chick trading was at its peak. Things were moving.

Ambassador Henderson was kind enough to say, on August 28, "both Iran and the United States are indebted to the labors of Point 4 particularly during the recent crisis." This work, he said, "notably strengthened the friendship between the United States and Iran and furnished incontrovertible evidence of good will on the part of the American people...." Our staff had had its baptism of fire. Its spirit was never higher.

Dr. Mossadegh quickly revised his government once he had won his demands. The rioting was held up as exemplification of the popular will. He made many changes in the Cabinet. The Cabinet Committee, with which we worked, had two new members at its next meeting. Dr. Mehdi Azar replaced Dr. Hessabi as minister of education, and Dr. Saber Farmanfarmayan replaced Dr. Maleki at the health ministry.

Publicly, at least, a great din was made against Ghavam. The fury of the uprising in the streets, regardless of how it had been incited, had been directed against that helpless old man who, though named prime minister, had been given few tools of government. A noisy search was made, but he was not found. Nearly everyone suspected that he had never left his bedroom. A law confiscating all his property was enacted to atone for the lawlessness for which he was declared to have been responsible. After General Zahedi became prime minister more than a year later this law was repealed. Ghavam was free to open his door again, but by then his long life was nearly done.

For about thirteen months from this time, Iran ran downhill. Dr. Mossadegh, trying desperately to hold a hopeless position, began systematically to take apart the country's institutions as counterstrokes to opposition to his policies. First he ordered the Army reduced, redeployed and dispersed. Many officers suddenly found themselves at the end of their careers. Then Iran broke relations with Great Britain. Later the prime minister dissolved the Senate. Then Dr. Mossadegh's supporters—the majority of the membership—resigned from the Majlis, leaving the national legislature totally impotent. Now the minority had no forum in which to raise its insistent questions. Since the Majlis had delegated all of its powers to Dr. Mossadegh before its majority resigned, the country was governed by the prime minister's decree. At the end the Shah himself was under such severe attack that he left the country in tacit protest. Thus he let the people know that they must decide. Throughout this period the tides of violence kept rising, whipped by a frenzy of incitement.

There was a correlation between the extremity of the government programs and the degree of depression resulting from repeated failures to arrive at any solution to the oil problem. Without the oil revenues Iran was short forty per cent of her operating budget and a far greater percentage of her normal amount of foreign exchange. The economy, already at low level, was continuing to fall off. The depths to which it receded would be utterly intolerable in any but an economy close from the first to the subsistence level.

Mob action in July 1952 was accepted as an expression of public opinion. Organized rabble rousing fomented the demonstrations leading to the Thirtieth of Tir. Everyone took for granted that most of the demonstrators were paid. To the democratic mind it was a wholly new idea that this type of public-opinion poll could bring about such radical changes in the government.

By the usual criteria a revolution had taken place. Yet those who were in the villages every day reported remarkably little interest there in the outcome of this clash on which the responsibility for their government depended. The government was not so vital nor so stable a force in the national life as many other influences. Their culture, their religion and, negatively, the ignorance which opens the way for uninformed popular reactions play a more important part in shaping the lives of the villagers.

A common culture, rather than any strong feeling of national unity, binds the Iranians together. Strong as the force of religion is among the people, it does not unite them, for their religion is individualistic. Nor is race the factor. Iran contains a great admixture of peoples. Some Armenian villages settled more than three centuries ago by Shah Abbas the Great still hold apart and only grudgingly accept such tokens of amalgamation as domes copied from the mosques on their churches, but they mount crosses on the domes! Language provides no cohesion, for the people are multi-tongued and neighboring tribes may not understand one another.

It is the culture that lends unity, and the apex of its expression is found in poetry. The architectural beauty and fame of the blue-domed mosques, the workmanship, design and color of Persian carpets, the delicate tracery wrought by the silversmiths, the color and distinction of the fine tile, the miniatures, the mosaics —all these are considered important expressions of a common and glorious heritage. But not one is on a plane with poetry.

Saadi, Ferdowsi and Hafaez have places of honor and respect in Iran to which even Shakespeare could not aspire among us. Omar Khayyam, the only Persian poet known to most English-speaking people, the Iranians will admit was good, but not among the best.

"You know," they will explain, "the English translator, Fitzgerald, who prepared for you the *Rubaiyat* of Omar Khayyam, was more of a poet than Khayyam himself. No English translator has done justice to our best."

The highest compliment one may pay to an Iranian friend would be to call him a poet. Whether he writes or not, he will undoubtedly be pleased. One who fancies himself sensitive to fine writings will not consider such a compliment frivolously given. He will accept it as an indication of esteem, paid to one recognized as a marcher in the main column of Iranian cultural advancement.

Having learned this much about Iranians' pride in their poetry, I understood the reasoning of a village council in the town of Destgerd-of-the-Cucumbers. The mayor presented a petition asking for help in constructing a school.

"Destgerd has no school," the petition said. "Destgerd needs a school, especially since Destgerdi came from here."

We were standing in the shade of a mud wall, where the mayor and his committee had met us. The *kucheh* was too narrow to admit a car.

Dr. Moghadam whispered to me that Destgerdi was a minor poet of about 200 years ago. Of course with such a tradition this somnolent village and its few hundred unlettered farmers felt a special obligation. A school might uncover another poet among the urchins following the donkeys to the fields or splashing in the *jube*.

But pride in culture, we learned, is not a strong enough force by itself to persuade a people to advance their general living standards, and lack of a government held stable by political unity strengthens the very foundation of movements such as Point 4 and the Shah's land reform. These are washed by strong, fitful tides of individual ambitions, jealousies, suspicions and fears when offset by no underlying swell of common national purpose or destiny.

I came to have a deeper understanding of the dangers stemming from propaganda designed to undermine our work. Deliberately inflammatory, it was designed to accumulate and some day, within a mob, to burst into flames that would consume us. Agitation needed to convince no one, certainly not the majority, nor even a large number. Its only purpose was to prepare a background for the carefully incited fury in the streets.

Some of the propaganda stories were amusing. On September 25, 1952, *Besuye Ayandeh,* a Communist-influenced newspaper, reported a press conference of mine as follows: "On Monday, Mr. Warne held a press conference at his office. The purpose of the conference was to show that Point 4 was helping Iran, but Mr. Warne did not say that they have come for imperialistic and military purposes. He did not say that giving aid was only an excuse for carrying out other mischievous aims."

The reporter was right, I had not said any of these things. He had simply reported nothing of what I had said.

Of the 101 newspapers publishing in Tehran, no more than three or four were even trying to be objective. Most of the rest were openly for sale to promote any point of view or conduct any form of blackmail. There would have been no limit to confusion, but three conditions mitigated it. Paper was scarce, editions were small and most people could not read. Any number of times various newspapers offered me their support for very small amounts of money or a little newsprint. I refused all such offers. My refusals always brought the threat, often carried out, to attack Point 4.

After the heights of emotionalism reached during July 1952 and in view of the number of verbal attacks made on foreigners, I was encouraged when six members of the Majlis came to me for long conferences on Point 4 programs almost immediately after Dr. Mossadegh's reinstatement. One of my callers was Motamed Demavandi from the city of Pahlavi in Guilan Province. A few days earlier he had raised his voice against Point 4 on the floor of the Majlis, in one of the few instances in which this had been done.

Ettela'at, leading newspaper in Tehran, reported the speech as follows: "Speaking of Point 4, Deputy Demavandi said, 'I have no idea as to what Point 4 is doing. All I know is that it has done nothing. If it is a propaganda organization it had better stop its operations. If it really means to do anything it must conform its activities to our needs.'" When Mr. Demavandi left my office after our conference he said he was moved to apologize and urged me to come to his town as his guest.

The Demavandi statement in the Majlis attracted attention in the United States. Several editorials asked whether our work was appreciated abroad. These American editorials, of course, were reported back to Iran. They made members of the government and other Iranians nervous, and we soon received a blizzard of appreciative statements. At about this time Dr. Mossadegh and I met again. He expressed gratitude for the malaria control project, which was in full swing at the time. I twitted him about his early tarantula comparison.

"I remember, Mr. Prime Minister," I said, "that one time you said Point 4 was like an Iranian tarantula—it jumps up and down and scares people, but doesn't bite."

Chuckling, he answered, "Now, Mr. Warne, we can say it has taken a little bite."

The anti-American and anti-Point 4 phases of the Tudeh agitation soon petered out. Our staff reported only one untoward incident in any village. Someone threw a rock at an audio-visual equipment truck of the Tehran regional team one evening in Yantabad Village. The mayor suggested that the team leave and not come back. The truck was to show a health picture and introduce a water cleanup campaign. Because a member of the health team was ill, no advance contact had been made in this village. H. A. Mathieson, then regional director, said that forty-nine other visits to surrounding villages had been made in the same week, several of them by the same motion-picture wagon. No other incidents had been reported. In Isfahan that week our teams made twenty similar visits. Here is a routine report of one of them written by K. David, Iranian technician:

On the third of August I went to the village Abar for film showing. On my arrival I met the chief of the village and arranged with him about the place and the show.
At 8 P.M. I started with the films "Dysentery" and "Cleanliness Brings Health" in the presence of about eight hundred women and eight hundred men and as usual before starting Mrs. Shrecer [a nurse] explained fully about the films. After the show I asked them if they had any questions, it will be answered and explained to them, but they requested that the film "Dysentery" to be repeated. So I showed the film again and finished at 10 P.M.
The people of the village were very thankful for the D.D.T. spray. They appreciated the results of it.

At this time Jonathan and June Bingham visited us from Washington. Jack was then deputy director of TCA. His work and his book *Shirtsleeve Diplomacy* have left deep impressions on our technical co-operation programs. The Binghams were well received by the Iranians. Though they had been several weeks on the road, they were ready to go right out into the field to see what really went on, despite the fact that the Thirtieth of Tir was not a month past. We took them to Isfahan and packed every hour of their visit.
On the night of August 24 we attended a showing of films at Falarbarjan Village, about twenty kilometers from Isfahan. Four or five hundred men and women, carefully segregated, sat on the hard ground for an hour and a half to see the two films and to hear the explanations that accompanied them. One film dealt with the fight against locusts; the other was about the importance of clean village water supplies. The crowd was intensely interested and better behaved than any American movie audience I

had ever seen. The viewers reacted audibly even to minor dramatic effects.

The film on water supply had been made in a village like Falarbarjan. Though slow-paced and crammed with informative monologue, it was especially well received. The introductory talk by a Point 4 Iranian sanitarian who described the film and told the audience what to look for was followed closely even by the several ten- or twelve-year-old boys who sat near us. After the picture had been shown, an Iranian public health nurse lectured to drive home the points it made. The villagers listened to every word. It seems to me the best way to appreciate the power of the motion picture is to sit in an audience that is seeing one for the first time. We talked about the experience all the way back to town, riding over rough roads, through dust so thick we could taste it.

Jack Bingham had seen some of the recent American editorials, and I had shown him a few of the thank-you letters our office was now receiving. We had discussed before whether we had the right to expect expressions of gratitude for our work.

"The only way these people can show their appreciation is to come to the show, sit through it twice and listen to the lectures," I pointed out.

"They're the ones we're trying to help," Jack replied, "and they are inarticulate."

As I bounced and coughed I thought, Their voices must be heard in what they do. They will be eloquent through their acceptance of new ways. When the program is appraised its acceptance by the people will be a sounder measure of its worth than the propagandist's belittling or the official's kind words of appreciation.

Six Farsa to Shalamzar

WHEN WINTER approaches, the nomadic Bakhtiari people move from the high Zagros Mountain fastnesses near the Khurang Tunnel, over Yellow Mountain to the warm desert foothills and the plains of Khuzistan. They were just beginning their autumn trek in October 1952 when I visited the area. I was en route to the tunnel, which, with Point 4 help, was then nearing completion.

It would be hard to find anywhere in the world a more colorful spectacle than the Bakhtiari migration. Their distinctive tribal dress, their great herds, flocks and clans, their picturesque camps and their complete good nature make one want to join this people on the move.

One of the men, who stood leaning a little against the wind, his black, wide-bottomed trousers flapping around his ankles, told me he would reach Mansurelaman, his winter quarters, in thirteen days. The women, some of them carrying babies in wooden cradles strapped to their backs, were herding donkeys, horses, oxen and cows. The animals were all laden with paraphernalia—a few chickens, a sheep-dog pup and, here and there, a little toddler who could not otherwise keep up with the march.

The older children urged the sheep and goats along at some distance off the trail. They avoided the roads and paths to seek a little grass farther afield. Shaggy, fierce dogs with their ears clipped to provide less hold in a fight herded strays back into line. The pack animals all wore bells to urge them to step along. Each man and every beast carried something. One teen-age girl bore across her shoulders a wooden plow, long tongue, single-

Six Farsa to Shalamzar

tree and all. The women wore all their necklaces and trinkets and several layers of clothing—all they had—since that was the easiest way to carry them. It was only the first or second day on the road for those we saw. The holiday atmosphere was strong, especially among the young ones.

The nomads number nearly one fourth of Iran's whole population. They comprise many tribes, of which a few—the Ghashghai, Bakhtiari, Kurds and Turkomen—are very large and constitute political units to be reckoned with. All the tribes have now been pacified, but many of the older tribesmen once fought in independent armies against the central government. Some of the younger bloods would not be averse to doing so again. These people hold strong loyalties to their tribes, loose-knit, cumbersome, tumbleweed organizations that they are.

The government has few programs that can reach these wandering people. They refuse to be tied to clinic buildings, schoolhouses and the clutter of civilization. They leave all dealings with the government to the tribal khans, who sometimes resemble mountain kings. Occasionally groups of tribespeople settle down in villages and abandon the nomadic life, like crystals precipitated out of a saturated solution. The khans explain that if their people could make a living on the land available to them they would all settle down, but, as things stand now, the treks are necessary. This is probably true, but there is still an infectious excitement about the trek that thrills all but the very old and the very young.

These tribes are not just tides of people ebbing and flowing over the landscape. They are not indiscriminate about moving into the high mountains or the low valleys to which they journey with the seasons. Each tribe's paths of migration are well known. And, similarly, the individual clans within the tribes have well-recognized summer and winter ranges, high or low. These patterns of geographical fixation were first called to our attention at the Khurang Tunnel. A Bakhtiari subchieftain called on us to complain that the tunnel had dried up a few springs that watered one of the pastures used by his clan. We told him that some of the water from the tunnel would be available to his people only a few thousand yards from their usual summer pasture.

"No," the man said, "We cannot consider using that side of the draw. It belongs to another clan."

Our engineers had to work out a way to divert enough water higher up the draw to refill the old water hole.

The Bakhtiari tent is typical of those used by most of the tribes. It is low, with one side slanting into the prevailing wind and a flaring opening opposite. The dark-brown sides are made of long strips of mohair woven on crude looms stretched flat on the ground. Piled inside are bags of grain to be ground for bread—usually the product of a field planted and cultivated on the summer range—sheepskins used as beds, pack saddles and other paraphernalia. The women cook over outside fires. Usually a litter of pups, a calf or two, a few chickens and, perhaps, a lamb or kid too weak to follow the flock stay with the children in the shade near the front flap.

We constantly received requests for special projects for the tribal people. The government had recently set up a special agency to deal with the problems of the tribes. The Iranian ministries now extended some services to tribesmen. Point 4 has cooperated in most of these and has assumed the major leadership in some. Our staff devised some special projects, among them a veterinary program and an educational program to serve nomads.

Dr. Glen Gagan of Utah designed what we came to call the nomadic school. Its equipment included a tent, special little desks for the pupils to hold on their laps, a set of books and teaching materials. There was even a small blackboard. The entire school made just one camelload for the march. Young men from the tribe received special teacher training. Eighty-four of these tent schools moved with the Ghashghai tribe the first year. I visited one on the day it first opened. It had been set up in the Ghasgouli Bozorg Valley. In the circle of squat, flaring Ghashghai tents the little school stood up like a steeple. About a dozen boys from six to fourteen years of age sat cross-legged on a rug. Each held his boxlike desk. Eagerness was on every student's face.

The khan said simply, "It is the first school we have ever had."

The veterinary service had been unable to move into the field before Point 4 came to Iran. Dr. Hendrik Verselus, our first veterinarian technician, found that anthrax was killing large numbers of sheep in the mountains. Tribal flocks were also plagued with intestinal parasites and liver flukes, which kept sheep and goats in poor condition, if they lived. Dr. Verselus proposed mobile teams to teach tribesmen how to treat their sheep. His suggestion was enthusiastically put into operation. Like Kentucky hill people, who sometimes resist the advances of government agents because they might be "revenooers," the mountain men of Iran were at first slow to accept at face value the offers of the government. The veterinarians might be tax collectors. But persuasion finally got the tribal shepherds to try their wares. Veterinarians could now move out of their offices and go by jeep or horseback to areas where they could serve most effectively. While some of the tribesmen were skeptical, most of them were very practical about the sheep doctor. Within a short time, some learned to use the vaccination syringe. Many were soon able to mix the medicines and dose the sheep themselves.

I asked a Bakhtiari near Yellow Mountain whether he had taken his sheep to be treated.

"No," he said. "If Allah wishes the sheep to be well, they will not get sick."

Several of his fellows protested. "Little worms cause the sickness," they explained. "It is not Allah's will that kills the sheep."

Demonstrations and education are slowly overcoming the old fatalism.

The Veterinary Bongah, inspired by the co-operative project, took a new lease on life. Its enthusiasm grew by leaps and bounds. Charts showed that the numbers of livestock treated were advancing in geometrical progression. In the fall of 1953 Dr. A. H. Ardalon, director of the Livestock Bongah, and I visited areas in which the tribesmen were treating their own sheep. In a dishlike valley about five miles across I counted two-score flocks awaiting their turn to come through the chute at the temporary veterinary station.

In the Ghashghai country in Fars Province bandits still roam the hills. They swoop down on the roadways and surround unwary motorists. Usually they abscond with the vehicle and with the clothing they strip from its occupants. On one occasion in 1953 a jeep carrying a veterinarian team from our Shiraz regional office was taken by such a band. About twenty men armed with war clubs and a few guns surrounded the jeep. The unfortunate team was made up of Iranians.

"You can't do this to us," one said. "This is a Point 4 jeep."

"Ah, you are Point 4?" the leader asked.

"Yes, we have been out in the mountains treating flocks."

"Oh, then you have the little pills they give the sheep?" the bandit asked.

"We have made a long trip, and there are not many left."

"Well," said the bandit, "give us the pills and you may go on."

From Isfahan to Shalamzar the road climbs through the foothills of the Bakhtiar mountains. Here and there it passes through vineyards and fields. Sometimes it runs along the banks of irrigation ditches. But mostly it winds through the desert. We were taking this road deep into the summer range of the Bakhtiari to visit an isolated valley.

"How much farther?" we asked.

"Six *farsa*" was the answer—six times as far as a donkey can walk in an hour.

Six Farsa to Shalamzar

And again we asked, as the jeep ground slowly over a talus slope, "How much farther?"

"Six *farsa*" came the laconic retort. It was to say, "Who knows?" None of the distances is ever measured.

Another time, as we bumped along a donkey path, seeking the river crossing between Shustar and Dizful in the Bakhtiari winter range, we shouted to a peasant plowing in his field.

"How far to the river crossing?"

"It is a long way," he shouted back.

"Have you ever been there? How far?"

"Yes, I was there."

"Well, how far would you think it is?"

The man had come near and stood gazing off into the distance in the direction we were going.

"Afoot it is about thirty kilometers," he said finally. "On a good horse not much over twenty. In that thing," he added, turning admiringly to our jeep, "it will probably be no more than fifteen."

But to us that day the way to Shalamzar seemed endless. The dust caked on the backs of our jackets and discolored our necks and hair. We made ourselves uncomfortable holding our breaths to avoid inhaling the dust at especially bad places in the road. Then more often than not, we found we must gulp some down anyway.

"How far?"

"Well, I should say about six *farsa* to Shalamzar."

At last the trail tortuously climbed a high ridge. Suddenly there opened before us a magnificent view of a long, flat valley a thousand feet below. A late afternoon sun slanted across the peaks of the Zagros Divide and filled half the valley with gold. Blue dusk was already deepening on the western side.

"Ah, Shalamzar."

And then we saw the manor house, surrounded by a few trees in a tiny village. Wreathed in misty smoke, it rose stately above the flat, checked fields. As the first evening lights flickered on, it seemed eerily misplaced in this valley, among these mountains, in this century.

"Ah, Shalamzar." Jamshid Samsan, our host, was speaking, "Mr. Warne, you would not think me a sentimental man."

No, I thought, I would not. Unusually tall and bronzed by his hours outdoors, Jamshid, who dressed in English shooting togs, was quick to spot and accurate to shoot the game that roamed these rugged mountains. I would not have thought him a sentimental man.

"Well," he said, "the great house of Shalamzar . . . It almost makes me cry to see it again when I have been long away."

"It's his ancestral home," Ardeshir explained to me. "His people tend their flocks in this valley. Oh, there will be great excitement in Shalamzar tonight. The master comes home."

It took longer than I would have thought to wind down that mountainous road into the valley. But finally we turned into a corridor of trees and entered the village which served Shalamzar. Men and boys shouted from doorways and ran after us a way.

The old guard who swung the gate opening the way into the great garden of Shalamzar was chuckling. "The master comes home."

Laid out in fine proportion, the formal garden held the manor house as a setting holds a jewel. Rippling streams pouring into a pool, and graveled walks and drives led to the door. The broad-faced manor house, whose high pillars rose from ground to roof, had, in Persian style, an unimposing ground-floor entrance. Here were rooms for the servants and overseers. On the second floor were the manor hall, the family quarters and the guest rooms, each of which opened on one of the wide porches running from end to end of the building on either side.

A stand and some basins stood on one porch at the head of the stair. Another old servant offered soap and poured water from a copper ewer. Here we scrubbed off the first layer of dust.

A few other guests had arrived before us. Several had not seen each other for many months, so there was much talking and laughing and catching up on news. I was shown to my room. There a small bed had been set up for my son Rob, then fifteen, who had arrived in a second jeep. School had not yet started in Tehran and he was taking advantage of a chance to see Iran with me.

Seeming to read my thoughts, my host said, "This is not a European house. It has no bathroom. The servants will bring warm water and basins when you need them. But on such a night as this, after so long a ride in the dust and heat, you will want to see our bath."

He clapped his hands and a servant dressed in wide-bottomed Bakhtiari trousers and brimless domelike tribal hat appeared carrying several big towels. Our host spoke briefly to him in Farsee and the man set off, motioning us to follow. We went along the porch and down the stairs to the garden. It was dark by now. The servant carried a lantern, which made flashing shadows along the narrow paths.

The servant led us through a door in the compound wall to a room used to store seed. Beyond that was a sheepfold, warm and heavy with good animal smells. The sheep and lambs plunged about to make a way for us. Beyond the next door was a marble-floored room with benches and shelves on either side of a door opening onto a broad, descending hallway. Down this hall, at several levels, I could see vats of steaming water. A real Persian bath.

Rob and I decided that we were expected to take off our clothes at the top level, wash our feet in the first vat and continue down to the deep, steaming pools below. The water in the bottom pool was deep enough to come to Rob's chin, but it was too warm for long sitting. The only light came from a gasoline lantern, but it was reflected from white-tiled walls. The place was brilliant. I remembered that our host had said his bath had only one innovation, a shower at the end of the line. It was icy cold.

A hunt had been organized for the following morning. When we returned to the house we saw a dozen or more of Shalamzar's Bakhtiari overseers sitting cross-legged in the cavernous rooms near the stairway on the lower floor. They were cleaning their guns, preparing for the next day's game. A huge charcoal brazier threw a red glow on their faces. In pale lantern light they looked as formidable as a knot of plotters in an Italian opera.

Back upstairs we found the hall a scene of great activity. Eight or ten retainers, all male, hurried back and forth between the dining hall and the kitchen with platters of food. The kitchen was on the other side of a door in the wall halfway to the end of the garden. The American colonial practice of keeping the kitchen at arm's length from the house is still followed in Iran when meals are prepared on open hearths—for the same smoky, smelly reasons.

The table was beautiful. The china was fine and old. The silverware was antique. By dinnertime, nine o'clock, so many of the clan had gathered that it would have been impossible for all to be seated. But it is customary at such large dinners for the guests to stand about the table. Sometimes one picks up a plate and moves across the room to talk to another guest, returning to the table for additional helpings. Except that I can never manage very well eating with a fork in my right hand and a plate in my left, I find a great deal to recommend this procedure, so like the American buffet. On the table were pilau and *fessenjen,* kabobbed chicken, roast lamb, flat breads of several thicknesses, mast and *duq,* a thinned yogurt usually served from a large bowl with chopped parsley and cucumber slices floating on the surface. Relishes included dill pickles and onions and large slices of Persian melons and cucumbers. For those who might not like

Six Farsa to Shalamzar

Persian food there were sausages and prepared cheese from the United States.

At Shalamzar, as in so many of the Iranian houses I'd visited, I found the carpeting the most outstanding feature of the *décor*. Shalamzar's carpets were made in the village in a private factory supervised during her lifetime by the lady of Shalamzar, Jamshid Samsan's mother. Though the furniture was not fine, some of the knickknacks, the ancestral portraits and the beautiful silken quilts were remarkably lovely.

This had been a long, hard day. After dinner we went back into the great hall for brandy and the thick Turkish coffee I never learned to like. Almost at the first mention of the hunt planned for early next morning, the party broke up. At Shalamzar's altitude even in the early fall the nights are chill. Old Iranian houses have no heating facilities so I was glad for the four-inch pile of blankets and quilts on the bed into which I scrambled as quickly as I could.

The noise of a truck grinding its way through the garden awakened me at early dawn next morning. My first reaction was surprise that a truck could have been brought over the trails we had followed. It backed up to one of the open rooms at the lower floor. A servant brought me a basin and ewer, and as I shaved on the porch I watched the Bakhtiari subkhans load the truck with tents, carpets and other gear for our noonday camp. From my porch I also saw the beaters ride off on fine horses. They looked like the spearhead of an advancing army leaving a bivouac, armed and ready.

It was late morning before we reached the hunting grounds. On the way we passed a number of villages. We had not seen nearly all the valley from the ridge the night before. It opened wide to the north and east. The valley tribe had been settled here for generations, depending on irrigation from the streams.

At last we saw half a dozen colorfully marked tents pitched on a long slope. Our camp had tents for lounging, a big, open one with a long, protruding flap for a kitchen and a great one for a dining hall. Other smaller tents were scattered here and there. The beaters had staked their horses in a string. Several of the guests were admiring them. I tried one, a beautiful black stallion, but I found that he neither knew English nor appreciated my western cowboy touch. Many Iranian horses seem smaller than one knowing their bloodlines would expect. But there are a number of fine stables of Turkoman Arabians, and now and then a horse fancier spies one that thoroughly lives up to his expectations. There were several such really excellent horses in this group.

The subkhans who were acting as beaters for the party rode into the far hills. We took jeeps up a draw in a quartering direction. In a saddle between two mountains we came upon a string of blinds about waist high, built of stones piled on one another. We had to repair the sections that had collapsed since the last hunt.

Before our party dispersed, the host repeated the rules of the hunt. All hunters were to stay behind their blinds. Once situated, we were forbidden to talk or make any noise. There was to be no shooting until the game drew near. If an animal approached, the men in the blind nearest it would, of course, have first shot.

We paired off and headed for the blinds, taking canteens of water with us. The sun was by this time beating down, and we knew we might have to wait for hours.

Jamshid Samsan and I picked a blind near the center of the string. It didn't need much repairing. At that altitude hoisting several tons of rock didn't appeal to either of us. We squatted down cross-legged behind the blind and laid out our guns. I had a very fine Belgian shotgun which one of the Samsans had lent me, and a short-barreled rifle that belonged to Ardeshir.

An hour passed. All the blinds were by this time completely

repaired. Every hunter had disappeared. Rob, I knew, was in the blind just to my left, and a little higher on the mountainside. He was armed with a .22-caliber target rifle I had given him for Christmas several years before. The subchieftain who accompanied him had an excellent reputation as a hunter, but could not speak a word of English. I knew there would be very little talking in that blind.

We waited well into the second hour. Jamshid dozed off. My eyes were tired from scanning the great, rocky mountainside. Several times I thought I saw something move, but what I took to be moving specks out on the mountain were only shadows formed as the changing light struck the peculiarly shaded rocks. I still watched carefully.

Down the mountainside came a pair of wolves, a huge male leading. The female leaped and trotted after. We had really come after gazelle and mouflon. The wolves, more canny and cautious than other game, were probably leading a general flight before the beaters. Apparently no one else had seen them. When they were within a few hundred yards I awakened Jamshid and pointed them out to him. He became as excited as I. We loaded our shotguns with heavy buckshot. The wolves came straight toward us. Jamshid jumped up and took two quick shots at the male. The wolf was hit, but loped past us. The female stood a moment, transfixed, then turned to flee. Too late.

I heard firing from several blinds now and wondered whether some other game offered. The male wolf had made his way toward the top of the mountain to our rear. He was hopelessly out of range. Puffs of dust kicked up in his wake as my bullets urged him across the slope.

All the hunters stood about, waving their arms. No other game appeared. We had frightened it clear out of the country with our fusillade at the wolves. We looked up and saw the beaters making their way down the mountainside. They said they had seen many gazelles and a few mouflon. When we asked where they had gone the beaters simply shrugged. One said, "The other way."

Two men insisted on taking a jeep to see if they could find the big wolf. I didn't see how a fatally wounded wolf could possibly lope up and across a mountainside. But after forty minutes they brought him back. My shots couldn't have made any of the marks on his coat, but Rob's .22 had evidently nicked him in the neck.

Iranian hunts are more than merely sport. For instance, our bag of two wolves in an hour would save as many sheep as an hour's work by the veterinary team on its way to this valley. Not that we had the protection of sheep in mind when we set out.

Back at camp a magnificent lunch had been laid out. Kabobbed lamb and gazelle which some beater had thoughtfully saved from an earlier hunt. We stretched out on carpets for siestas or sat on pillows in the shade of one of the tents. Someone started strumming a guitar. The music died suddenly in a great uproar from another tent, where many of the Bakhtiari sat about cleaning their rifles and shotguns.

"This is a really hot political argument," Ardeshir explained. "They're the Bakhtiari going against Dr. Mossadegh."

The loud debate continued. Ardeshir rolled to his side and leaned on his elbow, listening. "Some of them are for the government," he said simply. "But most of them are for the Shah and dead set against Dr. Mossadegh."

I recalled this dispute months later, when a Bakhtiari chieftain went to war against the Mossadegh government. He led a band of armed men partway down these mountains. An Army task force met him. I learned little more of the action but I did discover that some of the men who had argued in the tent that hot afternoon were in the chieftain's band.

Night fell before we returned to the garden of Shalamzar. One jeep lagged far behind. We were gathered in the great hall explaining away our bad luck to those who didn't make the hunt when it finally straggled in. One of the brothers Samsan rushed into the hall carrying a two-foot sword, a black teapot and a few other trinkets.

"Where on earth did you get those?" someone demanded.

"I took them from a robber," he said, still visibly excited.

He had trailed our procession, he explained, in order to help if anyone had trouble. As he passed through a village perhaps seven miles back down the road a peasant had flagged him down, shouting, "I've been robbed."

Mr. Samsan took the man into his jeep. Badly shaken, the peasant explained that the robber had threatened to slit his throat with a sword. He had stolen the poor man's donkey and his water jug. Mr. Samsan forced his jeep across the fields and through the ditches. Not far beyond the place in the desert where the robbery had occurred the headlights pinpointed a man with two donkeys.

As the jeep closed in, Mr. Samsan rose to his feet and shouted the robber to a halt. He trained his rifle on the man.

"My peasant says you robbed him and that the donkey there on the left is his," the lord of Shalamzar shouted. "I have a rifle. Do not move."

The robber stood transfixed. The men in the jeep could see the sword shining at his belt. "Don't shoot," he screamed. "Don't shoot. I'll return everything I've taken."

"Shall I kill him?" the lord asked his peasant. "He's the robber all right."

"No," the peasant said, "He will give back my donkey. It isn't necessary to shoot him."

"Leave the things in a pile there by the ditch," Mr. Samsan commanded. "If you ever come back to a village of Shalamzar I shall kill you."

The robber ran into the wilderness leaving everything he carried behind. The peasant quickly identified his small possessions.

He took them and both donkeys. Still lying on the ground were the sword, the blackened teapot, and the few other trifles that Mr. Samsan was now showing about the great hall. With mock ceremony, he presented the sword as a trophy to one of the guests.

What affected me most about this incident was the unquestioning acceptance by peasant, robber, Lord Samsan and now his guests of the feudal proprietor's absolute authority within his demesne. To my twentieth-century Western mind this came as a shock.

I do not mean to be stuffy about this ancient system, which still prevails in about a third of Iran. Feudalism once covered most of the civilized world, but it has been superseded in most places by governments allowing more general participation.

The lords of Shalamzar were exceptionally kind and hospitable to me. I do not mean to imply even the slightest criticism of them. Their concern for their villagers is sincere. They have been educated in the best European schools, and they take their responsibilities at Shalamzar seriously. On that evening in the great hall at least one of them strongly and cogently argued for Dr. Mossadegh's recently instituted reform to increase the farmer's share of the landlord's profit. The prime minister had decreed that landlords pay from their share an additional twenty per cent to the peasants. Half of the increase would go to the individual peasant sharecropper. Half would be credited to a council elected by the villagers. Council funds would be used on projects designed to improve the community in which the peasants lived.

As an outsider I had thought my view of this very significant step would be more objective than the landlords'. I did not think them likely to support it, since it was well designed to hasten the day when the feudal system would disappear. It would create in villages an institution, the council, which eventually could provide the leadership, guidance and direction that were the only remaining justification for the landlords' existence.

But in the gentility of this drawing room all recognized and few disapproved of the fact that the ancient order was crumbling under its own weight. Many centuries had passed this isolated valley by, and, except for the Samsan brothers and a few of their friends who had come from abroad, only a handful of the thousands of valley people had ever been beyond the crest of the ridges on either side.

The major-domo of Shalamzar had been to Isfahan. He had heard of Point 4 too. He caught me alone and asked if I could not give him a job in the Isfahan regional office. To him, as to people everywhere in Iran, Point 4 looked like an avenue of hope leading into the future.

Mission/9

Yankee Go Home

This is not the story of the Iranian oil controversy. If it were, someone else would have to tell it. But just as the petroleum problem figured in the developing crisis that in 1951 had taken me to Iran, so it touched the program later from time to time.

The presentation on August 30, 1952, of the joint Truman-Churchill note proposing a friendly settlement of the Iranian oil problem was undoubtedly the biggest and most significant news in Iran in that period. Dr. Mossadegh had just reorganized his government after the July overturn. At the time it was clear to us that the definite reaction to this note would express the new official and popular reaction to Point 4 in Iran. Flat rejection of the proposal would not mean flat rejection of Point 4, of course, but it would end the salubrious climate in which our program had prospered. Settlement of the oil dispute was an obvious prerequisite to any long-range success of Point 4 or any other constructive program in Iran.

Hopes raised by the note were dashed when the Mossadegh government rejected it. In late autumn the British yielded to pressure and closed their embassy. There was a rather sad little picnic at Karadj to bid good-by to George Middleton, the chargé.

This was the season of portents. General Zahedi on the floor of the Senate had voiced some disapproval of the Mossadegh policies. The prime minister, in the midst of a conference on some other subject, turned to me and said he felt that Ardeshir Zahedi should not work in Point 4.

Yankee Go Home

"He is using his position in a co-operating agency for political purposes," he said.

"He has struck my father in his most sensitive spot," Ardeshir said when I told him what had occurred. Knowing something of the closeness between father and son, I knew this was true. It was a sad parting. Ardeshir insisted on going, but asked to be put on indefinite leave without pay. "I'll still have a tie to Point 4," he said. That is the way we arranged it. Opposition to General Zahedi became implacable and firm. Soon he had to take refuge in the Senate chamber for his own safety, though in doing so, as it turned out, he imperiled the Senate itself.

The withdrawal of the Bristish, against whom the full force of the general xenophobia had been turned, was apparently the signal for the beginning in earnest of "Yankee Go Home."

Point 4 was selected as the key target of the anti-American attack. A Tudeh newspaper called *Baba Adam (Mr. Man)* led off:

"The TCI (Point 4) lady typists will make friends with several Iranian men, and not just one, to improve 'stock breeding.'" The article included more suggestive and scurrilous items. It ended by saying that Point 4 would allow only papers that published news favorable to it to get newsprint. "More guns and tanks," the article declared, "will be sent to Iran."

This drew immediate replies. On December 26, 1952, *Iran-e-ma* said: "But we do not care for the Communist Tudeh party and its papers because it is clear that they are agents of a foreign country, namely U.S.S.R., and they aim at nothing but the domination of the U.S.S.R. over Iran."

Our program for the 1953 fiscal year had just been approved. Another $23,000,000 had been allotted late in December 1952 to permit us to enter project agreements.

Just before Christmas Dr. Mossadegh and I signed a revision of the country agreement which created the Iran-United States Joint Commission for Social and Economic Development. This was important because the new commission replaced both the throttled Joint Commission for Rural Improvement and the Iranian Cabinet Committee, which, while I sat with it, was not in the same sense jointly operated. The official co-operation, as this showed, continued to be good. One of the first projects to be considered in the new fiscal year was to equip and finance a program for the control of locusts during the approaching season.

From time immemorial locusts have each spring wafted out of Africa and leapfrogged their way in a relay of generations across the Middle East and into India. They lay their eggs in the ground and, if rainfall and other factors are favorable, the tiny young hoppers come boiling up in myriads to begin eating their way to adulthood. When they are about three inches long they develop gauzy wings. Then hordes of them take to the air and migrate generally eastward, helped along by prevailing winds. They fall to earth like a blanket, lay more eggs in different earth and start the process all over again.

Each year, as the season advances, plagues of these pests wing their way along the age-old route. They cross Iran in April and May. If rains at just the right time have made the soils at the relay points just soft enough and the desert and fields just green enough, great hatches occur. Under these ideal conditions most of the hoppers survive. Clouds of locusts appear in Old Testament fashion. This happens very infrequently, but the people of Iran have an atavistic fear each year that the advancing season may this time bring locust devastation. Even in years of normal locust infestation some fields and a few large areas are ravaged, stripped of all greenery by the ravening insects.

The United Nations Food and Agriculture Organization, Point 4 and other agencies have attacked the locust problem in recent years on a regional basis. The nations of the Middle East have co-ordinated their work. A regional FAO team has co-operated with them. A Point 4 regional organization was operating out of Beirut, Lebanon, under William Mabee of the

United States Department of Agriculture. Point 4 missions also assisted the agencies of the individual countries to carry out campaigns within their borders. Locusts are fought by poisoning the ground around their hatching areas and by spraying the crawling hoppers from midget planes flown three or four feet above the ground in crop-dusting fashion.

The locust-control project was one of the first we undertook in Iran. In 1951 Point 4 had bought six little planes and donated them to the Agriculture Ministry. These, with crews trained by Point 4, became the core of the ministry's locust-fighting army. Each year the locust fighters had keep the depredation in Iran to a low minimum. Everyone, however, felt that more new planes were needed.

Funds were allotted by our Washington office to meet the needs of the plan presented from Iran. In December 1952 we signed a locust-control project agreement for the next year. Our latest program plan included the purchase of an additional half-dozen small planes equipped as sprayers. A combination of events was to make their purchase most embarrassing a little later.

Russia also had an interest in the regional locust-control program since several Soviet provinces at times are invaded by pestilential flights from Iran. The Russians offered to send ten spray planes to help out. A year earlier a flight of Russian spray planes had spent a few weeks of the locust season in the remote area of Iran east of Kerman.

Meantime earnest efforts to reach an agreement on oil continued. Ambassador Henderson took the lead, despite the rejection of the Truman-Churchill note and the departure of the British. In the early part of January 1953 the prospects for a settlement looked brighter every day. Finally it seemed that a tentative agreement had been reached. All that remained was one last conference between Dr. Mossadegh and his advisors on petroleum. Apparently they fell out, because the next day negotiations collapsed. Arbitrators could find no way to reopen the discussions for a year. Almost two years passed before an agreement was finally reached. During this time we had some very difficult days.

At about the time the oil negotiations were broken off, I belatedly learned that the Congress had included in the appropriation act which made our funds available a provision that none of the money could be used to buy airplanes. We had to back out of our agreement to supply new planes for Iran's locust-control program.

Point 4 field work continued, indeed was intensified, during the early months of 1953, while the position of Iran continued to deteriorate and the "Yankee Go Home" campaign reached its highest pitch. By January 31, 1953, a statistical study showed thirty-five separate program activities were under way in the Tehran region alone. There were, besides, twenty-two in the Isfahan region, twenty-one in the Tabriz, twenty in the Shiraz, nineteen in the Caspian, fourteen in the Kerman, twenty-four in the Rezaieh, eleven in the Meshed, ten in the Ahwaz and twelve in the Kermanshah.

But street demonstrations called *chalooks,* a Farsee word meaning crowds, broke out frequently in the cities. Professor Hoyt Turner, our education director, during these tense days visited one of the Tehran schools using our new teaching methods. He asked about the activity of an unusually noisy playground group and received the amazing reply, "Oh, they are practicing at demonstrating."

They take their politics seriously at an early age in Iran. This apparently, was a kind of civics class.

"Yankee Go Home," to look at the anti-American campaign a little more closely, is a slogan by which Communist sympathizers have expressed their opposition to American postwar programs in Europe, Africa and Asia. The slogan is supported

Yankee Go Home

everywhere by propaganda aids. Picasso's *Dove of Peace*, for example, is engraved on a card bearing a similar message in whatever language is locally spoken—Farsee in Iran. The campaign was inspired by outsiders in Iran as it had been in France, Italy, western Germany and elsewhere. It builds on whatever it can find for a foundation.

"Yankee Go Home" in Iran got under way in earnest at the time the British were expelled. Earlier, only an occasional sign had appeared on a wall. With the British gone a carefully nurtured distrust of foreigners was directed against the Americans, the largest foreign group left in the country. Point 4 was the most vulnerable target. If it had been eliminated the campaign would have been intensified against other Americans. And if the Yankees had gone home the campaign would have been directed against another group until it had reached its major objective—the elimination of all foreign influence in Iran except that approved by those who directed the campaign. At that point antiforeign feeling would be suppressed.

"Yankee Go Home" expressed an antagonistic reaction to the efforts of the United States to help Iran. We believed that helping Iran to help herself would make peace more secure. We knew we would have to expect opposition from those who interpreted this objective as antagonistic to their ends. A campaign of propaganda fought our program of friendly, co-operative action. But our opponents' words did not seem very effective measured against our deeds. The converts propaganda made were far fewer than those who recognized the basic friendship behind the American co-operative program. The advocates of "Yankee Go Home" were a puny minority.

Of course the campaign was a source of some annoyance. But it also provided some merriment among our staff members. It was not pleasant, of course, to have the animosity of even a minority, but it brought its laughs. When some teen-age boys shouted, "Yankee Go Home" at one of our technicians, he replied, *"Inshallah* (if God wills)." He sounded so hopeful that everyone joined in the laughter.

Two or three boys called "Yankee Go Home" at a couple on the street. The husband said, "They didn't mean me, I'm a Canadian."

"They didn't mean me either," answered his wife. "I'm from Georgia."

An American who surprised a small boy laboriously spelling out "Y-a-n-k-e-e" on a wall offered him *bakhsheesh* (money as a gratuity) and bought his brush for *yek toman,* one ten-*rial* piece, about the value of a dime then.

The agricultural division debated adopting as its motto one of the signs which had a slight spelling deficiency. It said "Yankee Go Hoe." A regional director, tired of waiting for recruits, cried "Yankee Come Hither" by cable. In short, those who faced the onslaught did so with characteristic Yankee attitudes.

Our greatest worry was that Americans back home might misread the campaign as evidence of our program's weakness. It was, in fact, proof positive that the program was considered too strong by those who wanted Iran to renounce her co-operation with us. They wanted Point 4 to fail of its goal.

It is easy to be flip and editorialize against cramming United States taxpayers' hard-earned money into the pockets of people who only berate us for it. This brittle reaction seeks no answers to what may be behind a "Yankee Go Home" campaign. Nor does it ask what the alternatives may be, or who and how many are the vociferous critics and brickbat throwers. The absolute fact is that the vast majority of Iranians appreciate the American friendship and earnestly desired to co-operate in our program.

Before any American foreign-aid program is launched each recipient nation must make its request and accommodate itself to the requirements of United States. This help is not forced on anyone. Most host governments seize an ample number of opportunities to demonstrate in a dignified way their appreciation of what the United States is doing. For the most part their proclamations or statements are given very little publicity in the United States. But it is fashionable for some politicians, editors and other leaders of thought to stamp their feet and pound their tables in irritation if an expression of appreciation up to their standards is not immediately forthcoming after every publicized step in the progress of foreign-aid programs.

Right in the midst of the "Yankee Go Home" build-up Ahmad Fallahi, the governor of Mahallat, made this speech at the dedication of a livestock station:

According to the available evidence and its brilliant history the Iranian nation has once been the source of world civilization and has led many great countries of that time, but unfortunately, during the past two centuries colonizing powers have plundered our wealth, bereaved us of our possessions and have frustrated our efforts and struggles toward any progress.

The Iranian peoples are thankful toward the philanthropic government of the United States of America who with a view of assisting them has started its technical and economic aid with close and faithful co-operation with our national government. The population of Mahallat heartily appreciate your efforts for the development and improvement of our country. You are in fact representing the United States government in inaugurating this livestock station. Be assured that just as the Iranian people cannot forget the tyranny and oppressions of the imperialistic powers they will not in the same manner forget the genuineness of your friendship which they will always recall with the deepest appreciation.

A multitude of similar instances showed that our hand of friendship had been warmly grasped.

But let me get back to the story of the developments in the spring of 1953. Dr. Mossadegh proclaimed the construction of an "oil-less economy" for Iran. Through February he was faced with increasingly grave economic problems. Vexed at the fact that the Senate provided a refuge for General Zahedi, he decided to eliminate that body. Rumors began to fly, as the Senate became shaky, that the Shah would leave Iran "for a holiday" in Europe. Announcement of the trip was an obscure weapon of political retribution. Half the senators were appointed by the Shah. The rumors were interpreted as the Shah's protest against Dr. Mossadegh. Great crowds demonstrated against their ruler's leaving. Others paraded in favor of it. When they met, they fought. Once I caught a brief glimpse of Ardeshir, my first in a long time. He was swinging from the gate of the Royal Palace, exhorting a mob.

When the time set for His Imperial Majesty to make his trip arrived, Dr. Mossadegh called at the palace, on February 29, 1953, to bid him Godspeed. It was the first time the prime minister had left his house in months. What occurred during his absence was laconically reported in *Keyhan* on March 1:

DISTURBANCE AT THE HOUSE OF DR. MOSSADEGH—At a meeting of the Majlis the Prime Minister, Dr. Mossadegh, told the deputies about the recent disturbances and the attack on his house. He said:

"At 11 A.M. I went to the Imperial Court with the Ministers and there I saw a crowd.

"When I returned home I saw that my house was surrounded by the mob. Then an Army jeep with a number of people attacked my house. As I found myself in a dangerous situation I ascended a ladder and went into the Point Four premises which are next to my house."

That Point 4 compound was the Tehran regional team headquarters. It was separated from the prime minister's home by a wall ten feet high. Together the two compounds formed an "L." They had no common opening.

After his call Dr. Mossadegh had left the Shah's palace by a side exit. He had been home long enough to return to bed. When firing began at his gate on Kakh Avenue he was again in the familiar pajamas and bathrobe.

At 3:35 P.M. the members of Tehran regional team saw a ladder suddenly appear over the wall of the parking lot at the back of Point 4 compound. The prime minister, helped by one of his sons and Dr. Fatemi, his foreign minister, scaled the wall. Point 4 made the leads of many sensational news stories around the world, since Dr. Mossadegh, still in the same striped pajamas, chose to describe his climb in his appearance before the Majlis later that night.

A political settlement was reached. It was a Mossadegh victory. The Shah remained in Iran. The Senate disappeared. General Zahedi fled into hiding.

Except in a role of innocent bystander, Point 4 had nothing to do with the affair in which it thus obliquely figured. Our operations were afterward disrupted somewhat. A company of machine gunners moved into the regional office to help restore order in Dr. Mossadegh's compound. It remained for a few days to protect the prime minister. The captain politely invited the regional team staff to continue to use their offices and to step over and around any sleeping soldiers. They chose instead to crowd into the headquarters building with us until an uneasy calm returned and the soldiers departed.

We were learning to live in what Robert Louis Stevenson, in "Aix Triplex," called a "tremendous neighborhood."

The word was then received by me about the impossibility of using our funds for spray planes. With much embarrassment I now had to ask Dr. Siafollah Moazzemi, who had succeeded Engineer Taleghani as minister of agriculture, to sign a new locust project agreement with me. This one eliminated the planes and increased the number of trucks and other vehicles. Dr. Moazzemi, new in office and suspecting a hidden motive behind the request, was most reluctant. He expressed grave concern over the chance that a serious locust infestation might develop. If such a thing happened, he pointed out, the government would be roundly criticized for not being prepared. And already the government had almost more troubles than it could bear. My efforts to reassure him did not succeed very well. I showed him reports from Africa that hatches of crawler locusts had been light. I pointed out that Iran would have the help of the regional team of locust fighters. Then I reminded him that Iran still had four small planes in good working order. In the end Dr. Moazzemi signed the revised agreement, but he was not happy about it.

The Iranian government almost immediately accepted a Russian offer to send planes and technicians to fight locusts. This time the Russians were stationed at the Shiraz airport in populous Fars Province. They were there during the days of mid-April that were to prove so trying.

Keyhan, a responsible newspaper with a record of fair treatment of the news, reported that "the Foreign Minister last week asked the Soviet Ambassador to give further aid for the locust campaign in the southern part of Iran. Among the many countries which undertook to give aid in the locust fight Soviet Russia was the only one which performed its undertakings in full. . . . Political circles in Iran pay special attention to the issues concerning the United States, and the Iranian Government's request for further aid from Russia. The Soviet Government will probably give the requested aid as well as other aids at a time when Iran is disappointed by the West." The foreign minister who made that request was Dr. Fatemi, who in a few months would be calling for the establishment of a "republic." He later was convicted of treason and executed by a firing squad.

The Point 4 help in the 1953 locust campaign was much more significant than the Russian aid. Our team in Khuzistan, with two regional planes and four Ministry of Agriculture planes, controlled a serious outbreak, the only one in Iran that year. The

Russian planes were not well adapted to low-level spraying, but that deficiency made little difference, since there were few locusts to be sprayed in their area.

The comic-opera aspect of the affair of February 28 soon gave way to grimmer realities. Civil unrest deepened. Demonstrations grew larger and more frequent as the prime minister pressed his contest with the Shah. He now asked more and more insistently for control over the royal estates. Showings of strength became more violent when it was reported that the extreme nationalists were welcoming Tudeh support in the streets.

A mass demonstration was staged in Shiraz on April 16. The demonstrators' orders were to march to the telegraph office and file a wire supporting Dr. Mossadegh's position. Throughout April similar "shows of popular support" occurred in Tehran. We closed our Sepah Avenue office early on April 17 to get our people off the streets. Late that afternoon I received a telegram from E. C. Bryant, provincial director at Shiraz. A mob had wrecked the Point 4 office there the day before. The inflamed rioters had turned from the telegraph office and crossed the street to the Point 4 headquarters in the Municipal Building, another wing of which housed the police station. Only an Iranian watchman was on duty. He was beaten and overrun. The local authorities had made no effort to halt the attack.

Ambassador Henderson and I called at the prime minister's office to protest. Dr. Mossadegh told us that martial law had already been declared in Fars Province. A new governor general and a new military commander were being sent at once to restore law and order. He besought us not to halt Point 4 work in Shiraz. He also tried to discourage me from flying south. When he saw he could not he asked that I take Engineer Abolghassem Radjy along to report for him. Mr. Radjy, deputy director of the Plan Organization, was one of my closest friends.

When we left the prime minister's office an employe met us

in the street with a telegram telling of another attack. Americans in Shiraz had been driven from their homes and were taking refuge in the Garden of Heaven, headquarters of the Ghashghai tribe.

Accompanied by a few others, Mr. Radjy and I took off as early as possible the next day. We arrived in midafternoon after a very rough trip. E. C. Bryant and Dr. A. S. Lazarus, virologist of our Health Division who was in Shiraz to set up a trachoma laboratory, met us at the airport. Mr. A. Mirurand of the Shiraz branch of the Bank Melli introduced himself. He said that the prime minister had cabled to designate him our host. He had quarters for us in his rooms above the bank. He told us we had been preceded two hours before by an Iranian Army plane bringing some officials from Tehran. These, it developed, included Mr. Saba, the new governor general, and Brigadier General Mir Jehengari, the new military commander.

Several of the Russian spray planes were parked on the airport apron when we arrived. They looked like training planes.

"They can't be safely flown very close to the ground," E. C. said. "They spend a lot of time here at the airport."

"Did the fliers have anything to do with your troubles?" I asked.

"No, not that anyone could see. Tudeh students from the medical school first turned the mobs. These fliers are under strict military discipline and are marched around in a group. They seldom have any freedom."

As protocol demanded, we went immediately to military headquarters. Here we found that we had stumbled in while the command was passing. From there we proceeded to the office of Governor General Nakhjevan. We found Mr. Saba sitting with him.

Governor Nakhjevan, apparently unaware that he was about to be replaced by his other guest, said that he was exceedingly sorry for what had happened. He insisted that he had the highest regard for Mr. Bryant and the excellent work of Point 4. He had not wanted to permit the demonstration to take place on April 16, he said, but he had been instructed to do so. An investigation had been started, he reported. Already thirty-two arrests had been made of those who were believed to have been responsible for the violence directed at Point 4 and the Americans. Governor Nakhjevan added that nearly everyone welcomed the Americans in Shiraz and approved of the Point 4 program, which he hoped would be resumed right away.

E. C. Bryant asked our military guard, four soldiers in a jeep, not to follow us to the Garden of Heaven. I soon saw why, for there we met the Ghashghai warriors. There was no one in our car whom they knew. Fifty or more of them were drawn up at the gateway. They wore striking gray felt hats with rakish, outsize earflaps erect on either side. Most of them were armed with stout war clubs three or four feet long. Many of these had ironspiked heads weighing about two pounds. The manner in which these clubs were brandished showed that we were not to pass until authorized. And the speed with which the guard was reinforced from inside the large garden indicated that only a major force could get through if it were not wanted. A few of the warriors carried guns—there was even one carelessly slung submachine gun—but the war clubs seemed a little more menacing. These were hill people. The faded clothes and weatherbeaten faces gave evidence of long marches in the sun. They were convincingly determined in mien. The fact that the Ghashghai had guests who did not wish to be disturbed pleased and impressed them. These tribesmen were keyed up and itching for a fight. I had no desire to oblige them unless I might be counted on their side. When the second car, carrying E. C. Bryant, arrived the scene changed magically. The gate was flung open and we were grinningly saluted. We passed through to a hearty welcome at the old manor house. The American families were in the great hall upstairs. We were quickly taken to them. All our people were there, surrounded by beds and baby bottles. Through the window I saw many warriors in the garden.

Bryant, who had had long experience with the Red Cross before joining our staff, said, "We are even beginning to smell like a refugee camp."

In spite of their discomfort the people were in good spirits. I told them that the prime minister had expressed his deepest regret and that the governor had assured us order would be restored. I promised that Ambassador Henderson and I would find room in Tehran for anyone who wished to leave Shiraz but emphasized that we wanted the program to continue.

They would stick it out.

Most of the ten American families lived at the edge of town, near the Garden of Heaven. Bryant had scheduled a meeting at his house for 10:15 A.M., April 17, the day after the offices were ransacked. Some soldiers under a Captain Yekzeban came at about 10:30 in response to a request Mr. Bryant had made of the governor. The staff meeting had begun when Mansour Bahmanbegi, Mr. Bryant's Iranian assistant and a member of the Ghashghai tribe, rushed to the door shouting, "There are about 500 of them marching up the street."

From the door the staff members could see some of the mob throwing stones at houses along their way. Captain Yekzeban and one or two of his soldiers fired a few tentative shots over the heads of the mobsters who fell back only a few yards. Some taxicabs had been scurrying ahead of the marching throng like chickens fleeing before running boys, not knowing which way to turn. Mr. Bryant and the others put the women and children into the cabs, gathered up the remainder of the Americans and followed the only road open, that leading to the Garden of Heaven. The Ghashghai opened their manor house to them.

Traditionally the Ghashghai stands aloof from or actually opposes the city people in Shiraz. The tribal leaders had been on the outs with some of the townspeople, but with others they had found a common meeting place in their firm support of Dr. Mossadegh. The Ghashghai's support, though, was based more on opposition to the Shah than on alignment with Dr. Mossadegh's program.

In any event the Ghashghai seized upon the Americans' plight as a cause. Around a hundred campfires under the old trees in the vast garden, tribesmen gathered to discuss a frontal attack on the city. More and more fighting men came down from the hills. But the city mobs made no approach to the Garden of Heaven and the crisis passed.

When I had heard the details of Bryant's story I understood better the tension at the gates when we arrived at the Garden of Heaven.

Already General Mir Jehengari had ordered heavy guards at all of our installations. At the Bank Melli that night the general and Colonel Falzeli, military administrator under martial law, called on Abolghassem Radjy, E. C. Bryant and me.

"It would help to restore the general self-respect of the city," General Jehengari told me, "if the Americans would return to their houses. Most Shirazi are greatly shamed by what has happened. Also it would help to calm down the Ghashghai. We have restored order and I can assure you that there will be no more difficulty."

I turned to Bryant. "E. C., do you think that will be good enough for you?"

"If the General says he has the situation under control, we'll return to our houses right away."

I flew back to Tehran on Saturday morning. Ambassador Henderson and I arranged to see Prime Minister Mossadegh April 23.

The prime minister said that British agitators had been behind the Shiraz incident. I said we had reason to believe Communists had taken charge of the mob. The prime minister said that it was all the fault of the governor and the military commander in charge in Shiraz. I told him that Mr. Bryant had seen a telegram sent by the appropriate office in Tehran instructing the governor not to interfere with the demonstration scheduled for April 16.

Through our long acquaintance Dr. Mossadegh and I had up to this time always maintained a very friendly, rather bantering relationship. There was no levity in his manner now. I am afraid I was very serious too. Still, official co-operation and collaboration with our work continued until the very day his regime fell, a few months later. Indeed, the prime minister made some effort to make amends.

On May 4, 1953, for example, he started a letter to me: "Before taking up the subject of this letter I would like to express my sincere thanks for the TCI co-operation as technical aid extended in the last two years in connection with the improvement of reclamation and industrial projects."

The seasonal danger from locusts had passed and the Russian planes were withdrawn. It was, incidentally, only in the field of locust control that the Russians provided any assistance to Iran.

Following the Shiraz incidents the Joint Commission for Social and Economic Development met. At the meeting Dr. Moazzemi who had been so reluctant to sign the locust project agreement in February, said, "I want to add my personal appreciation in addition for the quick and effective help given by Point 4 in the locust campaign."

By May 11 E. C. Bryant could report, "We are very pleased that from a program standpoint we are at present time functioning nearly 100 per cent. The repair on the headquarters building is now all completed and there are no existing visible signs that this establishment was subjected to an attack."

Unrest was still evident in other quarters, however. At Kermanshah Homer A. Mathiesen, the regional director, reported two incidents. Four men had tried to create disturbances, first in his offices and later in his house. The police arrested two but didn't catch the others.

In the canyon above the Darband Hotel, a favorite walking

place, a Point 4 technician and his family had been surrounded by a group of rowdy hikers and forced to leave.

A group including some students confronted some of those participating in the graduation ceremony of a class of laboratory technicians at the Malariology Institute on the university campus. They plastered several with "Yankee Go Home" stickers. When Dr. Marcel de Baer, resident representative of the secretary general of the United Nations, said he was no Yankee the crowd jeered, "Frenchy Go Home."

Encouraging messages kept coming from rural areas, though. I received this one from Mazandaran Province on May 15, 1953:

We, the undersigned, on behalf of 5,000 inhabitants of Soldeh district, wish to express our appreciation for the goodwill, efforts, and also for the material, moral and educational assistance of the Point 4 Caspian branch, which by providing experts and engineers and spending considerable amount of money have made the construction of a new six-class school building possible. By placing the new building at our disposal they have saved our children from the previous one which was very old and miserable. We express our sincere thanks to all your staff, especially those of educational branch who have been forerunners in this benevolent act.

We also wish to thank in particular Engineer Juyebari, who has personally been in charge of the constructional operations, performing his duties in the best possible manner, a fact which proves once more your good intentions. We hope you will duly commend such employees.

But *Shahbaz,* an extreme leftist newspaper in Tehran, attacked Dr. Mossadegh for his letter to me:

The Prime Minister, in a letter to Mr. Warne, Director of TCI, has appreciated Point 4's so called industrial and development activities in Iran.

It seems that Dr. Mossadegh has forgotten that some time ago a TCI agent was arrested at a restricted frontier area.

We have time and again unveiled the evil objectives of this espionage center and we will continue our campaign until they are expelled.

Dr. Mossadegh had not forgotten, as *Shahbaz* charged, that one of our men had been arrested in a restricted area. No such incident ever occurred. A little later the same paper said:

"On Tuesday Mr. Warne visited the cotton demonstration farms in Ghamsar. The real purpose of the trip was to inspect the American military and strategic bases in the north."

This was another typical propaganda piece. Ghamsar is east of Tehran. So far as I have ever heard there is nothing at all of military importance in that vicinity. There were no American bases, strategic or otherwise, in Iran.

Incidents like those in Shiraz of course raise questions. Certainly a technical assistance program would flourish best in a stable political situation. Such a program seeks long-term objectives, the ultimate goals improvement of human living where development has been delayed. This means the slow and careful building of institutions, making physical improvements, designing and executing plans of social progress. At every step of every activity the program can be wrecked by wanton acts. Re-building requires patience and strong faith. In an atmosphere of confusion and misdirected energies tasks that require steady hands may be jostled awry and hard-won progress tumbled in the dust. When heedless action is taken by the very people who need help and for whom the labor has been undertaken it is most disheartening.

But in the completely stable political situation that would furnish an ideal setting for Point 4, it is unlikely that any technical assistance would be needed. Stability is usually based on relatively advanced social and economic development. The Point 4 program is almost necessarily conducted in a country where it is needed most and most difficult to perform. Iran was such a country. Its aspirations parallel our own, but centuries of development must be telescoped into years if it is to come abreast. Everywhere in Iran's slow march of progress there have been many temporary reverses, much trial and error. In the attempt to compress the centuries for Iran, the same erratic progression will be the rule. But the country will move forward. Even the backward step on April 16 in Shiraz was redressed to the positive side a little later.

"Yankee Go Home" was a facet of the contest of the day. It was the outcry of the very forces we were fighting in the locust project, as in all the other activities by which we tried to improve the lot of the Iranians. The confusion and real pain arising from the impasse on oil were the basic fuel on which the fire fed. The antiforeign agitation of reactionary religious figures created an atmosphere in which it could burn brightly. But the Yankees didn't even stop work, let alone go home.

Mission/10

The Fight for Life

Dr. Jahanshah Saleh graces his profession of healer. One of a group of distinguished brothers, he has several times been minister of health and was dean of the medical school at Tehran University. A dynamic leader of thought in Iran, Dr. Saleh had served on the original Joint Commission for Rural Improvement when the Point 4 program first was set up under Prime Minister Razmara in 1950. When he returned to the Cabinet in September 1953 he became a member of the Joint Commission for Social and Economic Development established the previous December. Immediately he went about the country to see what progress had been made in the improvement of rural health facilities and services.

After a visit to Mazandaran Dr. Saleh told the Joint Commission that the Public Health Cooperative (PHCO) had helped the Ministry of Health to progress from the "pill pushing business" to field programs of substantial character in pre-natal care, well-baby clinics, health education, sanitation and preventive medicine.

"I went into a school near the town of Amol," Dr. Saleh said. "I pointed at one of the little boys sitting on a bench by the door. 'Tell me,' I asked him, 'what causes malaria?'

"'A microbe,' the little boy replied.

"'How is it spread?' I asked the boy.

"'By the bite of the female Anopheles mosquito,' the boy replied instantly.

"'How do you recognize this, your enemy?' I asked him.

"'It is the one,' the little fellow answered seriously, 'that when she sits down she sticks her little behind up in the air.'"

"It is wonderful," Dr. Saleh repeated, "how much progress has been made. Until this health education work got under way the people in the rural areas near the Caspian didn't even know about microbes. They said some diseases were hot diseases and some diseases were cold diseases. They had no idea how to protect themselves and their children from infections."

Dr. Saleh went on to say that the school children had now learned about the Anopheles mosquito and the microbe from posters and little lessons given them at their school. Already they had carried the information home to their parents. The additional co-operation we received in the DDT spraying to control malaria was good proof of that.

As time went on the PHCO, staunchly supported by Dr. Saleh, did many more things that drew much favorable attention to the program. The Ministry of Health had begun a malaria control program before Point 4 arrived but at that time no other preventive medicine was attempted. Since the Ministry had no public health service, technicians from the World Health Organization laid out the plans, and spraying had begun. But the project ran into trouble. The DDT supply was soon exhausted. After the nationalization of the petroleum industry in 1951 the Iranian government was unable to supply the foreign exchange with which to buy more. One of the first things Point 4 did, while the rural improvement project was still in the planning stages, was to rescue the malaria control project. It immediately flew in DDT for emergency use and shipped a larger supply during the summer of 1951. When the PHCO was organized in the spring of 1953 the malaria control project was transferred to its jurisdiction. The dramatic story of Iran's conquest of malaria requires the fuller discussion included later in this chapter.

The PHCO is an excellent example of co-operative management of a technical assistance project in a field in which the host government has previously had no experience. The consistent policy of operating only with and through Iranian agencies couldn't be followed in public health, as well as in a few other areas. Iran had no agency with which we could work. The government had to create agencies when this was true. Thus the PHCO became the public health department of the Iranian Ministry of Health.

The Public Health Cooperative was administered by co-directors, one appointed by the minister of health and the other by Point 4. The health division of Point 4 automatically became the American complement to the health co-operative. The Iranian staff was recruited from experts Point 4 had trained in public health, from a group of officials of the Ministry of Health and from the force employed in the malaria control project. The WHO and Point 4 experts became advisors of the PHCO co-directors. The funds, supplies, and equipment allocated by Point 4 to its health division were the contribution of the United States to financing the PHCO. The Ministry of Health contributed to the joint fund the salaries of its personnel and other budget items related to the work. The Plan Organization, an Iranian agency which had as a part of its legal function the stimulation of work in public health, contributed funds directly to the PHCO. The Institute of Malariology at the University of Tehran continued to conduct the field surveys to determine areas of high incidence of malaria and to map out the spraying program for the PHCO.

Thus was quickly created and rapidly built an effective agency to carry on programs which were seriously needed in any rural improvement plan but which previously had not been included in the government's activities.

It was a fifty-fifty deal too, though of the kind in the story of the "fifty-fifty sandwich"—one horse to one rabbit. But in this case the United States contributed the rabbit. We recruited fourteen American technicians and advisors for the PHCO.

These could hardly be said to equal the 2,400 Iranian technicians, from doctors down to spray-pump operators, provided by the Iranian government.

When I saw how much was done through inspiration and training and a little assistance my enthusiasm for the PHCO program almost equaled that of Dr. Saleh on his visit to Mazandaran.

The PHCO organized itself to combat epidemic outbreaks of the many diseases that afflict Iran. So many times that it became commonplace the PHCO moved its specialized teams into an area to put down a typhoid outbreak.

A soldier died of typhus in a barracks near Meshed. The PHCO moved in with its clean-up team and flea killers and completely renovated the place. There was only the one death.

The group's most spectacular service to date came in December 1954, when virulent smallpox broke out near Tabriz. The disease had spread to the city before a small village was identified as its source. Each day the number of cases reported rose sharply. The number of deaths increased proportionally. In a campaign unique in Iran, the Public Health Cooperative's division of health education marshaled all its forces to support a vaccination program in Tabriz. Using every medium from silk-screened posters to the Tabriz radio, the technicians laid the problem squarely before the people of the city. The PHCO flew vaccine to Tabriz from Tehran. They set up vaccination stations in every gendarmerie post and every schoolhouse. Technicians converged on the capital of Azerbaijan to carry out the mass vaccination program.

In eleven days 210,000 men, women and children in and around Tabriz were vaccinated against smallpox. This number represented more than three quarters of the population of the area affected. The number of new cases began to drop off. The epidemic was brought under control with fewer than forty deaths. For his part in this campaign Dr. Harald S. Frederiksen of the Point 4 staff in 1956 received a Flemming award for outstanding work in the United States Federal Service.

The advocates of spectacular projects in preference to long-term technical assistance programs had proposed again and again that all our health funds be concentrated in the construction of a single large hospital. The services of the PHCO in a single month in Tabriz did more to help Iran than those of even a very large hospital could have done over many years.

In Iran, as in most underdeveloped countries, health statistics are inadequate. Reliable records of such basic information as morbidity, infant mortality and general life expectancy are nonexistent. Dr. R. Leslie Cherry, head of the health division in 1954 and 1955, believed that fifty per cent of Iranian babies die in their first year. Of those who live one year he thought fifty per cent would die before the age of six. The infant mortality rate may be even higher. Many boys certainly become heads of families at very early ages. Not just once or a few times, but many times, I have met village youngsters of fourteen or fifteen who accepted and were recognized as carrying full responsibility as heads of their families.

An eminent Iranian medical man once told me that heart disease is not a serious problem because, as he explained, "Most of our people die of other ailments before reaching an age when heart disease would be encountered."

Large areas of Iran are without trained physicians or other health practitioners. Old crones of the village become midwives without any knowledge of sanitation or training in their calling. They employ folk ways and folk medicines, the leaves, seeds, roots of plants that grow in the deserts or on the hills. I do not scoff at these remedies, for I know that some may have values yet unrealized. But I am reminded of an experience years ago in the Altoplano of Peru. A friend and I stopped in a village market place and looked over the wares of an old woman selling home remedies. She had dried leaves, seeds, roots and colored earths—a bounty. My friend had the sniffles.

"What," he asked, "would you advise for a cold?"

"Take aspirin," she immediately replied.

The people in Iran wear amulets and practice primitive sorcery. They burn *esfand* or spread the blood of a slaughtered sheep across the road. They hang a mirror in the path to ward off the evil eye. Thus the people seek protection.

But a village's first clamor is always for a doctor or a clinic to treat the sick. The sick die unless they are treated. No matter how accustomed the people are to being deprived they would make any sacrifice to protect the child who is left.

It is not so easy to demonstrate to these people that preventive programs save lives by keeping the people well. The experience in Iran testifies loudly to the wisdom and political fortitude of men like Dr. Saleh in the Ministry of Health. He and his predecessors, Dr. Farmanfarmayan and Dr. Maleki, stood by and supported the public health work. Certainly they were often under grave pressure to put all their resources into programs for treatment of the sick. The public health work justified their resolute stand. It was strikingly effective.

In a certain village there were no young children. A village leader explained to a visiting nurse from the nearest PHCO office that he had called her because all the babies born there died of the "stiff disease." This sounded like tetanus. The investigation the nurse ordered showed that the two village midwives, for reasons best known to themselves, were using cow dung to staunch the flow of blood after severing the umbilical cord. An Iranian health visitor trained by the PHCO put a stop to this dreadful practice at once. She showed the midwives how to sterilize a scissors over a candle flame and gave them other medicamentary instructions. Soon one of the village women bore twin babies. When the health visitor returned to the village after a few weeks she found the babies still living. This was an event of major importance to everyone in town. The health visitor was honored at a public celebration.

Point 4 public health technicians in Iran use demonstration and training as tools just as do technicians in other fields. In cooperation with the Near East Foundation the PHCO has for several years operated a school for sanitarian aides in a village near Mamazan. Here trained technicians and engineers instruct young men gathered from villages throughout Iran in sanitary procedures. The students learn methods of obtaining co-operation from villagers in programs of sanitation and clean-up. They are taught the techniques of constructing such simple facilities as sanitary privies and drainage ditches. They then break up into smaller groups and move into the villages surrounding Tehran for three months' actual practical field work in sanitation programs being conducted by technicians of the PHCO and the Near East Foundation. Thus a large body of trained assistants is being developed and village programs are being started in most regions of Iran.

Because of poor sanitation and the lack of orderly methods for disposing of human wastes, hookworm, roundworm and other parasitic diseases are prevalent in Iran. Intensive surveys made in some areas near the Caspian shore showed that as many as ninety-six per cent of the populations of some villages had worms. The construction of sanitary toilet facilities is one of the principal methods of cleaning up this dangerous situation. But the villager must be educated first. He must learn the reasons for constructing such facilities and for consistently using them. The villagers co-operated so enthusiastically with the program that they installed many thousands of crude latrines of a type approved by the public health experts. The latrine consisted of a cement block with a hole in it. On either side of the hole were foot rests. The villager dug his cesspool, fitted the slab over it and built a low mud wall around it for privacy. The hole had a

The Fight for Life

flat wooden cover. As the number of these installations increased the project began to take on some aspects of the famous Chick Sales.

As the newly trained aides spread the environmental sanitation program, so the health visitors carried to the village girls and women lessons in how to protect food from contamination. They taught the villagers the importance of boiling water for their babies. The women learned quickly how to wash babies and the importance of eating vegetables.

In the rural areas of Iran women traditionally are permitted few freedoms outside the home. When they encountered this tradition the health visitors had trouble recruiting village girls to their service.

Mrs. Helen Bakhtiar, a lieutenant commander in the United States Public Health Service, started a school for village girls near Ali-Shah-Avaz in the Shariar area. She had to beat the bushes for recruits. Finally one day her problem was solved. A particularly timid girl of about thirteen slid through the door and took a seat in the back of the room. She was the daughter of an influential Mullah in a near-by village. Once it was clear that the Mullah's daughter had actually entered the class other volunteers came.

Helen, being a wise woman, arranged to call at the Mullah's village to thank him for sending his daughter. She had met the Mullah before and had found him somewhat less than co-operative.

But when she thanked him now the Mullah said that he had been thinking over what Mrs. Bakhtiar had said about the importance of improving the health of the villagers. He had decided, he added, that if such work were to be carried forward among the village women, it could not appropriately be done by men. So he had sent his daughter to be trained.

Thus walls are broken down and light filters through.

Malaria was Iran's Number One killer. Yet in another five

years malaria should be under complete control. The chief credit goes to the national malaria control campaign, though assistance and support for it have come from many sources. Its story is dramatic and heart-warming.

The words of one epidemiologist tell what the program was up against at the start:

On the basis of malariometric and entomological surveys, reliable hospital information, and investigations made by British and American armies [during World War II] it is estimated that two-thirds of the villages in Iran are malarial. With the exception of uninhabited desert regions, hyper- and meso-endemic areas of malaria are found throughout the country regardless of altitude. Principal vectors are the Mediterranean and Indian faunal types *A. [Anopheles] Superpictures, A. Sacharovi, A. Maculipenas,* and *A. Stephensi.* Tertian, quartan and estivo-autumnal malaria occurs countrywide.

In simpler language it is probably sufficient to say that several types of Anopheles mosquito range over virtually all of Iran. Their bites spread malaria over most of the country. The disease has always been present. Serious outbreaks would sometimes claim nearly all of the people in a village and would disable so many that fields could not be harvested. Along the southern shore of the Caspian Sea, where the best land lies and where, alone in all Iran, the yearly rainfall is sufficient for the crops, some areas were so dangerously malarious that the people had abandoned them.

The Ministry of Health planned the campaign with the help of three WHO doctors, Dr. Gramicia, Dr. Giaquinta and Dr. Pampana. The program was launched in the spring of 1951, before the day of the PHCO. The members of the Point 4 health group at that time were Dr. Emil Palmquist and Mr. Fred Aldridge, sanitary engineer. Both had been with the United States Public Health Service for several years. The Point 4 program was at that time still in the planning stage. Only very limited funds were available. When the crisis over the DDT supply developed Dr. Palmquist worked out the plan to fly enough Point 4 DDT to the Iranian Ministry of Health to keep the sprayers busy until a larger supply could be shipped in.

That year the crews sprayed 5,194 villages. In view of the difficulties, it was an impressive achievement. But much more must be done.

One of my first problems when I arrived in Iran was to help plan how Point 4 could best assist in the 1952 malaria fight. This was just before the end of the 1951 spraying season. Fortunately there was enough DDT left over to start the next season's work in the south, where the mosquito season came earliest. The malaria control project was the biggest single Point 4 project. Its success justified its priority.

Our first substantial contribution dramatizes our commitment. Sixteen jeeps, ordered earlier, arrived just as spring approached. The morning we presented the jeeps to Dr. Maleki, then minister of health, was memorable. Tehran that winter had been turbulent. We had heard rumors that many of the malaria fighters were Tudeh party members. Although some wished the jeeps to be only mute evidence of United States interest and help, I decided that the Point 4 symbol should be emblazoned on their sides. Dr. Maleki was understandably somewhat nervous. Just a few days before another cabinet member had been seriously wounded in an assassination attempt. We inspected the jeeps, which stood in a long line at the curb in front of the project headquarters building. A heavy shower that morning had left them shining.

From the steps of the building Dr. Maleki and I each said a few words to the huskies who would take them over trails to the remotest parts of Iran. Incidentally, this was my first experience in Iran at such an affair. I detected nothing unfriendly. We were, however, almost overrun by the crowd that shoved forward to stand on the steps when the news photographers began to take pictures. As I left I spoke to several of the drivers and spraymen standing along the walk. They were pleased at the prospect of getting back to work.

In 1952 they sprayed 11,157 villages.

The project workers encountered several serious operational problems that summer. Supplying the spray teams was a continual problem in logistics. The DDT was all bought in the United States. Scheduling its purchase, shipment and arrival at Khorramshahr was difficult enough. But that was easy compared to the job of fanning the stuff out over Iran. We had to supply the *vaheds,* or groups of spray teams, as they moved north. That meant getting supplies to pickup points not accessible to trucks—and getting it there on time. This problem was solved by decentralizing distribution of DDT through the ten provincial Point 4 offices. This proved so successful that the next year the PHCO decentralized its whole operation.

Two strange facts combined to present yet another problem. In Farsee the same word generally describes both the mosquito and the housefly. It would be the same if English called them both "bugs" and did not differentiate further. The first year DDT was used it killed nearly all "bugs," the housefly and the mosquito. It even exterminated scorpions and tarantulas. But the pesky housefly is one of nature's most efficient adapters. In a few generations he adjusts himself to the DDT, which is only a new hazard in his environment. Thus by the second year the fly was ready to live with the DDT. Fortunately the mosquito is not so adaptable. Though he too may in time become immune, he will not develop his resistance soon enough to prevent the control of malaria.

Villagers all over Iran were delighted after the first spraying to be rid of their bugs. When the sprayers came around the second year, they were ready and happy to co-operate. But as

The Fight for Life

the season advanced and the houseflies multiplied, their joy became disappointment. Then they grew suspicious.

"The spraymen have sold the DDT on the black market and are using chalk," they said to one another. "The bugs are not being killed this year."

Reports hinting that the malaria control work was being sabotaged by dishonest workers began to appear in Iranian newspapers.

At first we could not understand the reason for these rumors. A hasty check showed that no DDT was appearing in the market places. Besides, reason told us that there was no market in Iran for hundreds of tons of poison.

Tests of sprayed villages showed a satisfactory DDT residue on the walls. And mosquitoes were certainly being killed. The sharp drop in the incidence of malaria in the wake of the sprayers proved that.

Finally the light dawned. At last we realized that the villagers' mistrust resulted from the survival of the housefly!

Now we faced a difficult problem in mass education. We attacked it with motion pictures. Point 4 contracted for films showing how malaria is spread and how DDT halts it. They pointed out the difference between a housefly and a mosquito and explained that while the housefly quickly learns to live with the poison, the mosquito does not. These pictures were made by the Syracuse University Film Unit, then under William F. Gelabert. At the start of the 1953 spraying season we sent film trucks to the villages just ahead of the sprayers. When they saw the movies the villagers were happy again.

That year 14,542 villages were sprayed.

One habit of the mosquito makes it possible to control malaria through spraying as was done in Iran. Here's the fatal flaw in his behavior pattern.

The chain of infection starts when an Anopheles mosquito

bites a person ill with malaria. The mosquito then becomes host to the parasites causing the infection. The same mosquito then bites a well person and passes the disease on to him. After feeding, the mosquito habitually flies to a near-by shelter to rest. The Anopheles that wants to rest is likely to be the one armed to spread the disease. A spraying campaign can cover the surfaces on which the insect will probably land. When it lights on a sprayed wall to rest after feeding the poison does its quick work. The mosquito that could spread malaria is eliminated. So the chain of infection is broken. But because the spraying campaign chiefly kills mosquitoes that have bitten people, the mosquito population may remain relatively high.

A scientific council organized early in the campaign advised and helped to co-ordinate the technical work. The directors of the Institute of Malariology at the University of Tehran were sent to the United States on Point 4 training grants. The Malariology Institute was responsible for training malaria personnel, laboratory technicians and epidemiologists. It also conducted surveys and planned control operations. Institute technicians systematically tested sprayed areas to determine the effectiveness of the residue. Chiefly by means of spleen tests they compare the incidence of the disease in sprayed villages and in those not yet reached by the *vaheds*.

The work of the institute won the praise and confidence of the WHO and Point 4 experts. During the 1954 season its technicians worked out a plan for dropping out of the next year's spraying pattern 1,000 villages in which results had been satisfactory. Operations might then extend to 1,500 previously unsprayed.

The institute staff immediately initiated a system of careful checks and controls in the villages where spraying stopped.

In 1954, 15,405 villages were sprayed.

The malaria control program set an annual goal of about 16,000 villages for succeeding years. Older, safer villages would be dropped and new, unsprayed ones added each year. In 1961,

The Fight for Life

the end of the program's first ten years, experts expect malaria to be under control in all areas of Iran.

Even now malaria is no longer the country's major disease. In villages where ninety per cent of the population had malaria at the outset of the campaign, the incidence has dropped to five per cent. In the campaign's fourth year I talked to physicians who practice in such towns along the Caspian as Babol, Lahijan and Resht. They told me that they seldom saw a malaria case. Before spraying reached their areas their summer practices had been made up almost exclusively of malaria victims. Doctors from Ghazvin and Kazerun have reported that the campaign is responsible for increases in population.

Lands that once had to be abandoned because they were malarial have now been reclaimed to farming. In the Shariar area west of Tehran landlords told me that several years of spraying had resulted in marked increases in production on their lands. This was true, they explained, because the villagers were in good health and so were better able to take care of their crops.

All over Iran, from Baluchistan to Azerbaijan, the villagers flaunt the DDT sign, the mark of the spray team, on their doorposts. I have seen it painted in red on every house in a village. In villages where a team was expected the people have proudly led me to the compound and showed me piles of their scant furniture, pots and pans. They had put them there as the motion picture suggested that they do. "It helps the spraymen to go faster," they explained.

The spraymen enter the village with their spray tanks on their backs, like the grim fighters they are. They move methodically from house to house, down every *kucheh*. They spray everything—houses and stables, occupied and empty. As the day gets hot the children and dogs that at first followed them curiously drop out of their train. They go on alone to the end of the town. Then they move on.

During 1952 and 1953 Point 4 provided all the DDT. In 1954

the UNICEF contributed a substantial amount, as well as some jeeps. In 1955 the Point 4 contribution was drastically lower. By that time Iran was able to resume buying for herself. Some evidence that one variety of mosquito was gaining resistance to DDT led us to add another poison to our armament in 1955.

Perhaps Point 4's outstanding contribution to malaria control in Iran was the organization of the Public Health Cooperative. The work of the PHCO has been a demonstration in the management of a most difficult and complex field operation. Its efficiency made possible the progressive increase in the number of villages covered until the annual goal of 16,000 was reached in 1955. Iranians set the new pattern of administration. No more than fifteen Americans were among the 2,500 engaged.

The malaria control program's outstanding recorded achievement was drawing enough support from all sources to continue on schedule through a period of deep depression and crisis. The United States and the United Nations specialized agencies do deserve much credit for this. But the faith and determination of the program's Iranian leaders must be equally honored. No one can estimate the contributions of such men as Dr. Maleki, Dr. Farmanfarmayan, Dr. Jahanshah Saleh and Dr. Torab Mehra, now with the Iran Foundation but director of malaria control work for the Ministry of Health in 1951.

A break in this sort of public health program does much more than simply waste time. It depreciates all of the work that has gone before and makes it necessary to do much of it over again. Though it sometimes seemed that such a disastrous break as this would be inevitable, it never came. Each emergency was met as it arose. One of the largest and most significant fights against disease in the world rolled along on its timetable during these difficult years.

Mission/11

Pure Water to Drink

TEHRAN WAS ONCE the largest city in the world without a sanitary water supply. There has been no recent count of Tehran's population, but it is believed to have grown to 1,200,000 persons. While the city's exact size may be disputed, the fact that it had no equal in its lack of sanitation was never questioned. In October 1955 chlorinated water flowed to Tehran's people through a system of closed pipes for the first time.

The "water-piping project," as it is known in Tehran, eliminated the city's dependence on open ditches in the streets. These *jubes* brought all water into the city and flushed away its refuse. The *jube* is a combination intake and open sewer. It fell to Point 4 to help to complete the water-piping project.

Reza Shah, father of the present King, is reputed to have started planning the project after his return from a visit in Paris. Reza Shah already has become a legendary figure. Many of the stories about him, perhaps already more than half fable, depict his strong personality and his prodigious ability to keep track of a million details. So colorful are the anecdotes that those who never saw him feel they knew him. This particular story may not be authentic but it nevertheless reflects something of this amazing man who did so much to modernize Iran.

Reza Shah, so the story goes, called his advisors about him. "In Paris," he said, "they have water in pipes, and it is carried throughout the whole city. The lack of such a system in Tehran is a measure of backwardness. Why should we not have water pipes?"

"Ah, Your Majesty, why, indeed?" his engineer echoed. "We

could pipe a complete supply from the Karadj River. The city lies well, here on the slope near the mountain. It would not even be a difficult engineering task."

"It is an excellent idea, Your Majesty," said the minister of health. "It could avoid much typhoid and other sickness."

"Well, then," said the King, "let us have some plans."

In a few weeks the advisors met again.

"Your Majesty, it will cost quite a great deal," the engineer said. "The water pipes will all have to be imported. A sewer network will have to be laid out. Then there must be a water treatment plant and a sewage treatment plant."

The Old King, as Reza Shah is more or less familiarly called today, became a little nervous about the cost. "You mention sewers," he said. "I haven't heard much about them. It was water-piping that I had in mind."

The experts went on to explain. The *jubes* served two purposes—bringing water in and flushing refuse out. In Paris, they explained, an underground system of sewers carried away the wastes just as another underground system of pipes brought water in.

The cost seemed alarmingly high. Reza Shah wished to find a practicable way out. Finally he said, "The people of Tehran sleep at night. The people of Paris do not always. But our people will not use water at night. Devise a pipe system that will bring them water by day, when they need it, and will serve as sewers at night."

Obviously the Old King's plan, which would have been scant improvement, was not followed. Many years later Tehran would have a sanitary water supply. A sewer system still remains for the future. The Second World War delayed the water-supply project. Under the direction of Sir Alexander Gibbs, Ltd., of London, consulting and supervising engineers, the plans were completed. When the war ended the pipe was ordered, manufactured and shipped. This proved most fortunate. The pipe

Pure Water to Drink

was on hand in Tehran when the nationalization of the oil industry shut off the flow of foreign exchange to Iran in 1951. Though other projects requiring imported supplies were forced to close down, work on the Tehran water supply never stopped. It continued through the very worst of the depression that followed. When other British citizens departed Iran the Gibbs Company engineers remained and quietly continued their work by tacit understanding.

One of my first impressions of Tehran was that purposeful work was in progress on the water system. Huge pipes were strung along many streets in 1951 and 1952. Great gangs of pajama-clad laborers worked with pick and shovel to bury them in deep trenches.

Having observed all this activity, I was much interested when Charles M. Jones, Point 4's chief engineer, told me that Engineer Mahkaday, managing director of the Tehran water-piping agency, wished to call on me to discuss his project.

Engineer Mahkaday got quickly to the point of his visit. "We have on hand," he explained, "enough pipe and fittings to complete the system inside the city and to build an aqueduct to the Karadj River. But we have not ordered the machinery for the water treatment plant. There is no longer any foreign exchange with which to buy it. In three or, at most, four years we will have the pipes laid. It will take that long to make and install the purification machinery. Without that we shall have only underground *jubes*. Water will still carry pestilence to unsuspecting people. Unless Point 4 will help I don't know what we'll do."

I had already been exposed to the skepticism with which many Iranians view the work on the water supply.

"Oh, it will never be finished," a friend said to me a few days before Engineer Mahkaday's call. "Since I was a boy it has been talked about, but the people are still using the *jubes*. My little girl had typhoid fever last summer. *Jube* water in the *umbar* (cistern). What else can we expect?"

"But, look," I pointed out to him, "the pipes are laid halfway down Pahlavi Avenue. Hundreds of men are working on the job. I have seen the plans and they seem good. The aqueduct is more than half done."

"This work has gone on for years," he insisted. "Nothing is ever completed."

In view of this background of skepticism the prospect of the water system's carrying polluted water when it was finished was particularly unpleasant.

A little later I sat down with Charlie Jones and Dr. Emil Palmquist, then chief of our health division, to discuss the matter.

"You've seen the ditches," Dr. Palmquist said. "Is it any wonder that half the babies die in their first year?"

Certainly I had seen the *jubes*. I had followed them clear through the city. They constituted an irrigation system. Water did not flow along all streets at all times. It was channeled through a system of gates, first down one street then another in a regular rotation pattern. A householder could divert water into his garden and *umbar,* say, during two thirty-minute periods every week. Anyone could use the free-flowing water that passed at the curb—not only could, but did.

At an appointed hour water would come gurgling down the street. Men stopped and washed their faces. Girls hurried out in their *chadoras* and squatted to wash the family dishes and pots and pans. A mother straddled the stream to bathe her dirty baby. A boy dipped panfuls and sprinkled the hot sidewalk. Women did their laundry. The hot donkeys were allowed to drink while their masters refreshed in the water the wilting vegetables they planned to market. A tea vendor with a charcoal brazier at the sidewalk filled a can with water. A barber on a stool at the wall fetched a cupful and was ready to lather the stubbly face of another customer seated before the cracked mirror he had hung from a peg.

Pure Water to Drink

As the canals ran deeper into the city the water grew turgid. Orange peels bobbed along in it. It bore all of the filth of the city. At the siphons that carried the *jubes* under the streets at each corner men were constantly at work with long-handled shovels and rakes fishing out stinking piles of refuse. Carts and trucks came by and carried the filth out to villages. There it was heaped in great mounds to be swarmed over by packs of homeless dogs and scratched about by thousands of crows. Then it would be spread to fertilize truck farms. For days after the job had been done one could identify a field so manured simply by driving past and sniffing.

Clear, fresh water gushed from a number of deep, flowing wells in public squares throughout the city. Though many came to them with jugs and jars, most of the well water went to replenish the flow and thin the consistency of *jube* water. This flow both diminished and thickened as it ran down from the canal at the north side of the city.

Traffic through the city was always impeded by the water carts, which were filled at the "Shah's well" in the central part of the city. On hot days this was the busiest block in Tehran. The well had a system of pipes with nipples which could fill twenty or more cart-tanks at a time. The vendors jostled so for position that a squad of policemen was always on duty there to keep order. Each cart was pulled by a single horse. Fully loaded the poor animal could barely pull the weight. The vendor would have to jump down and lend a hand at any little rise to keep from stalling. These carts had the right-of-way at corners, and an auto driver not infrequently had to cope with a water cart struggling across traffic at an intersection. The horse would strain and slip on the cobblestone pavement. The vendor and perhaps a passer-by, or even the traffic policeman, would put shoulders to the wheels. The carters sold their wares by the bucketful, but many could not afford even the pittance a bucket cost.

At the south, the lower side, of the city the population is most dense. Here the *kuchehs* form a labyrinth among mud walls and huts. By the time they have run this far the *jubes* are saturated with pollution. Women washed clothes in the soupy stuff as it trickled out toward Rey—clothes that never got white or clean.

At our conference, Charlie and Emil and I decided that if an appropriate project agreement was possible we would help Engineer Mahkaday with his water treatment plant. It was. Point 4 ordered the necessary machinery. In March 1955, on one of my last days in Iran I went with Engineer Mahkaday and Ahmad Hossein Adl, minister of agriculture and chairman of the Joint Commission, to inspect the water treatment plant, then rapidly being completed. We stopped too to watch one of six crews at work making house connections to the water system.

Mr. E. Dryer, Point 4's master plumber, was instructing them. "These men," he said admiringly, "have already got the knack. Six weeks ago that foreman there had never made a tap or fitted a joint. He had no tools. But look at him now. He's instructing the other men. These Iranians are very handy and quick to learn. This man is doing thoroughly professional work. He can't read or write, and I can't talk to him. But when I show him, he watches. Before long he can do it too. In six more months they won't need me."

"Oh, but we have 80,000 connections to make this year," Engineer Mahkaday protested. "Then there's all the work inside the houses!"

"Well, there are six men like this foreman already," said Dryer. "And I can train ten more crews in six months. I think they can do the job."

Since there will be no sewers for some years the open ditches will have to flow part time. Ignorance or habit will lead some to use the contaminated water. But our experience has already shown that when better health is the goal all Iranians are quick

Pure Water to Drink 157

to take up new ways. I doubt that even the fear some have expressed that chlorine will spoil the taste of the tea so dear to the hearts of all Iranians will long prove a deterrent to full adoption of the pure water supply. Taste too is a matter of habit. The people can lose their taste for tea made from enriched ditchwater and acquire one for tea made from chlorinated piped water.

October 28, 1955, as a part of the celebration of his birthday then just past, the Shah dedicated Tehran's water-piping project. Complete with treatment plant, it was now ready to serve the whole city. Someone thoughtfully sent me one of the thousand silver coins struck to commemorate the occasion. The inscription was "Water gives life to everything."

The Tehran water treatment project was classified as a public health undertaking. We concentrated one of Point 4's most formidable drives on sanitary water demonstrations in Iran. In another project Point 4 helped to complete a closed water system at Bandar Abbas on the Persian Gulf. We also instigated the drilling of eighty-four deep wells to provide pure water for scattered villages each with a population of about 10,000. In a self-help program villagers all over Iran dug scores and scores of shallow wells equipped with hand pumps.

Dr. Jamshid Amuzegar, son of a prominent family, was the only Iranian sanitary engineer in the country when we arrived. Even he was not then working in his field of specialization. He joined the Point 4 organization as the chief of the sanitary engineering division of the PHCO. In 1955 he became undersecretary of the Minister of Health, in charge of public health activities. He is dreaming of a school of sanitary engineering at Tehran University. It does not seem so remote a possibility now.

Dr. Amuzegar—Jim, as the Americans soon called him—took over from a former United States Geological Survey specialist the work of spotting sites for deep wells. His major objective was to stimulate broad interest in sanitary water systems throughout the land. To carry out the program Jim had to visit hundreds of remote areas. Ironically and almost at the cost of his life, Jim's own experience completely justified his work, for he contracted dragonulosis.

In this terrible disease thin white flesh worms grow in the human body. The disease is found today along the Persian Gulf but in few other places in the world. In its life span the parasite lives in two hosts. A tiny crustacean called a cyclops, scarcely as big as a pinhead, is the first stage. The cyclops lives in cisterns. When unsuspecting man drinks water from a contaminated cistern he becomes the second host.

In towns and villages along the gulf, like Bandar Abbas, water is extremely scarce. Rains fall but once or twice during the winter. Systems of dikes direct all runoff that possibly can be caught into deep, circular cisterns. These are covered with huge mud domes that look like gigantic beehives. Since these cisterns are the only source of water for human consumption the cyclops becomes a great problem. If the cisterns could be permitted to go dry, the cyclops would die and the circle of infection would be broken. But human beings could no longer inhabit the areas that the cisterns now serve.

To free Bandar Abbas from its dependence on the contaminated cisterns we launched our water supply project there. Before the water system was completed, I once watched the Bandar Abbas women flock to the *umbars* as evening approached and the heat abated. They carried on their heads large jugs, five-gallon oil tins and every other sort of container available. They came to fetch the next day's water. The *umbar* had four low doors. Buckets hung on ropes in the cistern's dark, dank recesses. With these the women lifted out and poured and splashed water into their jugs, cans and buckets. Sometimes a cooling quart or so remained in the bucket when the jug was full. As often as not it was poured over the head of some little boy or girl who had been waiting around in expectation. Some water unavoidably drained back into the cistern—water was too precious to waste.

Pure Water to Drink

This, however, was the source of the cistern's contamination.

The new Bandar Abbas water system drew on a deep well in a distant valley. A pipe carried the supply to a regulating reservoir near the town. A simple distribution system moved it to spigots along the main street. Within a year this system freed the city of the disease.

But other areas, especially Lar Province on the Gulf, were still contaminated. So Jim Amuzegar went south to try to locate sites for new wells. Weeks later he complained of painful burning sensations in both knees. Because the disease is rare in northern Iran, Tehran physicians did not recognize Jim's symptoms. As a result a severe infection developed. Jim nearly died.

Though I was extremely hot and thirsty I tried to refuse all drinks except tea when I visited Bandar Abbas, despite repeated assurances that the water had been boiled. But the human will is weak. I found myself half-unwittingly gulping down a cool glass of lemonade at the governor's house. I didn't get sick. Dr. Amuzegar, the principal opponent of the cyclops, was the only member of our staff who was its victim.

"I simply had the biggest roof in this case," Jim explained laconically.

When I asked for an explanation, Reza Ansari quoted the Persian proverb: "The man with the biggest roof has to shovel the most snow." Yes, Jim's exposure was greater, but he has reduced the travail of thousands of his countrymen.

One of Point 4's first acts was to begin the deep-well program. The contract for the first group of twenty wells was signed in 1951 before I left Washington for Iran. At that time, I must confess, we didn't fully understand the plan of operation. Signing the contract in Washington contravened a principle to which we otherwise adhered religiously. Our usual policy was to work out a plan with the proper Iranian authorities and to encompass that plan in a joint agreement in advance of any beginnings. But in those early days we felt a strong urge for action. As it developed, the whole thing worked out for the best, but not before I had suffered severe mental anguish.

The contract called for spotting the first well on February 1, 1952. The Country Agreement, without which we could not begin, was not signed until January 20. That was the day Chief Engineer Jones arrived in Tehran.

"Charlie," I told him the next morning, "we have exactly ten days in which to activate the deep-well project."

"What!" he exploded. "I don't even know the way to the office, let alone have any idea where to drill wells! No staff! I don't even know the man at the Irrigation Bongah. What's his name?"

"Dr. Abol Hassan Behnia," I replied, glancing at a note I had made. "He seems like a very competent man, but he speaks no English at all. You'll find him at the Ministry of Agriculture building. There's also a likely young Iranian engineer around here who can help you. Name's Jim Amuzegar. He speaks English well."

On the morning of February 1, I dropped by the embassy to see Ambassador Henderson.

"Now where is it," he asked, "that we are to—what did you call it?—'spud in' the first Point 4 well?"

"At Karadj, near the college," I said. "It's about forty minutes away. Charlie Jones is out there waiting for us with Jack Richards, the driller, and about half the Cabinet and the college faculty."

"And where do we go tomorrow to start well number two?" the ambassador asked.

"Out the other direction. It's a little farther and the roads are worse. It's in the Veramin Plain, at a village called Katoonabad. It's not far from Mamazan."

"Oh, I know where Mamazan is," said Ambassador Henderson. "That's where the Near East Foundation headquarters are."

Charles Jones, bless him, had done his job, as we learned at

Pure Water to Drink

Karadj. He served his country well. He was invalided home exactly a year later with a condition made serious by the dust and heat of Tehran.

Soon our men were spotting wells at widely separated points. Only two failed to develop water. Soon we were drawing up plans for the water piping. With the villages paying half the cost, and the PHCO the remainder under agreements worked out by Dr. Amuzegar, fifteen large villages now have completed sanitary water systems. Others are under way. This is in Iran where previously only Abadan, home of the oil refinery, had safe and adequate facilities. One among all the 101 places classified as cities! Many little villages have safe shallow wells and perhaps a single pipe running a few hundred feet to a central corner.

The day the water was turned on became in village after village the occasion for celebration and jubilation. I attended a few of these ceremonies. They are unforgettable. An occurrence at Zarghan, a village in Fars, typifies the popular reaction. Several of us were driving through and did not plan to stop. We had had a busy day attending inspections and ceremonies, including the turning on of the water at Marvdhast, some twenty miles north. It was hot and the road was dusty. We were all tired and longed to get back to Shiraz and a bath. At Zarghan three or four hundred men and boys had made a roadblock. Sweating but cheerful, they had been standing in the broiling sun. One group held up a large placard. The schoolteacher, Mr. M. Dara, could speak a little English. He stood well in front of the crowd. The placard, laboriously lettered in English, most of which could be read fairly easily with a little study, said:

The citizens of Zarghan offer their greetings to Mr. Warne, the Chief of TCI, on his arrival.

Peace be upon the soul of Mr. Roosevelt, the author of the idea of the Atlantic Charter, champion of the freedom of the people of underdeveloped countries.

Our good wishes to Mr. Truman, the founder of Point 4.

Our good wishes for the humanitarian nations of America which by the force of science and other actions is enabled to relieve the poor.

Mr. Warne, we offer our thanks and appreciation for the efforts carried out by Dr. [Moye] Freyman [our regional health officer], Engineer [Orris] Miller [regional sanitary engineer] and Engineer Khazai [Mr. Miller's assistant], and request you to give our recognition for this service.

Nothing would do now but that we trudge along for nearly half a mile to see the new deep well. The village elders explained on the way their system of water piping. Then they talked of other village needs. There was much racing about for the key to the pump-house door. When the elders led us in we found the diesel engine popping cheerfully. A large stream of clear, cold water spurted forth. I cupped my hands to take a few mouthfuls.

"But you are thirsty," the teacher cried. "We must have tea."

"No," I said. "As much as we would like to, we must not. We are very late and have engagements with the governor general and others in Shiraz."

We trudged back down the ditch bank. Women were washing clothes from the other bank. Small children were nakedly splashing about. Soon I saw trotting toward us from a village door a young gentleman with a tray of juice and glasses.

"At least we can have lemonade right here under this tree," Mr. Dara said.

I gave in. "Yes, it would be pleasant."

Seeing us stop, the man with the tray leaped across the ditch, scattering some sheep that had been standing with their forelegs in the water. He turned and filled his pitcher from the stream. He mixed the lemonade as he came forward slowly.

All the other Americans in the party, not having committed themselves, found suddenly that they were not at all thirsty, thank you just the same. Rather gleefully, I thought, they looked

Pure Water to Drink

on. I hope I didn't grimace. The stuff did me no harm, and it was refreshing.

Most of the inhabited centers on the Iranian plateau depend for drinking water on unique horizontal wells called *ghanats*. These are a heritage of modern Iran from a culture older than Persia. Of such antiquity that their origin is obscure, the *ghanat* is mentioned in the country's earliest writings. Today it remains one of Iran's principal sources of water both for domestic use and for irrigation. Perhaps the *ghanat* survives because the mechanical age has been slow in coming to Iran. Even villages irrigated by running water from local streams use *ghanat* water for drinking. An uncontaminated *ghanat* is as pure as deep-well water.

The most important cities of modern Iran—Tehran, Isfahan, Shiraz, Kerman, Yazd, Hamadan and Ghazvin—are situated on the dry plateau, which comprises all the central part of Iran. These cities have grown up in areas along the short, lost rivers, where the land has been irrigated and very intensively used. Only where some accident of geography has collected the runoff from great areas into a rare stream have large numbers of men been able to make their homes along these watercourses. Between the cities, where *ghanats* have been dug, villages have grown up. But these are sparse and isolated. The few streams dashing from the mountains have no outlet to the sea. They flow into salt sinks in the desert and evaporate. The plateau is a vast closed basin surrounded by rugged mountains, so ground waters have in many places been trapped in the sands. The *ghanats* tap these underground reservoirs.

Though statistics concerning them are incomplete, there must be about 20,000 of these ancient wells operating in Iran. Most of the towns and cities have many, and large villages often have more than one. The Irrigation Bongah has drafted rough specifications and water measurements on 4,073 *ghanats* some of which are found in each of the ten provinces.

The *ghanat* provides a means of skimming the ground-water table. It needs no pump. A discovery or mother well is sunk in the usual vertical manner at a likely place up the slope of one of the many plains receding from the mountains. It is not uncommon for these wells to be thirty meters, or more than 100 feet deep. They may, in fact, be much deeper. If the mother well strikes water—and it usually does, because *ghanat* builders are very skillful—the next step is to start digging at a spot down the slope from the well, but above the land to be watered. The channel is carefully aimed at the bottom of the mother well. The bottom of this ditch rises gently. Its pitch must not be so steep as to cause erosion when the water flows in it. The slope of the surface of the ground is much steeper and, of course, is not smooth. As it progresses the ditch becomes a trench. Soon the difference between the slopes of the steeper ground and the gentler *ghanat* makes the trench a tunnel. This tunnel is the beginning of the horizontal well.

The diggers drop ventilating shafts to the tunnel as molelike it progresses toward its goal. As a matter of fact, if there are enough men they may sink several shafts at once and work from several facings. These shafts are used also to lift out the excavated dirt, saving the long haul back to the mouth of the tunnel. The earth is piled in neat, low cones about the adit to keep surface drainage from entering the shaft and fouling the horizontal well with debris.

When the tunnel reaches the mother well water flows through it and from the *ghanat*. The upper end of the tunnel is usually buried a few feet in the water-bearing strata, which, like the ground surface, slopes off under the valley at a greater rate than the *ghanat*.

Ghanat digging is a highly skilled trade handed down for generations from father to son. The digger has no instruments but a rude level and compass. He tamps the earth he digs from the tunnel facings in leather buckets. These are lifted to the surface by cotton or camelhair ropes on crude windlasses. A man or boy

Pure Water to Drink

uses his hands and feet on the windlass as a squirrel does on a treadmill to provide the power.

If a serious ceiling-fall occurs in one of these wells the diggers usually bypass that area with a shoo-fly, or loop. If they suspect rock or poor earth underground they may use a dogleg instead of a straight line. Two mother wells are sometimes joined in a "Y" to a single-stem outlet tunnel.

Modern engineers with all the latest surveying equipment work in big shafts where they can stand erect. Even with electric lights and forced ventilation to help them they sometimes have bad moments as they bring together in the middle of a mountain two tunnels started from different facings. Will they meet? Will the tunnel have a crook in it? Will a hump in it impede the flow of water? What if they have miscalculated?

So imagine the plight of the *ghanat* digger in an unlighted hole, usually about twenty-five inches wide and forty inches high. His hole goes through earth and for the greater part of its length is not lined in any way. His only ventilation is created by open shafts along the route. He is working on a facing that is supposed to meet another facing. When the two are joined the tunnel is supposed to maintain accurately a slope that will sustain only a gentle flow. The completed tunnel must intercept the mother well below the water surface. This man does not worry about engineering miscalculations, because he has made no calculations in the first place. The *ghanat* digger is successful.

Though much of the passage may be unlined, when the tunnel penetrates soft spots where ceiling-falls or cave-ins are likely, oval bracings are inserted. These are made of clay baked like bricks. They look like horse collars, but they are larger. Each oval is five or six inches wide, and each will support five or six inches of the tunnel. The oval is standardized and can be mass-produced and used in almost any *ghanat*.

Strings of the mounds around *ghanat* adits are typical features of most Iranian landscapes. Uninitiated air travelers almost always ask curiously about the "small craters" strung along the edges of the valleys, curving up the slopes toward the mountains.

I remember my surprise one frosty morning when I saw a row of steaming adits that looked like smoking campfires or geysers about to erupt. I finally realized that the vapor from the relatively warm subterranean waters was condensing as it rose in the still, frigid air.

A strange fact is that fish live in the *ghanats*. A *ghanat* is not connected with any surface water except its own, and that is usually wholly consumed in the village or the fields it supports. There are many legends to explain how fish get into the *ghanats*, but their appearance in a new one is a puzzle.

There are many dead *ghanats* in Iran. Some of them have dried up because the water table has receded, but one near Isfahan has had a recorded flow for 2,000 years—and it is still operating merrily today.

Some *ghanats* have failed because of cave-ins. But a great one near the Afghan border has not even required cleaning in more than 100 years. This one is famous even in Iran. Its mother well is 400 meters deep—a quarter of a mile. Its horizontal well is forty kilometers long and big enough in diameter that a horse can be ridden in it.

Near Kerman the *ghanats* have to accommodate themselves to such gentle slopes that men must *kesh-kesh* the water from them. Using brooms in a pulling motion, they move the water along sluggishly. Otherwise it would stagnate.

It is not at all uncommon for a horizontal well to flow 400 gallons per minute. This flow is continuous, though it may dwindle in the summer during Iran's long seasonal drought.

A whole body of law dating back to earliest times has grown up around the *ghanat*. No one, for instance, can encroach on the *hareem* of a *ghanat*, a prescribed circle around an adit. Unused or "dead" land belongs to anyone who provides a well for its irrigation. The right to use the water rotates among the irrigators every eight days. The man who provides the water claims one-fifth of the crop.

Pure Water to Drink

Since the *ghanat* often flows more plentifully in winter, when water is not needed, than in summer, when it is more precious than gold, it is not efficient. But it is economical to operate, and requires little attention besides an occasional inspection and cleaning. Digging a *ghanat* in Iran today costs about the same as a deep well, pump and motor. The pumped well is more efficient in its use of water, since it produces only when the water is needed, but the pump is expensive to operate. This fact gives the *ghanat* undisputed advantage in the eyes of the Iranians.

The *ghanat* stands almost unchanged by technical advance. A local inventor is trying to perfect a mechanical digger. Some American technicians have toyed with the idea of lining the *ghanat* with a specially designed porous tile and putting a gate and valve on a long sleeve so the flow can be turned off when not needed. This might increase the amount of land that these wells could safely serve in any region by as much as twenty-five or thirty per cent. But this improvement has not had a trial. It might be too expensive or it might not work. William E. Wheeler is directing a Point 4 project in co-operation with the Irrigation Bongah to experiment with these and some other ideas.

Ghanats are found in other sections of the Middle East, especially in Iraq and Syria. Many Iranians believe that they are found only in regions where Persia has at some time been dominant. But the late Hall Paxton, who was American consul at Isfahan, reported seeing them in western China. And Dr. George B. Cressey, geographer of Syracuse University, who is studying them, reports some in northern Italy.

It is not unusual for Iranians to dig their unique wells under lands irrigated by others higher up the slope. In this way they recapture percolating waters for further use. In Ghamsar these overlapping hands of irrigation wells extend to the very edge of the salt desert, where nothing will grow. The *ghanats* at the lowest level drain away the saline waters and lower the water table of the outer fringe of sweet lands.

In November and early December of 1954, a freak of the

weather sent rain for twenty-one consecutive days to the Ziandehrud basin around Isfahan. It was a soaking, steady rain. The rainy season began unseasonably early in other parts of Iran as well, but the most rain for the longest period seemed to fall over the Ziandehrud. Even in the absence of sound weather records for comparison, it's fair to say that this was a very rare occurrence. Some mud villages became saturated and actually dissolved. Their little domed roofs collapsed and their walls were partly reduced. Ceilings in old houses in Isfahan also collapsed. Most significant, though, was the damage to *ghanats* in the valley. Of a large sampling inspected immediately after the great storm more than one third had been damaged. Many of these had collapsed. Some had been eroded into gullies. The collapses apparently occurred when the ground became saturated to depths below the *ghanat* lines. The earth simply squished the holes shut. Only the lower portion of a cross-section normally comes in contact with water.

I have mentioned the old abandoned villages sometimes seen in various parts of Iran. These, as I have said, look as if they had suffered heavy rain damage. This might have occurred after their abandonment. Deserted lands in some areas were formerly served by extensive *ghanat* systems. A falling water table may have rendered these useless, though evidence indicates that if this is so the water table must have receded rapidly after remaining constant for a long period. Responsible Iranian officials have theorized that the slaughter of most of the people by one of the numerous invaders probably depopulated these areas. The remaining men, they think, could not keep the *ghanats* in repair and so joined the nomads in the hills and unsettled valleys. This could be the accurate explanation.

Some of these invasions, by the way, were truly horrible. When the Mongols swept down on Persia from the Turkoman provinces their cruelty and efficiency in destruction left memories and marks that all the centuries have not erased. One proud

Persian city resisted the advance and was razed. Its mud walls and buildings were leveled and its site planted to barley. The Mongol commander is alleged to have sent word to Ghenghis Khan that if he came that way the following year he could pasture his horses where a great city once stood. The entire population of another place is said to have been slaughtered. The bodies were decapitated, the heads piled in a high pyramid before the main gate. But even these stories seem inadequate to explain all the blighted areas of the present day.

On the other hand, the explanation for both abandoned villages and deserted *ghanats* may be found in some long-past storm of a duration equal to or longer than that in the Ziandehrud valley. Some valley lands were idle and some villages were not rebuilt. Many of the wells inspected were beyond repair. There were not enough diggers nor enough capital to construct new ones in time to prevent "the droughting out" of some of the populated areas.

Deep wells are being introduced into Iran, though so far few are being used for irrigation. As the wells increase in number, engineers must be careful to avoid disastrous effects on *ghanat* systems, which cannot survive marked lowering of the water tables they bleed. Rapid seasonal drawdowns of the water tables sometimes accompany heavy pumping for irrigation in other areas of the world. This occurs even in places where there is no overdraft of the total annual replenishment of ground water and no permanent lowering of the water table. Seasonal drawdowns would have a grave effect on the flow of *ghanats* at the very time they are needed most.

The conflict between the old and the new is apparent in many situations in Iran. The *ghanat* and the pumped well. Only understanding and wisdom can avoid wasting the old simply to make way for the new. Practical solutions will use both the old and the new. Great strides have been made toward this end in Iran. But technical assistors beware! Oh, beware!

Mission/12

Opening the Windows of Heaven

RURAL EDUCATION in Iran was far behind even the standards prescribed by Iranian law. The rural census conducted in Fars Province under the Point 4 Public Statistics Cooperative project disclosed that ninety-seven per cent of the people were illiterate. In one out of every four villages the census takers could find no literate person. Though there were no reliable statistics on other provinces, we had little reason to believe a general census would show a much higher literacy rate in other rural areas. In the large cities the illiterates were proportionately fewer—probably they didn't number more than eighty in a hundred. Though the national law decreed universal education, no practical means of providing it existed. More than half of the villages have no schools.

The University of Tehran, now about twenty-five years old, is the only institution of higher learning that approaches Western standards. It has made good progress in its short life and promises to continue to improve rapidly. Iran also has several medical colleges and other specialized schools, but their work is not always of high quality. About as many Iranian boys and girls are sent abroad for their college work as are enrolled in Iran. Some of these youngsters are sent away while they are still in their teens. Many if not most of them spend six years or more abroad. French schools used to attract most of them, but in recent years by far the greatest number attend schools in the

United States. In 1954 in technical fields alone 1,157 Iranian students were doing college-level work in American schools.

Unfortunately a great many of the students who spend such long periods outside Iran become expatriated. This is one reason why I remarked earlier that one of Iran's principal exports is her best-trained young people. In their new homes they find opportunities they believe cannot be matched in their native land. They marry and have families. They grow away from old ways and fear the problems of readjustment. This is particularly true of those who marry abroad. It is difficult for the Western wife to find her place in Iranian society. It is even more difficult for the young Iranian women students who have been long away from home.

Many Iranians, even high government officials and men educated abroad, are not accompanied by their wives in society. It is not considered altogether polite to ask an acquaintance if he is married. A wife is a man's personal business. Some men have more than one, but there are not many plural marriages in Iran today. A man may legally have four wives but I met only one, a country man, whom I knew to have so many.

One of my good friends, an Oxford University graduate with a lovely wife and three boys, told me that his parents arranged his marriage. The arrangements were made after he returned from England, where he had been for eight years. He had never met his bride until the wedding ceremony. He admitted that before they were married he had managed by some little contrivance to see his future bride once on the street. She told me that she had not seen him even on that occasion. I've never seen a more successful marriage.

"These ways are not so strongly held any more," my friend explained to me, "but my mother is old-fashioned."

Iranian young ladies who have received good educations abroad are not encouraged very much to work and use their training when they return home. Point 4 proved a fashionable outlet for them. Many whose parents would not have permitted them to hold jobs elsewhere were allowed to work for us. Iranian parents liked the wholesome, matter-of-fact American attitude toward working women. A few remarkable Iranian women have completely overcome the obstacles of their culture. Iranian men with whom they come in contact through their work accept them on the same basis as the American working women in Iran.

One could hardly have counted the raised eyebrows in Iran (many of them on American faces) when, in March 1952, I sent Dr. Lucy W. Adams to Isfahan as provincial director. Behind all of the doubt was the question whether Iranians, whose own women were so terribly repressed, would accept her. And as a matter of fact Mrs. Adams' assignment was our most daring step. I am pleased to report that the faith that Ambassador Henderson, John Evans, then in charge of our field operations, and I had in her ability to meet this challenge was more than abundantly justified. It was soon apparent that she was accepted completely in Isfahan by high and low alike.

Dr. Adams has done more than anyone else in recent years to break the shackles off Iranian women. The Iranian working women rallied around her and a small group of women on our staff. Helen Bakhtiar, the nurse, Mrs. Bernice King, organizer of homemaking programs in girls' schools, Mrs. Helen Hunnerwadel, home canning expert, and Miss Luana Bowles, adult education specialist, played key roles. These women organized a seminar to discuss Iranian women's problems and to plan programs for them. In November 1954, the Empress asked Dr. Adams to explain the programs. She wanted to do her part to encourage it.

Three important new activities for women and girls were soon under way. The Empress herself organized girls' camps at a summer estate near Babolsar. A group of women, among them some American wives with experience as camp counselors, supervised them. Mrs. Curtis Spalding of the Near East Foundation staff organized home-demonstration work and adult education groups called "literacy classes" among village women in the Veramin district. Women's club work, supported by many American wives, was taking hold among Iranian women of prominent families. These clubs sponsored many valuable projects, including an orphanage.

Miss Bowles and I attended the graduation of a group of men she had been training for the Ministry of Education. Her students were now ready to organize a group of training schools for teachers of adult courses in reading and writing.

The minister, Reza Djaffari, handed out fifty diplomas in a program over which Miss Bowles presided. Mr. Djaffari made a glowing speech of appreciation of her efforts and the class roundly applauded her.

Several of the men told me that in all their education they never before had had a woman teacher. At first, they said, some in the class had been skeptical about Miss Bowles, but she had soon convinced them she knew what she was doing. "Now," one of the students explained, "we are much pleased with Miss Bowles."

I could see that they were. Her method with them was one with which American teachers had made us familiar. She'd stand for no monkey business and had the ability to back up her stand.

Deep-rooted habits were responsible for the men's original attitude. It's just that in Iran the woman's place is considered to be the home and her work the homely tasks. In the home and family the mother has a respected place and great authority. Daughters and sisters are treated well by fathers and brothers.

Never did I encounter an Iranian woman in a village public

meeting called for discussion. Even at public ceremonies the village women seldom appeared, though they sometimes watched at a distance, from the housetops, from across the river or from some other place of vantage.

There were some rare exceptions to this rule. At Mahallat when a new livestock station was dedicated half the square was reserved for women, who were there in numbers as great as the men. At Avonek when Mrs. Taleghani was in our party the women of the village came out en masse for the welcoming. Women of the upper class occasionally participated in discussions and public meetings. Sometimes they even accompanied their husbands on field trips, but this was not a general practice.

Realizing that these attitudes were strongly held and the result of long-established cultural patterns, I never took a picture of an Iranian woman without first asking her permission. Often she refused and I lost shots I wanted of women hulling rice, tossing wheat in a threshing circle, washing dishes in the *jube* or baking bread in an outdoor adobe oven.

"It is not right for a Moslem woman," she would explain.

Under gentle pressure from Point 4 little girls are beginning to be admitted into some village schools, though not in the same numbers as boys.

Long, patient work must precede the general change of attitude that will give women in Iran enough stature to permit them to contribute much outside the home. The work is only barely begun.

Dr. Adams had one advantage over the rest of us. She was the only Point 4 executive who could meet with the village women. Lucy would go among a knot of village women washing clothes in a ditch. In a moment other women would join them. They would test the material of Lucy's clothes, try her lipstick, show her how to wrap a *chadora*. Often they would even take her into their mud houses to exhibit their babies or show her how to mix a soup. But had a man tried the same thing, the original group would have melted away leaving the washing unfinished.

When in August 1953 Dr. Adams became program officer in Tehran and a member of the Joint Commission, I saw no evidence of any slight reluctance in any quarter to accept her. And Lucy never seemed embarrassed to find herself the only woman among a hundred or more men at some high-level official function. She was a member of the Joint Commission and was treated as such.

That time I went along when Khalil Taleghani took his wife to visit his ancestral home at Avonek we passed a boy driving a donkey in the opposite direction along the trail. On the donkey rode a very old woman. As we passed she kept up a steady stream of high-pitched chatter that seemed to be directed at our party. The Taleghan valley men who were accompanying us as grooms and guides turned their faces away to hide their grins. They seemed sheepish but tickled. My Persian friends from Tehran maintained a stoic silence.

Later, as we drank tea under a tree, I asked what had happened. Khalil explained that the old lady on the donkey had berated the two women of the party, Mrs. Taleghani and a friend, for the way they dressed and for accompanying their husbands on such a trip.

"Go back to Tehran," she had cried. "Where has the decency of our country gone?"

The men of the valley had reacted very much as little boys do when a mother has been rude to one of their companions. There was nothing they could do about it. They did not share the feeling, but they were a little amused and glad the scolding was not directed at them, as it might have been. Women, though seemingly repressed, have certain recognized rights in Iran. They exercise them strongly in the discipline of their children. Some of them, when they grow old, assume those rights with regard to all their neighbors. They are not denied the privilege.

At tea Mrs. Taleghani was pensive.

"One should not feel deeply such unjust criticism," I told her. "These people live in isolation. Their ways are the only ways that seem good to them."

"How you must have felt when people were shouting, 'Yankee Go Home!'" she said.

"I never let it get me down."

"This makes me feel somehow unwelcome," she said.

"On the contrary, you were warmly welcomed. Do you remember the greeting on the road by Avonek? What could have been more sincere? If you should stay here even these old women in *chadoras* would get used to your going about wearing blue jeans, a pretty red shirt and a big floppy straw hat. They simply have never seen anyone like you before."

"Did 'Yankee Go Home' ever make you feel unwelcome?"

"There was sometimes an unpleasant shock in it," I admitted. "But I soon remembered how kind and hospitable most of your people are."

Many of the Iranian students abroad, especially the girls, feared their homecoming. On trips to the United States I visited Iranian students on many campuses. Always they asked me anxiously, "Will there be jobs for us in Iran?"

Beneath this question lies a problem being recognized right now. It is presented by educated people in many parts of the world. In many underdeveloped and underactive countries they are not able to find enough to do. They go sour and feel aggrieved at social orders that do not use them.

But Iran's desperate lack of technically trained people creates opportunities there. Most of her returned students will be needed to participate in an economic development program now being financed by the resumed oil revenues. I tried to reassure these students by pointing out to them that no serious problem should develop in Iran. In spite of the fact that young Iranian engineers, doctors, agriculturists and educators, right after graduation may see more opportunities and jobs in the United States, their long-range prospects would seem better in their homeland.

One of the outstanding contributions made by Point 4 in Iran was the succor of the Iranian students in the United States. In March 1952 the Iranian government found it necessary because of its financial straits to shut off the use of foreign exchange for education abroad. Iranian students in the European countries were stranded. Many had to sacrifice the time they had already spent on their studies and quit. But we exchanged dollars for the *rials* of the parents of students in the United States who qualified. To qualify under our program a student must take a technical course related to Point 4 objectives in Iran. He had to accept a student's visa as a means of pledging to return to Iran. He was allowed to stay away from Iran for no more than six years. In accordance with a policy earlier established by the Iranian government the United States could provide dollars at a reduced exchange rate. We subsidized about forty per cent of the limited monthly funds permitted each student. Students who benefited have strong ties with America. Many will be among the leaders in Iran during the next quarter of a century.

Point 4's participation in this program ended with the 1955 academic year, when resumed oil production made foreign exchange again available to the Iranian government.

Many of the problems growing out of the spending of the school years abroad would be eliminated if Iran could further strengthen the University of Tehran and other institutions of higher education. Some families would continue to send their sons abroad simply because it has become fashionable to have a degree from an American or a French college. But fewer would go if local schools provided equally good educations.

With building up Iranian colleges in mind Point 4 earnestly co-operated in numerous projects. We helped to strengthen the Agricultural College and establish soils laboratories at the university; to create the Malariology Institute and the Institute of Public Administration on the university campus. Other projects included the Audio-Visual Institute, established in the university college of fine arts, and the virology laboratory at the Shiraz Medical Center. This also served the medical college there.

Other major programs were designed to provide high-level specialized training. One of these involved sending about forty students each year to American University at Beirut, Lebanon, for graduate training in nursing, engineering and agriculture.

But the largest and most elaborate of all the Point 4 training programs sent Iranian technicians to the United States for topping-off study, mostly outside of academic institutions, and practical field training. Each year approximately a hundred trainees gathered from a variety of fields were sent for from six months' to a year's specially designed training that usually included wide travel in the United States.

This special training program is, by the way, in force in all countries where Point 4 operates. It is perhaps the most popular activity and is surely one of the most effective in the entire program. In Iran our staff made deliberate attempts to select participants from many parts of the country. They tried to choose those who had demonstrated their ability to perform field tasks and other useful work. Agencies conducting projects selected the candidates in collaboration with the American technicians working on the project involved. Some were government employes; others were not. But for all we required assurances that on their return to Iran they would be used in the fields of their training. Since this training was not expected to lead to a degree, and since it might not include any actual work in schools, previous academic work was not so important a consideration as ability to absorb training. This opened the door for many likely young men and women whose social backgrounds had denied them much schooling.

Those coming home after such study tours were most enthusiastic. Their impressions and comment varied.

"I am not an educated man, Mr. Warne," one said, "but I was welcomed everywhere."

"I come from a third-class family, but my program was just the same as that of any other," another told me.

"In Illinois on the Day for Giving Thanks a professor at the school where I was visiting invited me to his home with several American students for a roast-turkey dinner."

It worked the other way too.

An engineer from a first-class family who had been sent to study maintenance of diesel locomotives had accepted an invitation to spend Christmas Day in the home of a shop foreman at the division maintenance center of the western railroad giving him a part of his training.

"The American workmen live well," he told me. "They have nice families. That foreman had a son at the University of Illinois studying engineering. He came home for the holiday and brought his girl. She was the daughter of a doctor in Chicago. In the afternoon a lot of the men in the shop drove up in their cars, not old beat-up jalopies, either. Some were brand new. See, here I have a picture of us in the shop."

He showed me a picture of himself and two typical American railroad mechanics standing beside a stripped-down diesel locomotive. They were all, the Iranian and the Americans, dressed in the peaked caps and coveralls of railroaders.

"This one here is the foreman," he said, pointing one man out to me. The man looked like the kind of fellow you would want to know. He may not have understood, I thought, what a lesson in American democracy he, his family and his men had taught. He probably had been moved solely by the urge to be kind to a stranger at Christmastime. I had to wipe my glasses, so moved was I by pride in our people.

These and other experiences made me more and more conscious of the strength of America. It is found, I think, in the fact that everyone can participate fully to the level of his endowment—men or women, rich or poor.

In Iran there is no caste system. It is possible to rise in the social strata. Some do and are fully accepted. The problem is that the opportunities to rise are limited by lack of educational facilities and poverty. Many who are gifted are not able to develop their talents. The talents are thus lost to the community and nation.

Of course not all participants put their Point 4 training to its intended use. We could hardly have hoped for a perfect record in selecting our candidates. And accidents or unforeseeable happenings accounted for some misfortunes. A shift in command in the agency to which a trainee was pledged might and sometimes did affect his acceptance on his return. But despite occasional failures, the training program in Iran was an outstanding success. It led to the modernization of the Ministry of Agriculture and to the establishment of the extension service. It helped to begin filling the need for public health technicians and administrators and for supervisors of educational projects. It trained specialists in fields of need from census to traffic control.

Each year the results were better, until in 1953 and 1954 there were 1,600 technicians in the Iranian ministries studying English so they might qualify for training grants if the selection board should allot places in their fields for which they might compete.

In my opinion Point 4's most fundamental work in Iran was that of assisting improvement in the country's educational system. This involved co-operation in a self-help program not only to build and improve schools but also to render them functional. This program's in-service teacher training project in four years gave special training to 12,000 elementary and secondary teachers, forty per cent of all such teachers in Iran. The project also trained and sent to field posts fifty-five rural school supervisors. Few elementary teachers had had more than nine grades of instruction. Many had had fewer. None had had any instruction in teaching methods. Summer schools for teachers, therefore, were of utmost importance in upgrading rural teaching.

On one field trip in a remote area I saw a lone rider approaching across the desert. He came up, dismounted at the place where we were watching some tribesmen demonstrate what they had learned about vaccinating sheep.

One of the tribesmen brought the visitor to me. "This man is a schoolteacher. He wants to talk with you."

"I have ridden for three hours from the village where I teach," the rider said when I turned to him. "I came to thank Point 4 for the school I attended at Isfahan last summer."

"Have you found the training useful then?"

"I had nine grades of school and I had five weeks of teacher training at Isfahan," he said. "These two have been of about equal value to me in teaching this year. But my school has grown. I had only thirty boys last year, but more and more keep coming. And this year we added some girls—we had none before. There are now sixty pupils, and I need help. Can you find another teacher?"

On a demonstration basis, Point 4 built 200 schools in widely separated villages. All large enough to carry on adequate programs. Each had windows and blackboards, a well and sanitary facilities. Another 200 were remodeled and brought up to standard. Villagers contributed the labor. Mud was the principal building material. The Ministry of Education adopted our plans and worked out a seven-year program to carry the work forward at the rate of 250 schools a year.

"You have opened the windows of heaven to us."

A small boy read as he stood one pace in front of his class at an improved country school where we were visiting. I was delighted to see that there were even a few girls, three or four among twenty or twenty-five students. But the small speaker commanded all our attention. His head, like those of his fellow students (except one girl's) was neatly shaved. His clothes were clean, and even here a hundred miles from Tehran, his dress was much like children's "Sunday best" in the United States thirty years ago—a jacket and knickerbockers of matching dark-colored wool. This was obviously a dress-up occasion. The boy read in a practiced, oracular tone, evenly emphasizing his words. He seemed completely self-possessed, but I noticed that he got a little mixed up and read a part of his speech twice. His teacher interfered when the lad started a third time:

"You have opened the windows of heaven to us...."

At the outset of our program the Ministry of Education had no centers for training rural teachers and but four vocational schools. In 1955 it had eleven teacher training centers and ninety-five rural schools in which trained instructors taught vocational agriculture. A plan was under way to add 400 more. In addition, seventy-two home economics departments had been added to girls' schools, some in every Ostan or province. Forty-two urban schools had industrial arts departments.

Two additional important steps deserve mention. A necessary and important work of modernizing textbooks had begun and several new books had already gone to schools. And the curriculum had been altered to allow a progression from a four-grade school to a six-grade school, and so on up the ladder.

Professor Turner of Georgia headed the education division. He had accompanied Dr. Harris to Iran in 1950 and had the longest continuous service in the Iranian Point 4 mission.

When Professor Turner went home for a three-month leave after four years in Iran, Reza Djaffari, then minister of education, said farewell with a graceful little speech. He hoped Turner would return quickly for "the co-operation between Point 4 and the ministry should grow stronger day by day."

Reza Djaffari closed with a quotation from the Persian poet Saadi:

> Oh, our beloved traveler, hundreds of hearts go with you,
> God bless you and return you safe and happy among us.

A Project, Full Cycle

THERE WERE few areas of Iranian life into which Point 4 did not extend. The cotton-classing project, a part of the agriculture, industry and training programs, typifies the sort of work that makes no headliner but contributes substantially to a people's welfare. Since it was completed in the relatively brief period of three years, I know at firsthand what it accomplished for Iran and for us.

A short time after I arrived in Tehran in 1951 Dr. A. F. Moffagham, at that time deputy minister of the Ministry of National Economy, called on me.

A serious problem had been encountered, Dr. Moffagham said, and he hoped that the technical co-operation offered by this new Point 4 agency might be of some assistance in solving it. I told my visitor that problems were our business.

"Iran, as you know," he explained, "is woefully short of foreign exchange. We are having to curtail many of our most treasured plans because foreign exchange is no longer available to finance even necessities."

Inability to sell the nationalized oil had cut off Iran's major source of foreign exchange in 1951. The country began to feel the pinch within months. Even before the end of the year chaos seemed only weeks away. The people and agencies I mentioned earlier were at that time making various efforts to settle Iran's dispute with Great Britain and turn on the oil again. One by one their efforts failed. In the meantime, while waiting for the happy day when the affair would be settled several agencies were trying to find other means to obtain foreign exchange. When Dr. Moffagham first called on me Dr. Mossadegh had not yet developed his concept of an "oil-less economy."

The prime minister had asked him, my caller said, to try to stimulate the exports of other commodities. Iran fortunately had had good rainfall two years in succession. As a result at the start of Iran's foreign exchange crisis, she found herself in the fortunate position of being able to sell abroad 50,000 tons of cotton. This year having been another good crop year, Dr. Moffagham explained, she again had surplus cotton available. But now the foreign exchange requirement was even more acute. When Dr. Moffagham paused I nodded that I understood. He continued.

"Foreign buyers will no longer take our cotton."

"Why?" I was honestly surprised.

"The world market is not quite so short this year. Shipping costs from Iranian ports are not as favorable as those from some others where cotton is available. But worst of all," he said, "there was a good deal of complaint from textile manufacturers, especially in Belgium and England, about the Iranian cotton they bought a year ago."

Dr. Moffagham explained that in Iranian bales cotton fibers or staples of varying length and varieties were mixed. The quality of the baled cotton was perhaps not always accurately stated. Complaints about some of it alleged that it had gummed up mill machines and stopped the whole manufacturing process.

"What I want you to do, Mr. Warne," he said, "is to bring a cotton-classing expert from the United States and station him at Khorramshahr. There he can sample all the cotton that we export and certify the grade of each bale."

"Oh," I said, "but I don't think that that will be good enough. I believe the trouble must arise long before the bales reach Khorramshahr. Anyway it would take months to find the kind of expert you describe and get him here."

Greatly disappointed, he said, "I don't see that this is too much to ask. Our situation is extremely urgent. Yet you say it will take

A Project, Full Cycle 185

months to get a man here and you protest against the procedure."

"Well," I explained, "I'm no expert in cotton classification, but I believe the problem is not quite what you suspect. Our study of your cotton producing methods seems to show the trouble goes clear back to your fields. Then I think it's aggravated in your ginning processes. If the cotton in the bales is as bad as the reports from the manufacturers indicate the mere stamp of a cotton-classing expert on it will not help you sell it."

"But, Mr. Warne," Dr. Moffagham insisted, "we must sell our surplus cotton this year. The revenue in dollars and pounds has never been so badly needed. You know we can't provide exchange to the sponsors of our students abroad. We've even had to deny exchange to some whose doctors advise them that their lives may depend on going to Switzerland for medical attention. And besides that, useful projects have been shut down for want of machinery that can't be made in Iran. An entire industrial plant has been crippled because it can't buy repair parts that have to be imported. We must sell that cotton now."

"If indeed it must be sold," I told him, "you'd better start dumping it for whatever you can get without bothering to wait for a cotton-classing expert. In the circumstances he won't be able to help you very much anyway this year."

Dr. Moffagham, who became and remained my good friend throughout my stay in his country, indicated now that he thought I was being deliberately unco-operative.

Finally I said to him with some heat, "This isn't a new problem in Iran. It has just suddenly developed into an urgent one. And ours isn't a miracle mission, but a technical mission."

Then we both calmed down and talked over the problem. Dr. R. W. Roskelley, then head of the Agriculture Division, and Dr. George Stewart, head of the plant sciences branch, had been in to talk with me a few days earlier. I told Dr. Moffagham that they saw the need to improve the cotton production through the selection of pure seed. Cotton varieties planted close together cross-pollinate quickly. As a result mixed varieties and varying staple lengths soon prevailed in every field. In all Iran at that time almost no fields produced uniform cotton.

I told Dr. Moffagham that our men were testing seed, planning to multiply the best varieties. Engineer Mostafa Zahedi, undersecretary of the Ministry of Agriculture, was much interested in a cotton improvement program. With Engineer Zahedi, Dr. Roskelley and Dr. Stewart had talked to Leslie Lane and Silvino da Silva of the Point 4 Industry Division. These two men were studying methods of handling the cotton after it left the fields. I had called in Mr. Lane, who explained that Mr. da Silva and Mr. Mansour Kazemi, his Iranian assistant, had visited several cotton gins near Tehran. They had found that the gins were not being properly operated. The speed was not properly adjusted; the machinery was not accurately set. A great deal of cotton was damaged in ginning. The Plan Organization, Mr. Lane believed, must first improve the process at several gins it owned and then help the private gin owners to do likewise.

All the elements these men were considering, I said, were also involved in selling the surplus cotton abroad.

"Well," Dr. Moffagham said, beginning to see some of the complexities of the situation, "you will try to help us?"

"Yes, of course I shall," I promised him.

During the spring of 1952 we developed the program into projects. Dr. Roskelley and Dr. Stewart worked out a plan with Mr. Zahedi to propagate tried, pure strains of cottonseed. Mr. Lane worked out with the Plan Organization a program for giving technical instruction in gin operation. Together these two divisions worked with the Ministry of Agriculture and with Dr. Moffagham's Ministry of National Economy to plan the organization of a cotton-classing school. For this school Point 4 would bring from the United States two expert instructors.

In my weekly report dated December 8, 1952, I said:

At long last we have started our class for cotton graders and classers in the Ministry of Agriculture auditorium. We have

A Project, Full Cycle 187

done this with the assistance of Messrs. E. McInnes and Charles H. Etheridge who arrived here on ninety-day detail. There are seventy-five Iranian students in the class and the probability exists that afternoon classes of an equal number will be required. The material presented in these classes is being retained and can be used in future presentations. At the opening session, Mr. Lane spoke briefly emphasizing the responsibility of cotton classers, stating that their integrity would greatly increase the value of the exported cotton and the acceptability of this cotton in foreign trade.

I was chagrined when Dr. Moffagham departed from the government before the first class was organized. But the wheel turned a full circle before the story ended, Iranian politics being what they are. Dr. Moffagham was again undersecretary of the Ministry of National Economy at the end of this project.

The necessary instruction materials for the cotton-grading class had been imported from the United States. They were prepared by the United States Department of Agriculture.

Messrs. McInnes and Etheridge near the end of their stay in Iran reported that several of the students had shown remarkable aptitude. Those enrolled had been recruited from government agencies and private gins.

In spring 1953 one of the graduates of the cotton class was selected to go to the United States for one year's field study. Young Mr. Azizz Bayan soon found himself installed as a student at Oklahoma A&M at Stillwater. His training, like that of the other trainees, cost Point 4 approximately $5,000, including transportation. He was at the time he left an employe of the Ministry of National Economy, which continued his rather small salary during his absence. His Iranian salary went to support his wife and child while he was abroad. Mr. Bayan had no independent income. He could not have gone to the United States if his ministry had not continued his pay. Although his English was not very good, Mr. Bayan studied intensively from the day he was selected. By the time he left Iran for Washington for indoctrination and completion of his study plans he was doing pretty well. At Oklahoma A&M he continued to demonstrate his unquestionable ability and his high aptitude. He soon was able to compete successfully with the American students.

Early in 1954 a review of the cotton improvement program showed that the amount of pure strain seed available had been increased more than ten times. At Ghamsar the Ministry of Agriculture had produced in villages under its direct supervision two crops of pure seed since it had undertaken the project in 1951. These villages had increased their yields and had so improved their quality that increased returns from this cotton more than repaid the cost of special care the program required.

The 1954 review also revealed that the cotton gin improvement had paid. Many of the men who took the first cotton-classing course had returned to their gins understanding for the first time the importance of proper operation in maintaining satisfactory grades in cotton. These men had helped to improve ginning practices in several regions.

Dr. Moffagham, Mostafa Zahedi and Point 4 technicians Mr. Pat Regan (Dr. Roskelley's successor) and Mr. Ray Stickney (Mr. Lane's successor) met together and decided that the Ministry of National Economy, assisted by the Ministry of Agriculture and the Plan Organization, would organize a cotton-classing course. Mr. Bayan, who had just completed his training and returned to Iran, was chosen to direct the course. He would use the same teaching methods and materials that Eugene McInnes and Charles Etheridge had brought and introduced. Mr. Bayan was familiar with them both through his work in the original course in Iran and through his intensive study at Oklahoma A&M. Little additional help would be required of Point 4.

Still the work of improving Iranian cotton had not been completed. About nine tenths of the old seed still had to be replaced. But when the 1954 crop had been ginned there was enough pure seed to plant about half Iran's 1955 acreage. In one more year the old problem should be eliminated with the old seed. Of course there is no surety that the varieties again will not deteriorate,

A Project, Full Cycle

cross and mix, or that the gins will always be operated properly.

Our technicians had turned their attention to the problem of organizing with the Ministry of Agriculture its new extension service, which would be available to teach the growers the importance of keeping their cotton uniform. The technicians went one step further. In co-operation with the Ministry of National Economy they worked to interest dealers in seed certification. A new model gin was erected at the Agriculture Ministry's Veramin station to abet continuous improvement of ginning practices by training operators and by demonstrating the importance of good machinery well maintained.

On a cold day in December 1954 I went to the formal opening of the new cotton-grading class. The scene was a loftlike building belonging to the art school of the University of Tehran. Three or four of us in the crowd had attended the first meeting. A new class of about fifty alert and eager young men marched in. They had been recruited from the government departments and from the government-owned and private cotton gins.

Dr. Moffagham, Engineer Zahedi and I congratulated one another when Mr. Bayan took over and the government of Iran began to help to improve and stabilize the quality of cotton.

When I left Tehran I received a letter from Mr. Bayan. One part of it touched me very deeply. I had once said in a discussion at the Iran-American Society Institute that some day he might be known as the "father of cotton grading" in Iran. He explained in his letter why he was especially grateful to Point 4. He did not know, he said, whether he might in time have the honors I had mentioned paid to him, but he wrote that if he did it would be only because Point 4 had trained him. He went on to say:

"People like myself who have no 'party,' riches or family background to help them but who earnestly desire to better themselves look up to Point 4 for light and guidance."

Those of us who conduct such programs (as Point 4) may forget that we are helping to lower some artificial barriers, but the fact is never overlooked by those with whom we work.

From Peasants to Freeholders

IN SEPTEMBER 1952, project agreement number thirty was executed. It set up a plan for co-operation in the Shah's crownlands distribution plan.

I recall that the Cabinet Committee meeting to consider the agreement was held in the circular office of Engineer Zanganeh at the Plan Organization building. Summer hours, to avoid working in the worst heat, were still being kept. Thus we met at 7:00 A.M. Hossein Ala, minister of court, was to sign the agreement with me if the Committee approved it. As we began I recalled my first meeting with the Shah when His Majesty had commended this project to me. Mr. Ala, former prime minister and one-time ambassador to the United States, in his usual courtly manner thanked Point 4 with generous mention of many special efforts put forth.

Paul Maris, then about to retire from the United States Department of Agriculture, had come out from Washington. He was to work with us and with Amlock, the crown agency that supervises the royal estates. It was then responsible for carrying out in about 3,000 villages this program designed to make freeholders of peasants. Hossein Ala, who became prime minister again in 1955, now in 1952 sat as head of a distinguished policy board guiding the land distribution. This committee supervised what seemed to me to be the most impressive agrarian reform in Asia.

Within a few weeks after my arrival in Iran I accepted Mr. Ala's invitation to visit Davudabad in the Veramin plain. Here his board interviewed the peasants, studied their claims to farms and reviewed and confirmed the list of those who would receive the land, which the engineers had laid out in plats. The preliminary findings of qualified investigators guided the board.

Old and grizzled men, boys of fourteen, the Mullah, sturdy sons of the soil—each in his turn appeared, stated his qualifications and answered a few questions.

"Your name is Ali Akhoosh?"

"Yes, sir."

"How long have you farmed in the village?"

"All of my life. My father and his father, the old, old man I remember—they, too, though they are gone now."

"Do you own oxen?"

"Not a whole ox, sir. I am not wealthy. I own an eighth of an ox. With seven others, I own an ox. We use him in turn."

"Do you have a family?"

"Yes, sir. I have a family, but only one wife. Not two like Hossein who was just here. But my wife is young and strong. We have a son."

"How old is the boy?"

"His mother still carries him in her arms. But some day he can work, too."

"Have you anything you wish to say?"

"I want some land. I live here. I work hard. May Allah bless His Majesty."

"Thank you, Ali, you may go."

The farmer bowed his way out, still twisting his knitted cap. His chapped heels showed as he shuffled along in his *givehs,* so broken down at the back that nothing much remained but a covering for the toes of his sockless feet. He was clapped on the back by his fellows who crowded around the door. The gendarme smiled a little in spite of himself and the exalted company he was guarding, mostly for ceremony. It amused him to see how pleased and excited the farmers were.

The next man Mr. Ala ordered called was the Mullah. This interview was about the same as the other. He, too, felt he was qualified for a farm. But he had one additional claim.

"The holy place," he said, "I tend it too."

"You tend the holy place?"

"Yes, sir. It should be placed in my keeping."

"Are you an educated man?"

"I can read, sir. I taught myself. I can keep the records."

When he was excused he left with dignity. There was no scuffling with him in exuberant congratulation at the door. The crowd made a way for him to walk through.

While the board conducted interviews all over Iran similar to these Paul Maris studied the plans already drafted for the program. In his report to the board he stated that if the distribution continued at its current rate it would take centuries to complete. But with help it might be done in nineteen years. The villagers would need some supervision. Paul's report suggested that one per cent be added to payments made for the land to finance this. Since the villagers needed a source of credit the report proposed that Point 4 and the Crown organize the Development Bank. Mr. Ala's board saw the wisdom of these proposals. Now the project agreement won approval of the Cabinet Committee.

Later in the fall of 1952, we gathered for a formal ceremony in the building that the new Development Bank was to use. The tension in the city necessitated extreme precautions to protect His Majesty. Tanks were parked to block side streets. Most of the ministers were present for the signing. The Amlock board was in charge and Hossein Ala was master of ceremonies. Because Mr. Ala was so short the microphone had to be raised and lowered after each speech. This brought a smile or two. It was about the only humor to crack the solemnity of the occasion.

At the close of the ceremony the Shah asked for me. "United States help in this program through Point 4 is greatly appreciated by myself and by Iran," he said. Gravely serious, he then added,

From Peasants to Freeholders 193

"This program cannot be permitted to fail. Your interest in it is most encouraging."

"The United States is honored to participate in Your Majesty's program to promote the welfare of the people in the crown-land villages and to help them become freeholders," I replied. "I assure you and Iran that we will continue to co-operate in this noble work. The program certainly shall succeed."

My assurance was shaken within a year. The program was halted by the pressure of Dr. Mossadegh. In his last extreme effort the prime minister tried to separate the crown lands from the Shah's control. The land distribution program was a principal motive for his proposed action. "Our government," he said, "cannot provide similar opportunities to all peasants who want them."

Though the law to increase the peasant's share of any profits from the land he tilled looked in the same direction as the Shah's land distribution program, Dr. Mossadegh feared the latter and favored the other.

By that time Point 4 was irretrievably committed to both programs. Both were valuable. I was very greatly relieved, therefore, to see the Shah's program resumed after the Zahedi government came to power.

In August 1953, I went again to the Veramin plain. With me on the trip were Paul Maris, now with the Ford Foundation, and Kenneth Iverson, also with that group, Dr. Lyle Hayden and Mr. Curtis Spalding of the Near East Foundation and Harald Larsen, John McCauley and Robert Minges of our staff. We met with the first board of directors of the new co-operative organized among the freeholders of the first nine villages distributed by the Shah among his peasant tenants.

The Ford Foundation provided money to build a school building at Mamazon. In this school the Near East Foundation trained village workers. Point 4 and Amlock together provided the supervision and made loans through the Development Bank.

At one village we asked one of the new freeholders whether he thought the trained village workers could be dispensed with.

"You would not send a flock into the hills without a shepherd," he replied.

This seemed to be the whole answer. As Paul Maris noted, even the most up-to-date farmers in the United States welcome the shepherds of research and extension.

In October 1953 an impressive ceremony at the Marble Palace in Tehran marked both the Shah's birthday and the resumption of the distribution of land. Titles to the lands they worked were distributed to 1,600 villagers of Takistan.

Iran had just passed through a crisis which we have reviewed in detail. The Shah had made his brief flight and Dr. Mossadegh was gone.

In the cold drizzle that fell during the ceremony I was warmed by the feeling that the simple rural people of Iran were repledging a faith restored by the monarch's bestowing his lands on his people. Many a rustic was literally struck speechless and returned to his place in the hollow square unable to open his mouth at all in the presence of His Imperial Majesty. Only four of the scores who tried got out any words at all.

One stammered out parts of what sounded like poetry. Another shouted, *"Zendeh-Bad Shah-in-Shah Iran,"* the traditional salute to the king. On August 19, 1953, it had become the rallying cry of the people who rose to restore the Shah to his throne.

One peasant, after gasping a few times, began a speech. "Your Majesty," he said, "I have three daughters but no sons."

Whatever the poor fellow had meant to say beyond this simple statement he then forgot completely. The Shah stood expectantly for a few moments waiting for him to continue. Then to end the man's confusion his ruler simply and gracefully wished him well.

"Our ancestors took to their graves the hopes which you have realized for us today," one gnarled peasant told His Majesty. The old man tore a strip of green cloth from the talisman marking him a pilgrim to the shrine at Meshed. He clumsily tied it to the Shah's wrist, then walked around him saying, "May any evil intended for you repose on me instead."

At the village of Fariman, about two jeep-hours from Meshed, I saw a remarkable demonstration of the effectiveness of all the patient work with the rural people. Here in 1954 the farmers had recently received their land from the Shah. At the time of my visit they were beginning participation in a farmers' co-operative which would provide a means for them to work together. A large group of dignitaries had driven out to Fariman with Provincial Director Richard Bernhart and me to observe their election of officers. Among them were His Excellency Mostafa Gholi Ram, governor general of Khorrasan, and His Excellency Ali Motamedi, head of the shrine of Meshed, which is supported by many dedicated villages in the vicinity.

John McCauley of our staff had sent to Fariman Mr. M. Emami, a brilliant young Iranian he had trained as a co-operative organizer. Mr. Emami showed that he had taught the people well. Only a few weeks before, they had been peasants. Now they were earnestly turning to their adventure in the new estate of freeholders.

The rural people of Iran have had no tools for community action. Among them exists no tradition of self-determination and co-operative action. Democratic processes do not function. As a consequence opportunities for individual growth are few. In a country in such circumstances as Iran's it is hardly surprising that the processes of self-government are somewhat less than wholly efficient. No more than seven of every hundred people can read or write. Many live in villages so isolated that they have almost no contact with the outside world. More than half the country's population is outside the range of even the most rudimentary schools. There are no publications of national circulation. The range of radio is too limited to reach much of the country and there is not enough power in the countryside to support receiver sets. Only 101 of thirty or forty thousand centers are sufficiently large to be classified as towns, and the governments of these are administered from a central department in Tehran. Iran's government floats like the marshmallow on a cup of cocoa. His Imperial Majesty the Shah is the symbol of authority. The cohesive force he symbolizes is pride in a great common culture.

All these factors tend to limit participation in government, as well as all other constructive efforts, to a proportion perhaps no greater than ten per cent of the people. These are, for the most part, members of a group of families which traditionally have held property, position and influence. These people, of course, educate their children.

At the outset we in Point 4 saw that a wider participation in all the country's affairs would be essential to our long-range economic-development program. This participation would give us a broader base from which to draw additional leadership and would provide the widespread energies we required. With this goal in mind we began basic projects in education, in land distribution, in community development, in agricultural extension, in training village workers, in organizing co-operatives and in generally encouraging private enterprise.

Until it is possible to institutionalize democracy at the lower levels of society and throughout the length and breadth of the land, Iran's situation will probably remain as it is at present. It is difficult to explain the problem except by contrasting it with the situation in our own country.

Self-determination and local responsibility are the hallmarks of American civilization. Pioneers carried the tradition of the town meeting with them as they moved westward. They had the will and the ability to organize themselves to meet their problems on every frontier. They believed in group action, democratically governed and co-operatively carried out, disciplined by

From Peasants to Freeholders

the power of public opinion. They carried the beliefs they expressed in barn-raisings and quilting bees through every process of government to the constitutions which made states of new territories.

In trying to explain this to Iranian friends unfamiliar with American political traditions I often enumerated some of the institutions through which my father, a farmer in the Imperial Valley of California, worked with his neighbors on problems they faced together in what then was a pioneering community. My father was a member of the irrigation district, managing the canal that delivered water from the Colorado River to irrigate the farms of the neighborhood. He was active in and Mother served on the board of the rural elementary school district. Father once served as president of the board of the Union High School District at Holtville. He was an elector in the county, state and national elections. All of my family participated in a nondenominational rural church that had been organized in our schoolhouse. Father was a member of the County Farm Bureau and attended the meetings regularly each month. He belonged to the Imperial County Fair Association. He helped to organize the Imperial Valley Milk Producers Association, a co-operative creamery, and was a member of its first board of directors.

Each of these institutions, most strictly local, played a part in our community life and its development. Scarcely any problem faced by an individual, a family or the community could not logically be brought before one of them for consideration and appropriate group action toward its solution.

Some mighty oaks grew out of the little acorns these people in my home community planted through exercising the democratic process. The first public meeting I can remember attending was one of the Farm Bureau. My father took me when I was hardly more than nine years old. The meeting, I recall, was held at our schoolhouse at Alamo. I was so thrilled that my hair seemed to stand on end when Mark Rose, one of the farmers in our community, stood up and discussed a plan to build a great dam in Boulder Canyon of the Colorado River to protect the valley from flood and insure a continuous water supply. No one had to explain to a child living on the last ranch under the High Line Canal, eight and a half miles from town, the need to solve the problem of drought and flood that the Colorado River visited upon us with the seasons.

Boulder-Hoover Dam is now known around the world. Even my Iranian friends could understand the significance of the action to tame the Colorado that grew out of the group determination of such farmer organizations as that one. As a filip to the story, I always reported that my first job with the United States Government was in the Bureau of Reclamation, the agency at the time—now more than 20 years ago—building Hoover Dam.

Governor General Ram spoke briefly to impress upon the Fariman villagers the fact that their monarch had given them an opportunity which it was up to them now to seize. Only they could make that opportunity yield them a better life.

When my turn came to speak, I tried to make clear that the new co-operative would prosper and be useful in direct relation to the support and thought that they, its members, gave it. It was theirs, I told them, not Point 4's or their government's. The co-operative was a responsibility which they must accept and carry.

These people we addressed were illiterate. Of course they had had no previous experience with meetings of any sort. Mr. Emami could not find one of them who could read the charter. They did agree that it had been read to them several times. After Mr. Emami had read it aloud once more they adopted it.

Mr. Emami had one of the village officials call forward a group from the prospective membership. He put the group through the co-operator's catechism.

"If I am a Jew and you are a Moslem," Mr. Emami asked one of the villagers, "can we both be members of the co-op?"

"*Bali* (yes)," was the immediate answer.

"If I have ten sheep and you have but five, how many votes do each of us get in the co-op?"

"*Yek* (one)."

"Correct again," said Mr. Emami.

So it went through the whole list of questions.

The Iranian officials present at Fariman were greatly impressed by this evidence that the rural people could be led to organize for constructive activity in their villages. In the group of observers were many of the leading Mullahs and most of the principal landowners of the neighborhood. Dick Bernhart explained to me that these people were greatly interested not only in the co-operative itself but also in the peasants' success as freeholders. Some of the landowners, including Ali Motamedi's Shrine Land Agency, were already casting about for ways and means to distribute their lands. The Shah's example was being watched with interest.

During the first week of July 1954, after the oil negotiations had been begun, the Shah made a very powerful plea for social justice and unity in Iran before the Iranian Senate at his court. His address as reported in *Farman* concluded:

"Now that the oil tangles are gradually being solved, we should by unity throw away our differences and take long steps for the improvement of our social, cultural, economic and financial situations so that the future generations will think highly of their forefathers."

Reza Shah urged the houses of Parliament to endeavor to enact laws to raise the general level of living without favoring any class.

"At present all classes of the people with the exception of a limited number are in an undesirable plight," His Majesty continued. "Landowners, and especially landowning magnates, should take practical steps for the security and peaceful living of their peasants." He warned of many dangers "as long as the tillers of the land, the farmers, are not certain that a suitable life" is in store for them.

Following this stirring address the Majlis passed a bill to distribute among the peasants the so-called "public domain" villages owned by the central government and operated for revenue devoted to special purposes.

Very early, shortly after she first went to Isfahan, Dr. Lucy Adams had brought up the problem of the "landlordless villages" in the Ziandehrud basin. The term itself was a shocker—the problem of the landlordless village! That the discovery of such a problem was amazing illustrates some of the twists that cultural shock will take. To anticipate problems of the landlord-owned villages wasn't too difficult, though except for a few "company towns" nothing even faintly resembling them exists in the United States. But to understand the problem of the village *without* a landlord we had first to understand the landlord system and what it meant in Iran, to discover that the landlord served a vital purpose in the structure of the feudal society.

Dr. Adams' initial report on the problem said:

In parts of the Isfahan Ostan the breakup of the landlord system is apparent. Generally speaking, only the smaller villages are landlord-owned. Almost all of the larger ones are predominately in small ownerships. Here the economic problems are the familiar ones of units of land too small to support a family supplemented by some kind of hand industry, yielding a few *rials* per day per worker. Able-bodied men are deserting the villages for the town to find steady employment and leaving their families behind. There are not always enough people left to take care of the lands, therefore they cannot keep up the *ghanats,* and so on in a descending economic spiral spelling the breakdown of feudalism.

Disappearance of the landlord presents its own problem. The landlord represents direction, credit and some measure of organized activity. In most of the small ownership villages there is no satisfactory landlord substitute. The more enterprising peasants extend credit at ruinous rates of interest. There is no one to whom the man in distress can turn as he can to the landlord, at least when the latter is in residence.

From Peasants to Freeholders 201

Creating satisfactory landlord substitutes is a service Point 4 could extend to numbers of villages as we are doing in connection with the distribution of the Shah's land.

A little later the opportunity to undertake something in this field presented itself. Point 4 set up its most elaborate project in co-operation with the agency created to administer the act to increase the peasants' share. This act was, of course, the Mossadegh law decreeing that landlords must pay to the peasant farmers ten per cent of the former landlord revenues from villages. You will doubtless remember that another ten per cent of profit went from landlord to a council chosen by the villagers themselves. Point 4 was interested in these councils. They might provide the beginnings of a grass-roots democracy.

Dr. Ahmad Hossein Adl, later to be minister of agriculture, had had a major role in drafting the act. He had then stood as the bulwark against efforts of landlords to wreck the measure. In May 1954, after the law had been in effect a year, Dr. Adl and I visited the twenty-three public domain villages in the Ghamsar area owned and supervised by the Ministry of Agriculture which was now in his charge.

In the twenty-three villages, all with active councils, lived an estimated 10,000 persons. Of these 1,400 to 1,500 were classified as farmers—heads of families actually tilling the soil. A few heads of families were storekeepers or worked at some other trade. Their number was unknown.

Using only their ten per cent of the crop profit paid by landlords, the village councils collectively had:

1. Constructed thirteen water *umbars* with filtration chambers at an average cost of 84,000 *rials* each.
2. Built (using the Point 4 design) two modern bathhouses with showers. Each cost 160,000 *rials*.
3. Converted two old pool-type bathhouses to showers for 50,000 *rials* each.
4. Built one six-classroom school—160,000 *rials*.

5. Built three four-classroom schools—120,000 *rials* each.
6. Repaired four old schools, putting in windows—30,000 *rials* each.
7. Built eight mortuaries, each designed to serve more than one village—35,000 *rials* each.
8. Built ten bridges—50,000 *rials* each.
9. Built one new mosque for 70,000 *rials* and repaired an old one for 2,000 *rials*.

Dr. Adl and I met with many of the twenty-three councils. We found them made up of typical countrymen. The ministry had given them support by providing an energetic young engineer to be their liaison with agencies that could offer them technical assistance in such projects as, for example, designing the shower baths. In co-operation with the Emron Bongah, the development agency set up to administer the village council program, Point 4 was training more men to serve as technical liaisons in other areas.

Perhaps the most valuable techniques America has to offer underdeveloped regions are those that make our own democratic processes work. The great strength of the United States lies in the astounding ability to find leadership in the intelligence, initiative and energies of *all* her people. It has been widely said that democracy is valuable in spite of its inefficiency. Inefficient? No other form of government yet devised has been capable of using so fully the skills of so large a percentage of the total population. I'd call that efficiency.

Rural Iranians are a sturdy, industrious, intelligent people, loyal to God and Country. A continued failure to use such human resources would handicap all types of developments in Iran more severely than would locking her petroleum permanently in the ground.

The village-council program was aimed especially to help people to help themselves. Encouraging progress had been made by the end of the second year. Tens of thousands of councils had been formed. A fair proportion of them had already begun to function. The political opposition from landlord groups did not seem likely to reverse the trend toward rural advancement.

At a village in the valley of the Golpayegan River I met with my first village council. The village was a bleak little place built of mud. In one courtyard two barefoot men with their pajama pants rolled up to their hips were mixing adobe and laying bricks, each about eleven inches square, out to dry in the sun. Into the thickening mud they tramped wheat straw chopped in four-inch lengths.

Almost no other material than adobe had been used in any building in the village. The houses were of one, or at most two, rooms. Each had a thick, high mud wall surrounding its compound, which was usually a bare space of hard-packed earth—a place to keep the sheep at night or the donkeys after work. Each house backed on either the great wall that surrounded the whole village or on another wall that ribbed it along important *jubes* and *kuchehs*. Since there were no wooden rafters to bear the weight of the heavy mud roof, the ceilings were domed to make a supporting arch.

Some compounds I saw were fouled with dung. A few had shallow, uncovered wells. The houses had no windows. Often a grate stood sheltered in a corner against a wall of the compound. Before a number of these grates I saw girls hardly more than babies squatting to stuff straw or dried weeds into a fire under a blackened kettle.

In larger villages a series of squares or a complex of irregular compounds merely increased the number of dark rooms, dismal stables and folds, barren yards. As the size of a village grows the likelihood increases that at least one man will have enough money to build a home of baked bricks. These houses take on additional elegance and signs of more gracious living as their owners climb the scale. Windows are added and more space. A truly fine house may even have a second floor or a porch.

In just such a fine house as this we met that first village council. Its compound had not only a well but also a little pool with three peach trees growing near it. The house was raised off the ground. A wide porch stretched across its front.

"Make this your home away from home," said the man who led our party to the house.

As the day was warm, the conference was held in the compound by the pool, where there were a few straight-backed chairs and some boxes on which to sit. The council was composed of three men, but the Mullah also attended. He, being the only one who could read and write, had prepared a petition for consideration by the Emron Bongah and Point 4. It asked for:

1. Construction of a school, which is highly needed by our rural people.
2. Modernizing the old-fashioned reservoir bath to prevent disease.
3. Construction of a modern slaughterhouse to eliminate hazards of poor sanitation and erection of a livestock-feeding station.
4. Repairs to and completion of the clinic to provide equipment and drugs needed and the assignment to the area of a good physician.
5. Exchanging bad seeds for good American seeds.

The petition added that the farmers of the area had after great effort established a primary six-grade school. But it had many defects. Therefore, the council requested help to complete the school and provide facilities for the people. It also asked at the same time that the Bongah inform all inhabitants about the measures that would be taken. Seyed Yadollah Moinaddini, the Mullah, had drafted the petition. The others had added their thumbprints.

We placed proposals such as these before the Emron Bongah, which examined them and looked into the village's financial capacity. If the petitions were approved the Emron Bongah would loan the council money from a fund co-operatively established by Point 4 and the Plan Organization.

Mission/15

Sands Run Low

IN JANUARY 1953 the Joint Commission was organized to replace the Cabinet Committee. Throughout the first six months of the year it met weekly. This was a time of gathering storm for Iran's already battered economy. But regardless of the turbulence our program moved steadily forward.

The sixty-ninth project agreement—one for a demonstration of methods of curing and packing dates—was approved on June 30. This agreement completed our second annual program. The United States had placed a second allotment of $23,000,000 in our technical program. The project agreement just signed was the fortieth added in the 1953 fiscal year. Some of these substituted for projects now inactive, but we then listed more than 55 active projects. Even a partial naming of these inevitably gives this page a dull, statistical look. Perhaps by this time you have learned enough of Point 4 operations to realize the importance of each to the continued life of an old culture. New projects included improvement of law enforcement services, launching a series of river basin surveys, demonstrations in wool sorting and scouring, establishment of a bureau of standards and an agricultural extension service. We had also begun a program of training in labor relations, established a public statistics co-operative and audio-visual training programs for schools. Our personnel had worked to improve the National Iranian Railroad and to train its employees. We had conducted demonstrations of automatic looms and modern weaving practices and had worked with skilled Iranians to improve the hand-weaving industry.

Point 4 had also begun to develop fisheries industry in the Persian Gulf and had set up demonstration and training centers for farm machinery repair. Our experts had given training in highway maintenance and demonstrations of low-cost housing. Literacy training for the gendarmery was in progress. We had helped create several experimental farm machinery co-operatives and conducted demonstrations and training in canning plant operation. Nearly all of these projects drew Point 4 into new areas and new relationships with the people of Iran.

Not all of the activity that affected the program in 1953 took place in Iran. President Dwight D. Eisenhower took over the reins in Washington on January 20. Through the spring and early summer preliminary steps were taken to reorganize the foreign operations of the United States Government. Our Technical Cooperation Administration, which had been joined to the State Department, was replaced by the independent Foreign Operations Administration under former Minnesota Governor Harold E. Stassen. The new organization was responsible for all types of foreign aid, not just technical assistance. At first the change made no difference in our operation in Iran. But Dr. Mossadegh immediately began to feel out the new American administration.

On May 28 he wrote to President Eisenhower asking our government to help Iran market her oil or, if that was not possible, to give economic aid to combat "the present dangerous situation in Iran."

A month later Dr. Mossadegh wrote me a letter saying he hoped that "the benevolent intentions of the American nation" might be reflected in an even larger Point 4 program in the 1954 fiscal year. Engineer Zanganeh, then chairman of the Joint Commission, wrote in the same vein.

Keyhan on June 30 editorialized: "A few days ago Dr. Mossadegh sent a letter of appreciation to Mr. Warne.... We hope that in the new fiscal year the Director of TCI will obtain more funds and will take new measures for the improvement of the country's economy and for helping various Iranian institutions."

This concerted effort did not please the antiforeign Tudeh papers, which lambasted the prime minister for his letter. *Keyhan* retorted to them, "Such men are hotter than the Soviets."

The awaited reply from President Eisenhower was published on July 3. The President assured Iran that technical and military assistance would be continued in the fiscal year ahead at a level comparable to that of the past two. He expressed the hope that "before it is too late" the government of Iran would take such steps as were in its power "to prevent further deterioration."

Tensions rose and disorders increased. The Tudehists now openly participated in demonstrations and were apparently welcomed. Despite the rising storm our program continued to develop under almost anxious co-operation from the Iranians. New projects were moved up to the starting line by willing hands. Great solicitude was shown for our safety, especially for mine.

Radio Moscow beamed inflammatory broadcasts to Iran which referred to me as "Warne, the imperialistic warmonger." The broadcasts described the Point 4 program as an effort of the United States "to establish a new colonial regime" in Iran.

I had grown used to this treatment. Nearly two years before, when I had been in Iran scarcely long enough to be able to find my way to the office, I was urgently summoned late one night to the telephone in the office of the Darband Hotel. On the wire was an Iranian friend whose sincerity I did not doubt.

"Hello, Mr. Warne," he said. "I am calling you from the prime minister's office. Police have uncovered what is believed to be a plot against your safety, and the prime minister insists that I warn you not to go out without protection. Tomorrow two plainclothesmen will be assigned to you."

"I doubt very much whether anyone is that much worked up about my presence in Iran," I protested.

"Well, some religious fanatics here have tried some assassinations, and some of the Tudehists are still around. Even with their party outlawed they haven't been stamped out altogether."

"But such a violent reaction to our work!" I exclaimed. "No group with any sense of responsibility would try a physical attack."

"But," my friend pointed out, "fanatics, either religious or political, may not feel any responsibility."

The next day Hossein, my driver, introduced two young policemen in civilian dress and informed me that these were my bodyguards.

"My what?" In spite of the conversation of the night before I was astonished.

"Your bodyguards," Hossein explained, "the ones the prime minister's office called you about last night."

"Well, what am I to do now?" I had never been guarded before and was uncertain of the etiquette involved.

"One of these men will always ride with us in our car," said Hossein. "If you are not planning to go out at night tell the one on duty and he won't wait around any longer."

As time ran on I got used to having a bodyguard seated stolidly in the right-hand front seat of my car or waiting in the lobby of whatever building I happened to be in. I got used to taking care of them too. If I went on a trip I found their hotel bill added to mine. They eventually came to be known within my family under the generic name "Daddy's private eyes." This term young Margaret inelegantly bestowed upon them one and all, without distinction.

It was impossible at the time and is difficult now to tell where genuine concern ended and harassment began.

The police knew where I was every minute of the day and night. They knew whom I met and with whom I talked, what my habits were and who came to call at my gate at night. My "private eyes" seemed to pay no attention to these details but later when opposition was building up against the Mossadegh regime

Sands Run Low

one of my friends told me differently. The friend was out of sympathy with the good doctor but nevertheless had informants in important places in the government. "The secret police had a report in the prime minister's hands this morning," he said, "that my car was parked at your gate between ten and eleven o'clock last night."

But these messages were not always read at once in the prime minister's house. Though I made every effort to give advance notice when I was preparing for a trip I now and then found Dr. Mossadegh most reluctant that I should go. "Preparations should be made," he would say. "I did not know about it."

The first time this occurred was in late October 1952. I had been planning to go to Tabriz, the capital of Azerbaijan, for many weeks. I had been importuned to make the trip by the governor of the province, by members of the Majlis from that region and by many others. A chartered plane was warming up on the apron at Mehrabad Airport and my party had assembled there when I received a telephone call. It was from one of Dr. Mossadegh's secretaries.

"But Mr. Warne," he said, "it would be unsafe for you to go to Tabriz at this time. The prime minister forbids it for your own safety."

I could get no further explanation. I was compelled to make some very lame excuses to the people preparing to welcome me in Tabriz.

On another occasion several months later I had completed arrangements to drive to Isfahan and Shiraz. This was to be a trip of inspection. Functions had been arranged in several places along the way. The Iranian members of the Joint Commission gave a dinner for the Point 4 staff on the night before our departure. As I was leaving my house to go to the Darband Hotel, where the dinner was to be, my gateman brought me a note in Farsee. The insignia on the envelope told me it had come directly from the prime minister's hands.

When I got to the hotel I showed it to my host, a cabinet member. "This came just as I was leaving home," I said. "I haven't had a chance to get it translated."

He took the slip of paper out of the envelope and read it carefully by the light of a Japanese lantern in the garden. "The Prime Minister does not want you to go to Shiraz tomorrow," he said.

"But I must!" I protested. "The people there are expecting me. And I've notified all of the officials here. Everyone knew I was going, including you and the rest of the cabinet."

"He simply says that he does not want you to go because he considers it unsafe," my host explained.

I persuaded him to telephone the prime minister's house and remonstrate with him. When he returned to the garden he said that the prime minister had decided that I could make the trip but that he would send a squad of soldiers along with me.

At four o'clock the next morning a jeep drove up to my gate carrying a corporal and four Iranian soldiers armed to the teeth. They told my gardener that they were to escort me to Shiraz.

At lunchtime my car stopped at a roadside teahouse near Dellijan, where we broke out some C-rations. When we were about through eating we saw a jeep approaching pell mell. It carried our guard. We flagged it down and ordered lunch for the boys. They trailed us into Isfahan that night by forty-five minutes and pitched a tent under our window in the garden of the Irantour Hotel.

They sent an emissary to see me. "Would it not be possible, Mr. Warne," he asked, "for you to trade for a few days a Point 4 carryall for this army jeep so my boys can keep up? If the prime minister finds out they're lagging so far behind he won't like it."

The next morning we provided the soldiers with a car drawn from Point 4's Isfahan compound. Throughout the trip the soldiers stayed with us, bringing up the rear of our caravan. They all tumbled out whenever we stopped. They were always both

Sands Run Low

cheerful and dutiful. On the last scorching day of the trip, as we crossed the salt desert north of Qum, we stopped to let the motor cool and the caravan catch up. The soldiers were again in their jeep by this time. We had taken it slowly and they were not too far behind. Even so, the pace was furious for the little car. The boys looked very hot and dusty.

"Corporal, you and these soldiers have done a good job," I told them. "We're almost home. You can consider yourselves dismissed and go straight to your barracks. I am pleased with the way you carried out your orders and I shall report it."

I gave each of them a hundred *rials*—which, I learned later, equaled several months' pay for a common soldier in the Iranian Army, and took their snappy salute. There had not been any incident on the trip that required any special protection.

Indeed, at the village of Khupayeh the people resented the soldiers and took their presence as in some way critical of themselves.

"Tell Mr. Warne," they instructed a messenger, "that the villagers of Khupayeh invited him here and that we will protect him."

I tried to explain that I had not asked that the soldiers accompany me and that I felt no need for protection. I was especially anxious not to offend these villagers. The Khupayeh weavers constituted an important unit in the new project to improve the hand-weaving industry, vital to the economy of some areas. Their plight had interested Point 4.

Khupayeh is a forlorn-looking village. Its *ghanat* has failed. Once more populous, it has 3,000 residents today. Of these 800 are employed at hand looms, weaving cloths of various kinds. Only two hectares (a little less than five acres) of the fields that once surrounded the place are now irrigated for farming. The people have perforce turned to other means to earn a livelihood.

The way the town is situated provides the clue to the fate which has befallen it. It lies on the rising plain, far out toward the desert from the thread of the dwindling Ziandehrud River. Its *ghanat* must have been precarious from the start. Khupayeh was the first to feel a slight lowering of the plain's water table. The disaster struck the village many years ago.

Under the glaring summer sun which beats on Khupayeh its shortage of water is obvious. Not only is the agricultural area constricted almost to the point of disappearing, but the town itself is dust-dry. It has hardly a sprig of green anywhere.

At the dark moment when the farmland dried up someone must have brought strong leadership to the village. Its people's success at turning their hands to the looms attests to that. Yet I was shocked at the dark, dusty holes in which the weavers work. I couldn't help wondering why the ingenuity that beat back fate had not carried the industry a few steps further ahead. Many of the weavers are only boys. Peering through the lint-laden air of their workrooms I wondered whether there might not be a grim explanation for this fact.

Still the town is sparked with ingenuity and spirit. Its people built a fine modern school that uses every technical aid it can to improve its instruction. At the time of my visit Khupayeh had recently completed a new health center. But the village still has bad luck. No site for a deep well could be found, so the people must depend on a shallow one dug by hand.

Mr. M. Yussefy, the chairman of the weavers' union, was the leading spirit in the drive for the co-operative project to better their condition. He led us through the village's winding *kuchehs*. Our soldiers, who had heard the messenger's greeting, remained at the roadside while we went from one workshop to another. Finally we came to Mr. Yussefy's home, a modest house in a bare, sun-baked compound. The room into which our host showed us had no furniture. Sitting cross-legged, backs against the wall, on a fine Persian carpet we fingered and tested cotton, woolen and feltlike fabrics, the products of Khupayeh's handcraftsmen.

Mr. Yussefy introduced his committee, modest, sturdy, weatherbeaten village men. We talked of their ambition to get better looms and to pool their resources so they could co-operatively buy better yarns. They especially hoped to work out a method for the weavers to sell their products without each one's having to take his bolt to Isfahan, nearly a hundred kilometers away.

We also debated at this time whether the weavers should plan to dye their own threads and yarns. Most of the committee favored this, since they disapproved of the quality of some of the colored yarns they had recently bought.

A major point in our discussion was how to curb the strong individualistic tendencies of the people to avoid shattering the co-operative.

"If the looms are placed together," a committeeman said, "the weavers will work together. They cannot learn to work together each in his own dark cell."

Units of this project similar to the one at Khupayeh were being established in Isfahan, Kerman, Yazd and Nain. With Point 4 help the weavers were able to buy improved looms of Japanese design. On these looms they were able to make better cloth faster. Our technicians recommended community weaving rooms to provide more healthful surroundings.

After our hasty visit much more study went into the organization of the project at Khupayeh. In the end the men of the village built a community weaving room. They set up their buying co-op too and joined together to market their goods.

"It is the duty of patriotic Iranians and good Moslems to pay gratitude," Mr. Yussefy wrote to me when his weavers' union was operating under the project's improvements.

The spirit of the Khupayeh villagers impressed me. It had kept them from faltering in the face of great adversity. It was reflected too in their reaction to the guards Dr. Mossadegh had sent with me. It was to prevent just this reaction that the Point 4 people in Iran made every effort to avoid having to appear in the villages with military escort. The presence of armed guards seemed to speak more of force than of co-operation.

Wherever I went in Iran, I found that Point 4 was known and I was recognized. So perhaps if there had been any undercurrents of violent opposition in the countryside the "protection" would have proved useful. But I must admit that the only time I was involved in an incident came after my "private eyes" had been withdrawn. My usual reception was one of welcome.

On one occasion, for example, my party entered the Lavison Valley in the Elburz Mountains over a difficult donkey trail. I had not ridden for a long time and welcomed a halt at a teahouse. We sat in the shade while our mules were watered and tea was prepared. A young man approached us.

"I believe you are Mr. Warne of Point 4," he said.

I looked up quizzically, then nodded. So far as I knew no one in this valley knew I was there. I had intended only to pass through to a still higher valley.

"Must you pass through immediately?" he asked. "I would be pleased to gather some of the men of the village together to greet you."

"No, I'm sorry," I said, "I must be in the Lar valley by nightfall, and it's already late."

"You will permit me then," he said, "to extend to you our welcome on behalf of those who are absent. This valley too has many problems I should like to call to your attention. There is a sickness among the flocks. I think the water is polluted. The school is inadequate. The people here are poor. They have no money with which to buy the things that they need."

I made a note to have a veterinarian team look into the sickness of the Lavison Valley flocks. I had heard that hoof and mouth disease was endemic to these mountains.

On another afternoon we stopped to look about in Destgerd-of-the-Grapes. Almost immediately men began to assemble.

Sands Run Low

Soon a village leader came. He was an old man with snow-white hair. His long whiskers had been dyed pink with henna. He stood respectfully before us, holding in his hand the hat he was obviously long-used to wearing, perhaps indoors as well as out. Through his thin hair his pale scalp gleamed in sharp contrast to his weatherbeaten face. He spoke a few words of welcome and said that he regretted that we had not let the villagers know we were coming. He assured us of their earnest hospitality.

The old man talked then of the problems of his village. Many of the children were ill. There was no school. The sen bug was taking the wheat. He believed, our petitioner told us, that these things would warrant our attention. Again he welcomed us, then concluded by saying that he and his fellows looked hopefully toward the future.

At Chadegan in the autumn of 1952 we received a truly impressive reception. This village is in an isolated valley which has a population of, I suppose, 150,000. By improving a donkeypath, removing rocks, filling in old ditches, and clearing stumps the villagers had made a passable road twenty-two kilometers long so we could drive clear into Chadegan. Two days earlier Mr. Amir Moazemi Daliri, a village leader, had asked us to arrive at noon. He rode fifty kilometers to meet us. At the gate stood a village woman holding the welcome brazier. She showed us how to sprinkle *esfand* into its smoldering fire. Around the corner we came upon a throng of thousands. Men and boys filled the narrow square and the road. Women and children covered the housetops for as far as we could see. Again the cheering. And again the greeting ceremony by the village leaders. This time a formal petition had been drawn up and was presented.

On another trip in January 1953 we reached Khoshkrood after night had fallen. Several hundred men led by five Khadkhodas met us a kilometer from the village. The desert night was biting cold. The road was lighted only by three or four lanterns and the stars. Men and boys were drawn up like soldiers on either side.

A typhoid epidemic had broken out here five weeks before, and one of the three Point 4 mobile health units had been assigned to Khoshkrood. Its efforts had halted the spread of the scourge that had taken twenty-one lives. We had come to inspect the work and to observe the making of a film to help teach other villages how to combat typhoid. We were escorted between the lines to resounding cheers. Despite our protests the villagers sacrificed two sheep and spread their blood across our path. The Khadkhodas urgently invited us on foot to lead the villagers into town. "It is the custom," they explained.

Our procession proceeded with a lantern at the front. In the village the women and children were drawn up in columns as the men had been. Additional sacrifices were made, again over our earnest protests. The cheer, now familiar, was for *Asle Chahar*.

It was at Khoshkrood that I learned about the bridge of Sarat. According to folk tradition this is the bridge of separation between heaven and hell. Souls cross it to heaven or are stopped there, according to their desserts. There on the bridge witnesses may testify to one's earthly performance. This testimony determines whether one passes beyond the bridge to eternal bliss.

Dr. Moghadam told me the legend of the bridge to explain an incident of the evening. There had been much speech-making in the road. At one point a very articulate but rough-looking peasant rushed forward, clasped my hand and delivered, in mixed Farsee-Turki, an impassioned oration on the needs of the village. He thanked Point 4 for what it had already done and enumerated additional needs, especially a water supply and school improvements.

He concluded by saying, "And if you do these things, I and the people of Khoshkrood will await you in the dark of the eternal

Sands Run Low

night as we have met you in the darkness of this evening here at our village gate, and we will not permit a bar to be placed in your way on the bridge of Sarat."

At Khoshkrood I learned another important lesson—without heat the rooms of a mud hut get desperately cold on winter nights. We could keep warm only by going to bed almost fully clothed. And even at that my knees ached for an hour. We who have grown used to living in heated rooms and even riding in heated cars find it hard to remember what an enemy of comfort—and even life—bitter cold can be. Iranian villagers must spend about a third of their time and energy searching for fuel to burn against the winter's need. Hillsides for miles around are stripped almost unbelievably clean of all plants and brush that can be burned. But it is never warm in these mud houses once the cold sets in.

Flying on a clear winter day over Iranian villages in the high plateau, I have seen many of them completely blanketed in untracked snow. Not a visible wisp of smoke rises. In bitter weather the people stay close to home and use devices like the *corsi*, which keeps the whole family warm.

A *corsi* consists of a brazier of charcoal embers placed under a low table, which is then covered over with blankets. I was introduced to it by Dr. Gholam Mossadegh, son of the prime minister, whose wife rightly thought I would like to try one. The *corsi* almost filled the room it occupied. Cushions were placed around it. I left my shoes at the door and shoved my feet under the blankets to the heat. It was snug and cozy and most welcome to me.

I mentioned that one of the objects of our visit to Khoshkrood was to check on the progress of Point 4 film being made there. The audio-visual center of Syracuse University made in Iran, under a Point 4 contract, scores of films to assist in our educational and training work. The center also trained Iranians to make these kinds of teaching aids. The young men working in the motion picture project had to devise new techniques to appeal to unsophisticated audiences as those in the back-country villages. Slow pacing was required as well as recognizable scenes and properties.

A few times we tried showing pictures made in America, but the background scenes were so strange to the Iranian audiences that they rendered even the message unbelievable. And while American audiences understand such camera tricks as close-ups and superimposing, the villagers of Iran do not. In one American show, designed to persuade its viewers to rid themselves of mice, the camera so focused on a mouse that he filled the whole screen so that the enemy might be dramatically identified. One peasant, seeing this, was heard to say, "No wonder they think mice are dangerous in America. So big! The mice in our wheat stores in Aliabad are so little that they are harmless."

That morning in Khoshkrood the film unit photographed some scenes for the film on typhoid control. We followed the movie crew down the long flight of steps to the *umbar* which was the town's only source of domestic water. Its contamination had been responsible for the typhoid epidemic. The mobile health team's first move had been to chlorinate the water.

One of the doctors showed us through a door into a one-room home. Stretched out on a rug in a corner was a man from a village six miles away. His family had brought him, very ill, to Khoshkrood when they heard the news that the health team was there. He was suffering from double pneumonia, but had been safely set on the road to recovery. People from sixty-one villages came to Khoshkrood to see the doctor during the five weeks the team was there.

Friendly experiences in the villages were, as I have said, the rule. The one untoward incident I mentioned earlier occurred near Hamadan. This was a deliberate effort to embarrass or intimidate me.

I had gone to Hamadan in May 1954 on the invitation of Mr.

Sands Run Low

Abolghassem Panahy, then director general of the Plan Organization. His unexpected death, which came a month later, saddened all Iran.

The Plan Organization had completed a small but modern hotel at Hamadan, the site of Avecenna's tomb. The millenium of the death of that great savant had inspired a celebration which brought learned men from all over the world to Iran. The hotel was built to house these distinguished visitors. The Shah himself stayed there on the last day of the celebration, when the group participating in the celebration moved from Tehran to Hamadan.

Mr. Panahy, his family and some friends were going to Hamadan for the weekend, taking advantage of the fact that the Monday following was a religious holiday.

"Why don't you come along?" Mrs. Panahy asked me. "Hammadan is an historic old town. It is very high, so it will be cool and lovely up there. We will have picnics in the fruit gardens on the mountainside. I'll even show you the carvings of Darius on Mount Alband."

Her husband joined in urging me to make the trip. "The capital will be completely closed down over this holiday," he assured me. "You could drive back on Monday afternoon and be here when your office opens on Tuesday morning."

It was a wonderful holiday at that. The weather was all it had been advertised to be. The hotel was very comfortable. We visited Avecenna's tomb and the famous old shrine where Babataher Oryan, a famous poet, was buried. This tomb was in a Mosque at least a thousand years old. We also visited the Jewish shrine, where a functionary who looks almost as ancient as the hewn-stone door leading into the sepulchre retells to visitors the Old Testament story of Queen Esther, who with Mordacai is buried there.

"Tomorrow morning, before you start back for Tehran," Mrs. Panahy said, "we shall climb up to the inscription of Darius."

She was an excellent hiker and had been there many times. To save time we borrowed a jeep to take us as far as it could. To reach the inscription we used the road which two thousand years ago ran from Hamadan, Darius' summer capital (Ecbatana), to Tooysergan, over the shoulder of Mount Alband. Most of this old road had been used for many centuries only by donkeys and flocks. The inscription was up near the snow line, close to the crest of the road. Reza Ansari, my good young friend and assistant, went along.

We did very well in the jeep. By turning and twisting, dodging washed-out places and fallen walls, we drove to within a few miles of the carving. As usual on holidays, many hiking parties of men and boys were bound for the mountains. At one point the trail peters out into a canyon through which a plunging stream has obliterated all sign of the ancient track. Here, about half a mile from the inscription and about a thousand feet below it, the inevitable teahouse awaits the traveler. There we rested for ten minutes.

There must have been fifty men and boys in and about the teahouse. Some obviously planned to go higher, while others prepared to go back. Although few women and fewer foreigners must have stopped at this isolated hostelry, we attracted little attention at first. Then a group of about a dozen arrived, and I heard the word go around that Mr. Warne was there.

We began the last of the climb, not hurrying because of the altitude and the rough going, but not stopping either. Within about 200 yards of the carving we were passed by a hiking party of young men and boys. They were taking a slightly different route and were having a little better time of it than we. There was no marked trail on this part of the mountain. When we came up to the inscription we found this group was there ahead of us, waiting. Paying no attention to the fellows, mostly teenagers, I scrambled up through them to get to a vantage point from which to take a picture. Mrs. Panahy stayed below. From a rock down beneath me somewhere I heard her call to me that after I had looked at the inscription from where I was I could come down and get a good picture from a place she had found.

At this moment I heard angry voices, including Reza's, behind me. I then became aware of some unspoken antagonism on the part of some of the boys near me. They did, however, get out of camera range and let me have a place with a secure footing. I took plenty of time since my film was nearly gone.

In climbing back down to Mrs. Panahy I passed again through the hikers. I noticed a young man who seemed to be their leader standing on a big boulder near by.

"Mr. Warne," he said, "did you take your picture?"

"Yes," I answered, surprised that he spoke English.

"You have made your picture. Go," he said shortly.

"I didn't know," I said, "that we were interfering in any way with you boys. I want to get a picture from down here too."

I paid no more attention to him but went on to the rock where Mrs. Panahy was sitting. While I was getting my camera ready the fellow again addressed me.

"Take one more picture and go, Mr. Warne," he said, with a slight change in tactics.

Mrs. Panahy said, "I'm sorry, but I don't think we should stay here too long. This is a Communist gang."

"Yes," Reza added, coming up. "That fellow wants to start something."

"I thought probably he did," I said, "but the younger ones have been acting well enough. They won't do anything."

I could see other hikers going on up the canyon past the inscription, but none stopped to join those already on the rocks behind me. I felt certain that the word had been passed around that this group planned to embarrass me. Most of the hikers didn't want anything to do with a scene.

I took another shot with the last frame in the camera. Mrs. Panahy, Reza and I stood looking at the ancient inscription for a while. We were much impressed by the care the proud king had taken to recess the carving to protect it from the weather.

The manner in which his son had ordered his own addendum carved also interested us. He had been very careful to keep lower and to the right of his father's inscription. We observed too that the stone had, in more than 20 centuries, weathered so that a flaw defaced but did not obscure the Darius plaque.

Going back as we had come, we passed the group of hikers again. When we were about a hundred feet from them the leader shouted what sounded to me like, "The young Communists of Hamadan say go!"

A sentence or two in Farsee followed. Then the leader struck up a Tudeh party song. I turned and waved to them as they sat on top of a big rock. Some were singing with the leader, who was marking time like a school teacher.

I found later that Reza and Mrs. Panahy took a very serious view of our experience. Some of the Farsee shouts had been more threatening than I had comprehended. But the fact remained that we were not molested. A few days later the police rounded up the leader. He was a teacher who had been discharged from his school for Tudeh party activities. No other incidents like that were reported from Hamadan.

But to go back to July of 1953, almost every day was a day of violence in the streets of Tehran. Dr. Mossadegh seemed to have no solution for his country's tribulation. Without oil the Iranian economy was stalling. Tehran newspapers headlined an interview in which Secretary of State John Foster Dulles was reported to have expressed anxiety that the "unlawful Tudeh party" was being increasingly tolerated in Iran.

The newspapers played up even more boldly a few days later an interview with Alayar Saleh, Iranian ambassador to the United States. Dr. Saleh said that extremist groups flourish where conditions are favorable to them. He blamed Iran's plight on previous British exploitation. He seemed to believe that without a great deal of help the Tudehists could not be put down.

The sands were running out.

Mission/16

Doors to Progress

"You have opened many doors to progress for us," said Ahmad Hossein Adl, minister of agriculture. This speech, made in autumn 1954, opened a conference on plans to integrate the Point 4 agricultural projects into his Iranian ministry. "It will be important," the minister continued, "for us to weld these new programs into the framework of the structure of the ministry."

In the field of agriculture we had done some of our most telling work. The jackasses, the baby chicks and the mobile veterinary teams were only the beginning of the livestock improvement program. And the work in livestock improvement was but a small unit of the whole agriculture program. Minister Adl's desire to "weld these new programs into the framework" of his ministry indicated Point 4's complete success. Our whole object had been to help develop new programs and to assist in strengthening the local institutions so that they could carry them forward.

"The longest journey in the world must be begun with the first step," Pat Regan, our chief agriculturist, said. "And we have made the first important step in the long journey of improving Iran's agriculture."

Even a compressed summary of all the details of the agricultural program would make too long an account. Plant science projects improved crop varieties. They introduced row culture and disease control and, according to Mr. Regan, "changed cotton, wheat, and sugar-beet crops from failure to abundance." Fifteen million animals were vaccinated under the veterinary project. And most of these were in tribal flocks, which theretofore had been altogether neglected. We imported new, improved Brown Swiss herd sires and artificially bred 35,000 cows by them. The first crossbreed calves to reach maturity more than doubled the milk production of their dams. The complete agriculture extension service established within only three years in the Ministry of Agriculture had trained 200 agents and established them in the field. Our experts demonstrated better uses of water and land. Point 4 introduced farm machinery and established training and repair centers. Under our guidance home gardens were planted by the thousands.

But most important of all, perhaps, was the program's revivification of the Ministry of Agriculture. Its succeeding ministers, Khalil Taleghani, Dr. Moazzemi, Mansour Atai and Dr. Adl, and Undersecretary Mostafa Zahedi sparked the Iranian leadership. A young department of the government, this ministry had been unable to get its programs off the ground. In 1951 eighty per cent of its total budget went for salaries. Its field programs never reached beyond the suburbs of the cities. But in 1955 the ministry was active everywhere. Point 4 assisted in all of its programs. By that time work on Dr. Adl's suggested incorporation of the new programs into the minister's own structure was well under way.

In addition to the other projects the Karadj Agricultural College had been remodeled. Dr. Bennett had said to me before I left Washington, "There is an Agricultural College at Karadj, near Tehran, which I hope you can make into an instrument of service to the rural people."

I would that he had lived to see the progress made there. Its farm machinery division now has not only farm machinery but also a practical course of instruction in its repair and use. Once it had neither. Its animal husbandry division now has a blooded herd of Brown Swiss cattle and a blooded flock of New Hampshire Red chickens. And the college can now offer instruction in animal feeding and care and a program of experimentation.

Once no courses like these were available. In nearly every phase of its work the college has made the same kinds of advances. It now can and does collaborate with the Ministry of Agriculture. And in its extension service the ministry has a transmission belt to carry the results of the college's work to all rural Iran.

A specific example of its work may best demonstrate the effectiveness of the new college and show how the co-operative technical assistance program brought about a change in the scope of its effect and influence. This example is found in Shahpassand wheat.

The college was in 1951 under the direction of Dr. Atai. He was later minister of agriculture, then again dean of the college. Sometimes the personnel shift in Iran's top-level administrative positions reminded me of the children's game called "Fruit Basket Turn Over!" Though I had been in Iran less than four years I had already seen several of my friends come back for second terms in particular and important places that, for one reason or another, they had left. Dr. Adl, sometimes called the father of modern agriculture in Iran, was another of these friends. I have already mentioned his various offices. He was eloquent and convincing in speech, and his dedication to the improvement of the rural life of Iran was widely respected.

Once when Dr. Adl, Khalil Taleghani, Dean Atai and I, all good friends, were together at a meeting I said I was honored to be among a group containing eleven ministers of agriculture. Dr. Adl saw at once that I was referring only to my three companions. Dr. Adl had been minister of agriculture in nine different cabinets! Asked how this came about, he explained, "I never would take any other ministry."

I would have to alter my joke if I wanted to use it today, for Khalil Taleghani in the early summer of 1955 began his second turn at the post, succeeding Dr. Adl. Together these three friends have now held the ministry an even dozen times.

But to get back to Shahpassand wheat and Karadj College,

Dean Atai had over a long period carried out experiments with wheat varieties. He hoped to develop through crossing and selection one that would better fill the needs of the Iranian farmers. Wheat is Iran's most important crop.

Iran is largely arid or, at best, semiarid. Only a narrow strip along the southern littoral of the Caspian Sea is humid. Here the prevailing winds meet the gigantic Elburz range and drop their moisture before they pass into central Asia. The Caspian front of the Elburz is covered with a virgin hardwood forest which has probably had no equal in the world since American settlers cut their way through the Ohio valley in the Northwest Territory. The bottomlands of the Caspian shore are fertile and intensively cultivated, but this region is the only one of its kind in Iran. Elsewhere wheat is the dominant crop. The rest of the land is so dry that farmers in most places cannot even raise a quick crop of winter wheat without irrigation. In such areas as Azerbaijan, hard against Russia and Turkey in the northwest, the villagers dry-farm by rotating planting and fallowing. Here the living is precarious. As in the high plains of the United States, in some years there is enough rain and in others there is not. Crops are good or they are fair or they fail according to the fickle weather.

Dr. George Stewart, agronomist and a principal member of our agricultural staff, prepared statistics on farming in Iran. He used the best information he could obtain after several years in the country. The cultivated area, Dr. Stewart learned, equals twelve per cent of total land area. Of the cultivated portion only a little more than one third—not quite five per cent of Iran's total acreage—is cropped annually. Eighty-eight per cent of all the land is uncultivated. Of this sixty-eight per cent is used for grazing, though a third of this is only slightly grazed. This third may be used only for a few weeks at favorable seasons each year. Two per cent of the total area of the country is in woodlots. Of the cultivated lands cropped each year two thirds grow winter wheat. Cereals are the only crops grown in every Ostan. Most of these are consumed directly by people. Very little of the cereal crop is fed to stock. And while Iran usually has enough grain for her own use, she seldom has much for export. An increase in the wheat yield, it can be seen, would be of transcendant importance to everybody in Iran.

Because of the wheat's importance to Iran, the major experimentation at Karadj College had been with this crop. Dean Atai had developed the new variety called Shahpassand. Trials had demonstrated that it would produce about forty per cent more grain per acre with no more effort or, more important, no more water. But having completed this much research, the college had turned to other studies. Shahpassand wheat had never been grown more than forty kilometers from the college.

One of Point 4's first projects with the Ministry of Agriculture was to multiply the Shahpassand wheatseed and to distribute it to the villages. We planted fields on the ministry's farms to obtain the seed and we distributed it through the agriculture extension service. Each year for three years we traded 25,000 bushels of Shahpassand seed to farmers for their old seed, which was ground up and sold. In 1955 the new seed was being produced in all parts of Iran and the project was completed. The work done at the college for the first time was influencing the daily lives of the people.

Meantime at the college experimentation continued. The students crossed Iranian wheat with various strains and varieties that Point 4 brought from the United States. Dean Atai began to get first-trial results that stood in a fair way to surpass those of Shahpassand. The tests indicated that some of the crosses might have specialized values. One, for example, ripened very quickly and seemed as if it might be useful in areas where the irrigation waters flowed for only a few weeks each spring. The ministry and its extension service watched the wheat trials closely. They were ready to seize upon any new seed that could be approved for a specific use and use it as they had Shahpassand. The college had taken the place Dr. Bennett had foreseen for it.

The extension service was vital from the first. The story of the pistachio nuts at Ghazvin is a concrete example of the way in which it made itself felt.

Ghazvin is a historic city at the base of the Elburz Mountains. By car it is a little more than two hours west of Tehran. Long ago Ghazvin was the capital, and the Shah had his court there. Once when the Shah was visiting Europe a Hapsburg king asked him to come along to his lodge.

"There is a beautiful city near here," the king is said to have told the Shah, "and in it I have a wonderful garden. I would like you to accompany me there."

The Shah replied, according to the story that the people of Ghazvin still delight in telling, "In Persia I have a beautiful garden, and in it there is a wonderful city [Ghazvin, of course]. I invite you to accompany me there."

The irrigated lands about Ghazvin are extensive and gardenlike. The city retains tokens of its past splendor. A beautiful gate still stands, though there is no wall and though the main street no longer passes through the gate. The vineyards and the pistachio groves are very productive. The soil is good, but the water supply is now short. Perhaps long ago, when the Shah resided there, there was more water.

In about 1948 a terrible blight began descending on this garden. A small fly appeared and laid its eggs in the blossoms of a pistachio tree. The eggs hatched as the nut buds began to develop. The larvae grew in the fruit. The pests rapidly increased in number. By the end of three years Ghazvin harvested no nuts.

In 1953 during the blooming period the Tehran Point 4 team and the Ministry of Agriculture sprayed a few trees in the Ghazvin groves with a DDT mixture. Sound nuts developed on these trees. A year later the tree owners were invited to organize an area-wide spraying campaign.

The Farmandar of Ghazvin, Mr. Sadegh Navab, became an enthusiast of the program. He talked about it to everyone who would listen. Ministry of Agriculture personnel trained the previous year in spraying methods were prepared to help the tree owners. Point 4 loaned some spraying equipment and two jeeps. The tree owners bought the DDT. As it turned out they bore more than three fifths of the cost of the whole operation. Most of the rest was carried by the ministry, whose field staff organized co-operatively with our Tehran team.

In the second year of the program we carried forward some additional experimentation. That is, we sprayed some trees a second time on a test basis. Also some groves from which the male trees, which bore no fruit, had been removed were artificially pollinated.

The first year's work had demonstrated that in order to be effective spraying had to be done while the trees were in blossom. This meant split-second timing in order for the program to cover the whole area before the fruit set on.

As was to be expected, when the governor called the tree owners together some fell to arguing.

One said that his neighbors could just count him out. He would pay nothing for any such service as we proposed. Another said that while he would be willing to pay his share he felt that the small amount of spraying done the year before had not really demonstrated the worth of the undertaking. He was going along with his neighbors, he said, only because he felt that they expected him to. But the others, more than thirty men, seemed enthusiastic. Talking among themselves they finally happened on a solution.

They would spray all the groves except the one owned by the man who wanted to be counted out. And they would spray all the trees except the very biggest one in the grove of the man who did not really care.

In mid-July 1954, Undersecretary Zahedi and Ralph Workinger, then Point 4's Tehran provincial director, organized a field trip to Ghazvin. There a group of technicians met us. In the crowd were Jafar Rassi, head of the extension service, Engineer Abolhassan Fardad, Tehran regional representative for the Ministry of Agriculture, and LeRoy Bunnel, an agriculturist from Utah who was Mr. Workinger's appointee to the cooperating group.

We went first to the grove of the Doubting Thomas. It was swarming with little flies. Not one nut spike contained anything more than a few discolored, bitter nuts. I thought it improbable that any marketable nuts would mature on these trees. The ground was covered with shriveled and fallen husks.

Next the technicians took us to a grove that had been sprayed just once during the flowering season. The trees were heavy with ripening nuts. No flies swarmed there. We had to hunt to find any immature fallen nuts at all. Next we went to a grove that had been sprayed twice. Its crop was still heavier. Then we visited the grove that had been both sprayed and artificially pollinated. Here we saw a tree which its owner thought would prove champion at harvest time. He thought that it alone would yield nuts worth about $400. Our last stop was at the grove of the man who had grudgingly consented to spray his trees. On all but the single unsprayed tree he had a good crop. On this tree was nothing but shriveled nuts.

On a ditchbank in the bright sun we talked to most of the owners of the groves. Even the two doubters were present.

"How much better will the crop be this year than before?" I asked.

"Ten times," one said, but another retorted, "More than that."

"To what do you credit this?" I asked.

"To the spraying," one replied.

"Nine tenths to the spraying and one tenth to a late rain," said another.

"The artificial pollination helped my grove."

"Is the man whose grove we saw first here?" I asked. The man whose grove had not been sprayed at all was pointed out.

"What do you say," I asked him, "will you spray next year?"

"Bali, bali, bali," he said emphatically—"yes, yes, yes."

"I wanted them to spray that last tree in my grove, too," said the owner of the single fruitless tree we had seen, "after I saw that very few nuts were setting on it. But they wouldn't do it."

"Well," explained Abolhassan Fardad, "it was too late to do any real good by the time he changed his mind. By then the flies had gotten in their work. Anyway it was a good demonstration to him and the others of the value of the program. All of this man's other trees are bearing."

After our talk with the nut growers we went to the Farmandar's home for lunch. Mostafa Zahedi estimated the value of the pistachio crop around Ghazvin at about three million dollars. This success, he said, was an example of what could be done when people at all levels co-operate to help themselves. Only a little help had come from the Ministry of Agriculture and Point 4. Perhaps other beginnings were less spectacular, he said, but all over the country with crop after crop and in area after area farmers were reaping their own peculiar benefits.

I could hardly get out of Ghazvin. The Farmander and his people kept holding me. "If you can help a little, as you did in the pistachio project," they would begin. Then they would reel off whole lists of things that needed to be done.

Several things at Ghazvin were apparent to us. One of these was the value of the Tehran regional team's program to help the Ministry of Agriculture decentralize its technical work and mobilize a field organization. Another was the value of a demonstration followed up quickly by a full-scale self-help project. In Ghazvin this method had set off a significant chain reaction of self-improvement. The Farmander told me he believed this reaction would carry far beyond the spraying of pistachio crops.

Progress over the whole country has been spotty. Spectacular increases of as much as 300 percent in average farm income were recorded in some villages in the Veramin Plain. But many of our demonstrations both of improved farming methods and of consumer and marketing co-ops were concentrated there. Some other areas of Iran have hardly been reached at all.

The wheat, livestock and poultry improvement programs have had widest impact. Cotton too has shown marked increases in yield as a result of our work. Growers obtained up to fifty per cent more cotton than in previous years just by planting in rows to make irrigation, weeding and thinning easier. Two American cottonseed varieties, Cokers Pedigree and Lightening Express, had already been tried in Iran. They were grown in quantity under the program and distributed in the now familiar way of even exchange with the villagers. These varieties yielded, on the average, thirty-six per cent more cotton per acre. They brought a premium at marketing time.

Our original assumption was that in Iran, as in most underdeveloped countries, mechanization of the farms would be the most rewarding undertaking. Though in the beginning both the Iranians and the Americans who planned our program shared this assumption, the Americans were disabused of the idea first. Even so, machinery ordered in 1951, before I arrived in Tehran, caused some embarrassment in later years. Some of it, standard size for a small American farm, proved too big for efficient use in the tiny fields of the Iran villages. Many obstacles stood in the way of mechanization. Gradual improvement of both the social and economic conditions of the farmers may be required before any large-scale mechanization will be successful.

The obvious problems caused by the lack of mechanics and repair centers are complicated by a total ignorance of machinery on the part of the rural people. Many farmers did not operate on a money economy, but money was required for diesel fuel, gasoline and lubricating oil. It was obvious that we must meet other requirements, among them improved marketing, before

Doors to Progress

we could hope for mechanization on a large scale. Our most difficult problem, however, was still that the fields worked by individual peasants and farmers were too small to be worked efficiently by tractors.

Once I explained these difficulties to an American audience. I told them that the Point 4 program was not designed to bring Iran in one leap from the fourteenth century where it is now, both by the Moslem calendar and by its rural development, to the twentieth. But when I said that we must advance Iran through the lost decades step by slow step I was attacked.

"Why should the program stop short of the most up-to-date?" my questioner demanded to know. "If it does stop short, doesn't it in fact hold rural Iran back? What's the motive for that?"

I tried to explain that to achieve the results we desire would require much time. One problem opens into another. Economic problems impinge on social and political problems. Centuries might be compressed into decades, but not into a few days, months, weeks or even years.

"That would be revolutionary," I said, "and the Point 4 program is not revolutionary but evolutionary in its very concept. It takes time to work out, as the Shah is doing, ways to make freeholders of peasants without revolution. And it takes time for a crop-improvement program to progress with order. It must move first from better seed to a surplus to sell. This means money to spend for a simple tool, which may lead to still better yields. These, in turn, give the family more income than it needs for subsistence. Now, perhaps, there is enough money for a steel plow. Maybe in time a son of the farmer who began the evolutionary spiral can afford to buy a tractor. But we offer this method of advancement as an antidote for the method that promises pie in the sky but produces blood in the streets."

Dr. Adl as well as anyone else in the program understood the difficulties. His main hope was to stimulate the progression of Iran's agricultural improvement. He had a major role in drafting the law to increase in the peasants' share, which, with the village councils it set up, stood as one of the major social and political steps in Iran's recent history. Without this means of self-organization and without this incentive and reward many villages could not have been expected to advance.

Products of farming in Iran were most commonly divided in this way:

Twenty per cent went to the owner of the land and twenty per cent to the tiller of the soil. The man who provided water got another twenty per cent, as did the one who furnished oxen. Twenty per cent went also to whoever provided seed. Under this system the landlord sometimes got eighty per cent of the returns. His poor peasants had contributed nothing but their labor. In some parts of the country the basis of division was different, and sometimes the peasant got more than one fifth under the plan outlined above. If he owned his own ox, for example, or could save his own seed he could build up his share. The increase in the number of small landowners was changing this pattern.

As the Shah's land project had clearly shown us, it was not enough just to teach the farmers better methods to give them the new status of freeholders. They needed in addition access to credit and assistance in the art of working together and organizing their combined efforts. But when the needed elements were available the program's success was startling.

Our whole progression in the United States has been from the solution of one problem to the solution of the next. It must be so in Iran or any underdeveloped country trying to catch up.

Such programs as Point 4 should continue for a long period. Technical help will be needed to solve new problems as they arise. Great concern often has been expressed about the problems that will be generated by success.

"Already people are suffering from poor nutrition and even from starvation," a friend of mine once said. "Will the babies your health program saves live just to starve?"

Doors to Progress

This is the same concern expressed by Malthus in the eighteenth century. He gloomily saw populations increasing to the point where Mother Earth could never suckle her whole litter. The starvelings, thought Malthus, must always die.

"Look," said my friend as our conversation continued, "the emaciated hand of every beggar in Tehran proves this theory."

But archaeologists point to many convincing proofs that far greater numbers than there are now once lived in Mesopotamia and in the plains, valleys and plateaus of Iran. Their evidence also seems to indicate that the level of living was higher and that the people were then better fed. What was once could be again.

Point 4 technical experts showed that the productive capacity of Iran's land and water resources could be increased greatly just by introducing improved seed. This alone made cereal and fiber crop yields forty per cent larger than before. And our demonstrations indicated that such new cultivating practices as planting in rows and thinning and weeding cotton would yield at least another twenty-five per cent increase. Better water conservation practices could save about one third of the precious water used in irrigation, thus making it possible to irrigate a third more land.

It is much too early to think about large-scale or general use of fertilizer in Iran. The economy is still at too low a level for the farmers to get cash with which to buy it. As the rural improvement program progresses some fertilizers can be used in the relatively near future. In time they may be as broadly applied in Iran as in the United States. Judicious use of fertilizers to supply the various different soil deficiencies in each part of Iran would so dramatically affect both the quality and the quantity of farm production that its impact would be almost revolutionary.

Above and beyond these opportunities to increase the supply for a growing population one fact stands like a mountain rising above its foothills—the fact that the principal waters, the major rivers of the country are not being used at all. The Karun, which certainly at one time contributed to the support of an empire, is today almost entirely wasted into the Persian Gulf. Complete utilization of the rivers by irrigating the large areas of very high quality arid lands available would at once introduce the problem of marketing surpluses abroad. But if in the next decade the Karun and its tributary, the Ab-e-Diz, were harnessed to irrigate the Khuzistan Plain the extra produce could be frozen, canned, or dried and marketed in southeast Asia or western Europe, where food is needed.

Another strong retort to Malthusian arguments against our program in Iran is the probability of a lower birth rate in the future. As hazards to life are diminished the present extravagant rate of reproduction will no longer be necessary simply to replenish the race. But often before we have had the opportunity to bring this out in our discussions someone will introduce a new point of disagreement. A typical expression of this point came from a sincerely interested but puzzled friend of mine.

"The farmers of America are already plagued by surpluses that the government has to try to get rid of abroad so they won't flood out our own prosperity," he said. "So how can anyone justify using our technical know-how to increase food production in Iran? It seems to me that we're creating additional surpluses to compete with our own in world markets."

"Well," I began, "we haven't created the surpluses yet. There are still people in Iran who don't get enough food, let alone enough of the right kinds of food."

"But you're begging the point," the man interrupted. "In just a few more years, if you keep up this program, Iran is going to have to sell abroad."

I did have to grant him that point. Iran has had wheat to sell about one year of every five. In several recent years she has marketed cotton abroad. She still buys more cotton piece goods than she exports raw cotton, but I had to admit that this balance could be shifted. But this point, indeed the whole argument seemed to me irrelevant to the fundamental issue involved.

One person fears that such programs as ours will so increase

Doors to Progress

the number of mouths to feed that the world simply will not be able to fill them. Another fears that they will so increase the world's farm products that civilization will sink hopelessly in a flood of surplus wheat, cotton, beans and potatoes. Neither is ever convinced that the dangers he foresees may not be wholly real. I have seen exponents of these positive and negative poles of fear stand in the same circle to debate and have seen each leave the discussion shaking his head, still showing fright.

The raw and chafing truth is that in this world in the middle of this, our twentieth century, we do have surpluses of food at some points, starving millions at others. In America, where the population has increased more rapidly than in any other country, people are not starving but are better fed every year. This is true because in America technological progress has been most widespread. Scientific agriculture and scientific distribution and marketing are responsible for a better living standard than has ever before prevailed in the history of the world.

In my judgment—based on my own experience in Iran and on my decades of dealing with the problems of conservation, development and use of resources—the earth can be made to produce far greater quantities of her wholesome fruits than growing populations will require for many decades, even for generations to come.

Of course we will always have the problem of distribution, of leveling off the peaks of production to fill in the valleys. We'll always have to move surpluses from especially favored areas to places, perhaps far distance, where food is needed. But because we in our own age or our children who follow us will still have problems to solve should we accept calamitous counsel today? Should we abandon constructive programs? We have immediately at hand the tools to solve today's problems in Iran.

In the United States we have not turned back from the solution of today's problems because the solution might generate new problems for tomorrow. The automobile provided a new solution for our transportation problem. The automobile also created problems in road construction that have planners all over the nation scratching their heads in puzzlement. But no road designer has yet recommended that we return to the horse.

The only way for us to avoid our children's having to face tomorrow's problem is, I believe, to avoid facing today's. But if we do, our children will have to face the problem we did not solve. There will be no gain for them, only a failure for us.

One very early summer morning I was with a party driving east from Isfahan down the road which follows the Ziandehrud from village to village through the irrigated valley lands. On the road we encountered possibly hundreds of donkeys loaded with melons. They plodded along with sturdy patience, each carrying a bulging load of the fruit for which this valley is justly famed. The melons of Persia earn their reputation, and connoisseurs consider those of Isfahan among the very best.

As we went further from the city the number of donkeys with their melons did not seem to diminish. I grew more and more interested. I noticed that a man or a boy followed nearly every donkey. Some were driving two or, once in a great while, as many as three. The farmer or his oldest son was marketing the daily yield of his crop at the peak of the season.

"*Eeenyuh!*" the donkey drivers called to their donkeys, now and then prodding them with a stick. "*Eeenyuh!*"

Dust swirled about them. Each driver trudged along, giving his full attention to his tiny caravan.

"*Eeenyuh!*" The cry kept the little beast from falling asleep in his tracks. Sometimes a poke from the stick would make him trot a few steps. But really, this strange "giddap" served only as a bond to hold man and donkey together in the single purpose of covering the miles of dusty road.

We still saw donkeys trickle in from the byways and lanes to join the stream on the main road when we were as far as twelve kilometers from Isfahan. The farmer would take half a day, it seemed, to load up his donkey and market a dozen melons.

Marketing its produce is a great problem in a country with poor roads and a poor transport service. What we saw on the road that day spoke authoritatively to us of the need to improve the whole gamut of marketing facilities as we worked to step up the farmer's production.

In Iran many peasants live on a subsistence level. They produce hardly anything to sell for money. If the farmer can produce enough to have some left over to sell—and with very little technical assistance he can—he will begin a chain reaction of a hundred problems that didn't exist before. Means of handling, transportating and marketing, of processing, refrigerating and storing must now be found. And money in the hands of the farmer will also create problems in the manufacture, distribution and sale of all the things he will want to buy—shoes, lead pencils, newspapers, dishes. It will probably even mean modifying the national monetary system to provide enough currency for the farmer to have money to exchange. This last contingency may seem ridiculously far-fetched. But in the fall of 1953 the government of Iran did experience a crisis caused in part by the fact that the operation of the act increasing the peasant's share placed money in the hands of rural people, many of whom had never had any before. The people had no bank accounts in which they could deposit the money. They felt no immediate needs that any goods on the shelves in any of the little village stores could satisfy. So they put the money in a samovar and stood the samovar on a shelf. This, of course, slowed down the circulation of currency. Soon the Bank Melli had barely enough money in its vaults to cash government payroll checks. Until the crisis was resolved it kept people awake on two continents.

Some people have seriously argued when contemplating this appalling Pandora's box of troubles that the thing to do is to leave the situation alone and not even try to improve the farmers' production.

But, once begun, the work of raising the living level of all the people in an underdeveloped country can never be finished.

Once it is started it can never be stopped. Each problem solved will always create another. This point is nevertheless not a valid argument against technical improvement.

Men have argued to me that even the great and wealthy United States cannot afford to undertake programs to meet all of the problems that will flow out of this bottle once we pull the cork.

But though the social and economic problems encountered in efforts to improve the life of a people may follow one another they are not all encountered at one time. Thus we can devise orderly programs and keep them to manageable proportions.

As the months went by I had on many occasions to remind my Iranian friends that this should guide our efforts. They were often tempted to make one of two serious mistakes. One of these was to start too many things at once on too many fronts, spreading ourselves too thin to get any real impact anywhere. The other was to jump in and try to resolve some central problem without taking care of the preliminary and subsidiary ones.

Working out such a program as ours is like unpacking a trunk. The objective is to get the thing on the bottom. There are two ways to reach it. One is to grab the trunk, hold it upside down, shake everything out onto the floor and search through the mess. The other way is to remove the top layer, proceed to the second, the third and fourth and, proceeding in an orderly manner, to reach the treasure at the bottom.

In programming our technical improvement work in Iran we were guided by this second philosophy. Since eighty per cent of the population lived in farming villages, our basic program had to be rural improvement. There the fundamental problems were to increase production, to keep the people well enough to do their work and to train them in new methods. The program's entire structure was built on this base.

Though the doors to progress which Dr. Adl saw each opened on a corridor involving more work, he was not deterred. He wanted his ministry organized to open a few doors on its own.

Mission/17

Twenty-eighth of Mordad

FROM A HIGH window I observed a mob organizing to march down Shah Reza Avenue through the heart of Tehran. On both sides of every *kucheh* and cross street I could see the organizers at work, collecting young men and boys from the sidewalk crowds and rallying them behind banners in the alleys.

Now from the east I saw a growing band approach, banners flying. The marchers were chanting some slogan. The crowds in the alleyways swung in behind the column as it came by. The organizers marched at its sides like platoon leaders. As the mob went forward new elements fell into the swing. The organizers dropped off at street corners or melted into the crowds. If the mob met resistance, official or otherwise, very few of the organizers would be involved.

During the summer of 1953 the whole stream of activity seemed to be rushing toward disaster. Tehran was under martial law. A curfew kept people off the streets during most of the night hours. Tanks were often parked at key intersections, their guns unlimbered. Groups of soldiers were present everywhere. But no one interfered with the mobs.

The marching and shouting seemed to promise some climactic event. In a so-called plebiscite ninety-seven per cent of the vote cast supported Dr. Mossadegh in his harsh program. But some felt the plebiscite unfair, since "yes" votes were cast at one polling place and "no" votes at another. The polls for negative voting were surrounded by thugs. When they tried to reach the polls would-be voters experienced serious difficulties. Many were even stabbed. One young rioter threw some cabbages into a jeep and injured a young man from our embassy. The Iranian driver of the American naval attaché was flagged down at a street corner and stabbed in the shoulder. My own chauffeur was beaten, even though I did not happen to be in the car. In spite of all this I had the feeling that all the threatening agitation was not really designed at that stage to result in actual violence to the Americans and other foreigners.

Finally, in desperation, Dr. Mossadegh proposed to confiscate the Shah's estates in the name of the government and to use their revenues to finance his oil-less economy. As authority for the confiscation he cited the complete power the Majlis had granted him before its resignation. His action of course brought him into direct conflict with His Majesty. The controversy was developed skillfully, in true Mossadegh fashion, over several months.

Dr. Mossadegh argued that the royal family should be placed on a budgeted stipend to be made available by the government from year to year. He cited as an example the manner in which the British support their royal family. But intertwined in his campaign was the skillfully marshalled propaganda of those who would establish a "Peoples' Republic." In other chapters some of these have been mentioned. They are set down here in the chronological order of their climactic finality.

The Shah's precipitate departure from Iran was his protest against Mossadegh. It served as the final and determining factor in the fall of the Mossadegh regime. In those hectic closing days the foreign minister, Dr. Fatemi, made slashing personal attacks on the Shah.

The period from the Thirtieth of Tir to the Twenty-eighth of Mordad, 1332 (July 21 to August 19, 1953), was the most riotous I have ever experienced. Alarms during those weeks became commonplace. One after another my good Iranian friends closely connected with Dr. Mossadegh's regime came to tell me of some new plot involving violence to the Americans. More and more of my various far-flung staff members reported that they had been insulted by Iranians.

Even by day, Iranians painted the unlawful "Yankee Go Home" signs on walls near Americans' homes. Whenever I turned on my radio I heard antiforeign utterances. Many newspapers used most of their editorial columns to berate all foreigners. Some of the more radical Moslem groups were drawn deeply into the general disorder. Dr. Mossadegh contended, in fact, that most of the mobs in the streets were Moslem in origin and organization. But he had undeniably accepted Tudeh support.

Agitation was much less violent in the rural areas and many of the secondary cities. In many places there was none at all. Indeed, our field work continued without interruption. But in Isfahan and Kermanshah conditions were almost as riotous as in Tehran.

The Shah had gone first to Ramsar on the Caspian shore, where he had a summer palace. From there he fled the country in his private plane. Only after he had arrived in Baghdad was his departure announced in Iran. Before he left his own country he issued a *firman,* or royal decree, designating General Fazlollah Zahedi to replace Dr. Mossadegh as prime minister.

Rumors of that decree floated throughout Iran. It was never officially acknowledged by Dr. Mossadegh, and General Zahedi was still in hiding.

During the night of August 15 General Zahedi's supporters made a comparatively peaceful attempt to enforce the Shah's order. I knew nothing of it until the next morning, a Sunday. When I heard someone knocking noisily at my gate at dawn I flung on some clothes and went out. A much agitated Iranian friend told me that Dr. Mossadegh had been forcibly dispossessed of his office and was then in jail. General Zahedi, my friend said, had made effective the Shah's order appointing him prime minister.

Although this was not usual in Tehran a second house stood

within my compound. Commander Eric Pollard, the naval attaché, lived there. I hurried across the garden and knocked at Eric's door.

"Apparently something has happened," I told him. "A friend of mine just came by to say that General Zahedi is now prime minister."

We decided we'd better go immediately to the embassy in Eric's car. We stopped only long enough to observe the commander's naval tradition of a morning cup of coffee.

Before we finished our coffee another Iranian friend knocked at the gate. He looked as though he had had no sleep all night. "It's not true," he told me.

As we later pieced the story together from information gained from several sources, General Zahedi had indeed attempted to serve the *firman* on Dr. Mossadegh. A colonel of the Iranian Army had made his way in a tank from Tedjrish Square, north of Tehran, near the Shah's summer palace, to Iranian Army headquarters. Here he looked for the chief of staff, but couldn't find him. He must have intended to notify the chief that General Zahedi was prime minister in order to avoid the Army's mixing in if a fight developed.

When he learned the chief of staff was absent, the colonel turned his tank about in the street and made his way directly to Dr. Mossadegh's house, only a few blocks away. But before he could get there someone sounded an alarm. At the gate he met two other tanks, which trained their guns on his. A smart military guard was prepared to seize him if he made a move. There was no shooting. The abortive attempt ended at that point. Dr. Mossadegh described it officially as a thwarted uprising.

And now from somewhere deep in the mountains General Zahedi began to circulate photostatic copies of the Shah's *firman*. Although many people received them, they went especially to all military unit commanders. The already tense situation now seemed at its breaking point.

Twenty-eighth of Mordad

We continued to work at our headquarters office. I urged our people to keep off the streets unless their work required going about. Telegrams were often long delayed or lost as service was interrupted by violence. I resisted efforts to persuade me that we should close down "for a while" even though all of our installations began to look like armed camps. Dr. Mossadegh in his anxiety to protect us from violence continued assigning greater and greater numbers of soldiers to our guard.

In the midst of programming a conference in my office an excited messenger called James J. Goulden, my assistant. When Jim came back he explained that a truckload of soldiers had blocked our entrance. Jim had succeeded in persuading the young lieutenant in charge to move the truck so people could go in and out. Excited mobsters marched up and down Sepah Avenue. Jim said that the lieutenant had reported that his instructions were to keep the mobs out of our compound.

"Just as well bring the soldiers inside where we can serve them coffee," Jim said, then explained that we had a meeting in progress.

The lieutenant agreed to the suggested deployment and the immediate advisability of serving coffee. Coming smartly to attention, he said solemnly, "They will have to cross our dead bodies to disturb your conference."

Though most of us were only amused, I could see that Jim's report of the incident alarmed the newcomers. I foresaw that we could not long continue unless conditions improved.

One evening when I reached the relative peace of my home, Villa Panarama in Golhak, I found nine-year-old Margaret in the garden disconsolately trying to play with her big black Belgian poodle, Cookie. Cookie was a splendid dog, but he was lazy. He could stand only so much of Margaret's romping. He had dignity too, and when his little mistress dressed him up in doll clothes his loyalty would sustain him only so long. He was right now trying to hide in the hedge. I realized then how difficult it was for our families to be held virtual prisoners in their compounds. Our children could not go from one house to another to find playmates. Our wives could not go to the shops to do even necessary shopping. Social life had come to a stop. While everyone tried to maintain a good face, it was growing more and more difficult.

When she saw me Margaret gave up on Cookie and moved dejectedly down the steps to the lower garden. Trying to sound cheerful I said, "Anything happen today, Margaret?"

"No, nothing at all, Daddy."

"Oh, come now, Margaret," I urged, "something happened, surely?"

"No," she insisted, "nothing at all—just tanks running up and down Old Shimron Road, but they didn't shoot at anything."

Ambassador Henderson was expected to arrive from Beirut on August 18. We had heard at least a hundred reports that the Communists controlled the streets of Tehran. On August 17, they had toppled several statues of the Shah and his father, Reza Shah, from their pedestals. On the morning of the eighteenth I saw a truck dragging one of the great equestrian statues at the end of a wire cable. A loud, jeering throng ran along behind the truck, and a number of toughs rode on it.

The ambassador's plane was due at Mehrabad Airport early in the afternoon. The prime minister's office had telephoned to suggest that we keep our cars off several of the principal streets. After greeting Mr. Henderson and arranging to see him later in the evening, I deliberately drove through some of the proscribed areas, past the University of Tehran and near the Shah's palace.

For months I had been used to seeing tanks with their gunners at the alert and their cannon trained down the principal streets. I was well accustomed to meeting blockades of machine guns in approaches to such sensitive areas as the prime minister's house. Patrols, both mounted and afoot, were commonplace sights in the centers of busy streets. These didn't even interfere with traffic or halt the people's comings and goings.

Several times I had asked soldiers to move their machine guns so I could keep an appointment in a restricted area. For more than a year the security forces had not interfered with mobs except occasionally, in the most severe instances of disorder.

On August eighteenth the strength of these security forces was about as usual.

When I approached the circle near the university I saw that the heroic statue of Reza Shah, which had faced the street named for him, looking toward the heart of the city he had modernized, was gone. The pedestal, still in place, had been daubed with red paint. I could not read the slogans painted there, but Hossein described them as "Tudeh party."

At the entrance to one of the streets leading into the circle I saw a burly group of about fifty huskies smashing up a bronze statue. This was not the one that had stood in the circle but another, which had been dragged from a distant square. The gang, using hammers and sledges, made the bronze ring like a bell. As the hammers tore off pieces, members of the throng carried them away. No crowd watched the destruction. Only a few knots of men stood about the circle. With them were some little boys. I saw no cheer or exultation in these faces. They seemed to me to be grim and shocked.

Comparatively few people were on the streets. I did see some other gangs engaged in business like that at the circle. I watched one wheel into Shah Reza Avenue from a side street. Hossein pointed out another gathered about a roadblock near the military college. No one attempted to interfere with my passage.

I got the impression on my drive that the Tudeh mobs ruled the city and said as much to Ambassador Henderson when I saw him that night. He had seen the prime minister, who had assured him that he would make every effort to protect the foreigners in Tehran.

I reported to the ambassador that the Joint Commission was scheduled to meet at seven o'clock the following morning, Wednesday, August 19. Things were still moving ahead in

Point 4 as they had been when he left Tehran some weeks before.

We could count on even the mobs in Tehran not to vary the city's daily routine very much. In the early morning the streets would be quiet. No trouble would start before the traditional time for business places to open—in the winter eight o'clock and in the summer seven. Even rioters would observe the time-honored siesta from two to four each afternoon. And civil disturbances would break up for a fairly early bedtime.

Knowing this, I expected no excitement when I went to the seven o'clock meeting on Wednesday morning. And I was quite right; there was none. Along the streets shopkeepers stood before their doors debating whether it would be safe to raise their shutters and open for business.

Six members of Dr. Mossadegh's Cabinet served on the Joint Commission. All but one appeared that day. Dr. Sadeghi, the minister of interior, who was in charge of all law and order agencies, did not attend. Our business had to do with planning the coming year's program. The members were prepared to act. We settled to our work with no premonition that disaster was about to fall. Though we remained in session until ten minutes after eleven, we knew nothing of the nature of the excitement we could now and then hear rising from the streets. So used were we by this time to noisy demonstrations that most of us paid no attention to the occasional waves of sound that reached us.

Each new arrival at one of these meetings goes gravely around the entire circle to shake hands and pass a word of greeting with each who has arrived before him. I liked this custom. No conference in Iran can begin without these small formalities. An Iranian who fails to inquire politely concerning a business acquaintance's health would be considered gauche.

This etiquette made it easy for three of my Iranian friends to draw me aside for a quiet word of warning as they greeted me that morning. Each of the three said that he felt very much concerned for my safety and for that of the American organization I headed. One said that the prime minister had announced that he had unearthed a Communist plot to make Point 4 the next objective after the statues of the Shah.

"Mr. Warne," this man said earnestly, "you must be very careful today and tomorrow. The prime minister thinks you should close your offices for a few days. He knows you will not want to do this, but you know, Mr. Warne, the prime minister would never forgive himself if anything happened to you or one of your good associates."

"I can't be forever closing the Point 4 offices," I said. "The ambassador tells me that the prime minister has assured him he'll make every effort to protect us."

"We greatly appreciate the help of the Americans and Point 4," my friend continued. "And we will try to protect you. But right now things are unsettled. You will please study carefully what I have said."

As the morning wore on the noise from the street grew louder. At first we could hear only faint singing and shouting, which sounded as if it came from groups riding by the building in trucks. In an hour or two we heard a crescendo of approaching marchers. Then the noise died in the distance. But by eleven o'clock the uproar seemed continuous. We wondered if it were so all over the city and knew that something extraordinary must be taking place.

The only hint that any of us gathered about the table had of what was afoot came in a telephone call that summoned from the meeting Dr. Zanganeh, the director general of the Plan Organization.

When after a few minutes he returned to the table he said something in Farsee to his compatriots. Then turning to me, he said, "Mr. Warne, it is nothing. Some of the workers of the Rey Cement Plant do not want to work today. I told the police chief to put them in jail. You know we are trying to quiet these mobs."

I had never before heard of such defiance of authority by government workers, but if I thought of this news as portentous at all it was only subconsciously. Our meeting continued through a long agenda. We had had tea served twice. At eleven o'clock came Turkish coffee. We finally adjourned with many pleasantries and the usual formalities of leave-taking. Each man before he departed solemnly shook hands with all remaining.

As I was leaving my friend said again, "Mr. Warne, you will be careful."

With this warning on my mind I walked down the two long flights of concrete steps to the street. But I was not prepared for the tumult about the main door. A great crowd milled slowly—but aimlessly. I saw no particular violence and felt no particular hostility directed at me or my staff. Some of the ministers' cars nudged through the crowd and pulled up before the door for their passengers. I looked about for my car but soon gave up all hope of its being able to get to the door through the mob. Since my office was only a long block away from the Plan Organization building I preferred to try to walk it.

I did not see my friends from the Joint Commission again for a long time. Some of them never. Later I learned that several had been intercepted before they reached their offices.

I pushed through the mob to the Point 4 compound. Hossein was trying to follow me in my car. In the compound I found several Iranian staff members and several Americans waiting in high excitement. All day they had been getting telephone calls and notes from the prime minister's office urging that we close and send our people home. My principal Iranian assistant informed me that Dr. Mossadegh had said he couldn't bear the responsibility if we didn't.

It was obvious that no more work was going to be done that day. I sent word to all principal staff officers, American and Iranian alike, to meet at my house at Golhak at 4:00 P.M. for further instructions and ordered that all our offices in Tehran be closed and their staffs sent home. I told each officer to direct his people to stay off the streets as much as possible. My secretary, Miss Elsie Hartman, and I loaded her typewriter and enough supplies to set up an emergency office into the turtleback of my Chevrolet and began hunting a way to Golhak. At the embassy I was told that it was unclear what was happening. Obviously the largest-scale disorder yet experienced was in progress but no one there knew its nature. The government was in a state of near-panic. Tudeh groups had been beaten up in a rally for the Shah held at the bazaar early that morning.

I tried to make my way up Old Shimron Road, past the radio station. Literally dozens of busses struggled up the same road, loaded clear to the tops. On some bus tops stood as many as twenty men. The crowds in the busses were shouting and waving handbills that bore the Shah's picture. They permitted no car to proceed that did not have its lights burning. This, I soon learned, was a sign that the driver supported the Shah. This was the first disturbance I had witnessed in which the general public seemed at least interested spectators, if not actual participants. Clots of women and children gathered about every gate, many of them laughing and shouting. I noticed that many of the passengers in the busses were soldiers and policemen.

As we approached the radio station, two thirds of the way up the hill, I saw a huge roadblock ahead. Old Shimron Road was completely closed by a milling throng. The busses were turning, unloading and going back to town. A troop of cavalry from the guard station beyond the radio towers charged toward the mob. I expected a furious outbreak, but none came. The horsemen wheeled and helped to lead the mob's assault on the radio station.

I returned to the embassy and reported what I had seen. Next we tried the long way around to Golhak. At Tahkte Jamshid and Pahlavi avenues I could hear machine guns and rifles and even a few heavier pieces. It sounded as if perhaps tanks were shooting near the prime minister's house, about two and a half blocks away. Pahlavi was nearly deserted.

When Elsie and I finally did reach Villa Panarama we found that several of my staff, including two Iranian assistants, had beaten us there.

Word that General Zahedi was at the head of a movement to gain control was circulating pretty generally.

I was called to the telephone soon after I got home. Telephone service in Iran was rather uncertain at best, but mine was working on the afternoon of August 19.

A calm voice said, "Hello," and paused for my acknowledgment before continuing. "Mr. Warne, you will recall that we were to have a dinner party tonight at the Darband Hotel."

"Yes," I said, recognizing my caller as Dr. Gholam Mossadegh, the prime minister's son and social representative. "Yes, Dr. Mossadegh, I remember."

"Well," he said, "because of an unexpected happening it will be impossible for Mrs. Mossadegh and me to have the dinner. I am calling to tell you that we have postponed it for a few days. I shall let you know the date later."

I thought I could hear through the receiver the sound of shots at the other end of the line. I thanked the good doctor for his consideration in calling me and rang off. Dr. Gholam Mossadegh and his wife were among my favorite people.

Returning to the living room, I found that one of my Iranian assistants had on Radio Tehran. The announcer was calmly describing a musical selection about to be played. Suddenly a great uproar drowned out his pleasant voice. An excited-sounding man took over the microphone. He identified himself as one of the leaders of an assault on the station. "General Zahedi is prime minister!" he shouted. "Long live the Shah!"

In the next several minutes there was pandemonium. New voices would begin to say a few words but would immediately be interrupted by others. They must have been grabbing the microphone out of one another's hands. In perhaps half an hour someone called out that General Zahedi approached. Calm was restored in the studio. A quiet voice gave a brief description of the scene. Crowding close to the set in my living room, we heard it announce that the prime minister, General Zahedi, was standing erect in a tank coming up the hill to the studio door. Loud cheers rose in the background. Soon the general, whose voice I recognized, read the *firman* naming him prime minister. He promised to restore law and order and asked for the co-operation of the people.

The building of our Tehran provincial team was overrun by the mobs. It was stripped. I thought afterward that its fate had been sealed that February night when Dr. Mossadegh appeared on top of its wall as he fled from his house. Apparently the mob had determined not to let its prey escape by this avenue a second time.

Dr. Mossadegh's house was occupied before evening. He had escaped but was found two days later in a house two doors away. A body lay in the lower hall of Dr. Mossadegh's house when the mob broke in. At first it was generally thought to be that of his son. But in a few days young Dr. Mossadegh himself put an end to the mourning for him. From a hiding place he sent word that he was still alive. The dead man was the secretary Ambassador Henderson and I had met when the ambassador took me to pay my first formal call on the prime minister in Tehran. By nightfall of August 19 General Zahedi and his associates were in complete control of the capital. The general had requested the Shah to return. A very tight curfew was instituted at 8:00 P.M. The new prime minister was well along on his program to restore law and order.

Many died in Tehran that day—probably about 300. Similar violence occurred in other principal cities of Iran. Only at Kermanshah was the new regime's taking over delayed. The agitation, mob action and mass demonstrations to which we had grown so accustomed almost immediately became a thing of the past.

One amusing thing did happen on the afternoon of August 19. Melvin Johnson, who was then my reports officer, was taking Old Shimron Road to Villa Panarama during the demonstration before the radio station. He had turned on his headlights, of course, and had thus got through most of the roadblocks. But finally three young fellows flagged him down. He must show a picture of the Shah, they said, in order to pass. Mel didn't have one. The men climbed in.

"We will ride with you to the radio station," they said. "And we will provide a picture of the Shah."

One of Mel's new passengers took out a ten *rial* note, on which the Shah's picture was engraved, and held it against the windshield. He made motions which conveyed to Mel that he should provide a note as well. Mel felt in his pocket. All he had was a 200 *rial* note. It too carried the Shah's picture. The young man obligingly held Mel's note to the windshield beside his own. At the radio station the young fellows jumped out, taking, by mistake of course, Mel's 200 *rial* note and leaving the ten!

I mentioned the fact that several of the members of the Joint Commission were arrested. The incarceration of these gentlemen really was no reflection on them. The new regime felt it necessary to get out of circulation all who had been leaders in the old. One by one the members of the Mossadegh Cabinet who had served on the Joint Commission were released after several days. Most of them were permitted to resume normal activities outside of the government. I had great respect for these gentlemen. Their interest in our program never flagged.

One of the finest tributes Point 4 received in Iran was embodied in an action by the new Zahedi regime. Traditionally changes in administration in Iran are marked by complete rejection of previous policies and programs. Dr. Mossadegh had, as I have noted, refused to acknowledge or permit any formal reference to the first Point 4 country agreement, which had been negotiated with the Razmara regime in October 1950. Usually the more violent the change, the more violent was the rejection of the actions of the previous government. Knowing this I was greatly perturbed over what might happen to our work under the Zahedi regime. Here was a shift as sharp as that which had originally brought Dr. Mossadegh to power.

But General Zahedi appointed new members to the Joint Commission almost immediately. Only two weeks after the historic August 19 meeting that body reconvened with an entirely new slate of members on the Iranian side of the table. In an orderly way the Commission proceeded to the first item on its agenda—approval of the minutes of the previous meeting. My heart was in my mouth as I listened to the minutes being read. I had seen Iranian members balk at approving minutes of meetings they had not attended, saying that because they had not been there they obviously could not act. Several of the items of business transacted on the morning of August 19 culminated months of work. If they now were overthrown by refusal to accept the minutes it would take many more months to regain the lost ground.

Without a murmur the new members approved the minutes and, in the Iranian custom, signed the formal copies that were passed around the table.

There wasn't the slightest break in the continuity of our work thereafter. This I considered the highest tribute possible. The program was esteemed by Iranians above all local political considerations.

Mission/18

Rebuilding Iran

Ardeshir Zahedi came to me shortly after his father took office. He told me that the new prime minister was awaiting a call from me. I went with him to the general's office, in the wing of the Ministry of Foreign Affairs. Our reunion after many months was pleasant and cordial.

The day was extremely hot. The whole summer had been unusually warm. I found General Zahedi in khaki shirtsleeves. His tie was hung over the back of a chair upholstered in cloth of gold. He had taken his pistol from its holster and laid it on a corner of the desk. He was hard at work when I entered the room.

General Fazlollah Zahedi and I spoke, through Ardeshir, of pleasant afternoons we had long ago spent in the Zahedi garden in Hesserick, high on the mountainside overlooking Tehran. The summer house there was always cool, even on the hottest days.

Neither of us mentioned the trials and tribulations of the months since we had seen each other there. Part of this time General Zahedi had spent under arrest, the guest of the chief of police in the latter's office. He had been for a while in sanctuary in the Majlis building. The rest of the time he had spent in hiding. In the crucial days after the Shah had issued his *firman* and before General Zahedi had been able to effectuate it Ardeshir had somehow managed to make his way into the city. It was he who had had the *firman* photostated and the copies distributed. This much, but little more, was said of that hectic time. The general was eager to discuss the future.

"That is past," he reminded Ardeshir, who might have told me more. "Let us turn to the work ahead."

General Zahedi had a hundred things in mind—agricultural advancement, improvement of transportation and roads, resumption of the Shah's land distribution, a program similar to His Majesty's for the peasants of the government-owned villages, an extension of rural education.

I thought as I listened to him that in the optimism of the moment the new prime minister was underestimating the seriousness of some of the problems ahead. He was above all a soldier. And although he had served at various posts in the government he had not had much opportunity to deal with fiscal management. At that moment everyone underestimated the difficulty of Iran's financial predicament.

"I want particularly to complete the railroad," General Zahedi said. "It is disgraceful to have its two main arms outstretched toward Meshed and Tabriz but, after all these years, not reaching them."

On August 26, 1953, the day preceding my call, Prime Minister Zahedi had written to President Eisenhower. His message as printed in the Persian Press expressed gratitude for the assistance already given and for the contribution the American programs had made to raising the standard of technical knowledge in Iran. But the letter went on:

The United States aid being now contributed to Iran, although useful, is unfortunately inadequate in amount and nature to relieve Iran of financial and economic crises facing us. The treasury is empty, there is no foreign exchange available, and the national economy is deteriorated. In order to save Iran from such economic and financial chaos, we need urgent aids.

The prime minister promised that Iran would endeavor to use her wealth and resources to strengthen her economic position and would also strive "to improve Iran's international position."

He said that Iran wished to contribute "her share in the maintenance of world peace and the furtherance of good will in international relations."

President Eisenhower responded in a letter which appeared in the Iranian papers on the same day. The President wrote that the people of the United States continued to have "a deep interest in the independence of Iran and the prosperity and happiness of her people." After reviewing the Prime Minister's proposed program he said, "I can assure you that we stand ready to help you...."

Events moved at such a pace in September 1953 as to sweep me, for the time being, completely loose from my moorings in the technical co-operation program. An exchange of letters between Ambassador Henderson and the prime minister on September 1 placed the Point 4 program on its firmest footing. The letters acknowledged all the previous agreements, beginning with the one signed on October 19, 1950, by Prime Minister Ali Razmara and Ambassador Henry F. Grady. The notes that I had exchanged with Dr. Mossadegh on January 19 and 20, 1952, were also recognized, as was the December 1952 correspondence relating to all of the project and program agreements. This action by the general and the ambassador removed once and for all the cloud cast by Dr. Mossadegh's refusal to acknowledge the commitment of his predecessor.

When the Joint Commission met on September 2 Dr. Adl assumed its chairmanship.

But a new task now fell to my lot. I had to delegate to other members of the staff more of the responsibility for the basic technical program and spend more and more of my time wrestling with the job of resuscitating the almost completely moribund economy of Iran.

The letters of August 26 between President Eisenhower and the prime minister brought very quick action.

On September 5, 1953, the President announced that in re-

Rebuilding Iran

sponse to her request for urgent aid $45,000,000 had been made available on an emergency basis for immediate economic assistance to Iran. The announcement added that this allotment was in addition to the regular technical assistance and military programs.

The President's message said:

There is great need of immediate assistance to restore a measure of stability and establish a foundation for greater economic development and improvement in the living standards of all the people of Iran. It is hoped that, with our assistance, there will be an increase in the internal stability of Iran which will allow the development of a healthy economy to which an early effective use of Iran's rich resources will contribute.

On the same day General Zahedi expressed his thanks for "much-needed quick action in helping to overcome the financial and economic crisis." He continued:

My government will make every effort to alleviate the existing financial crisis of the country and will be enabled for a limited period of time to take urgent steps to put into effect programs designed to improve the living standards of the Iranian people. In the near future, if we carefully apply ourselves to these programs, we should also be able to make maximum use of our national resources.

Two days later I wrote a note to Dr. Ali Amini, minister of finance, who later was to engender an international reputation as the negotiator of the oil settlement. This note set the pattern for the use of the first of the emergency aid. It contained essential details of how the aid money was to be handled and used. In countersigning it, Dr. Amini made of it an agreement.

The next morning bright and early I called on Dr. Amini in his office. Since we had estimated what the first month's requirement would be I handed him a check drawn on the United States

Treasury for $5,400,000. This he took to the Bank Melli, the state bank of Iran. Immediately 508,000,000 *rials* were deposited to the Ministry's account.

Thus were three achievements recorded at once. The Government of Iran was able for the first time in many months to meet its current obligations. The Bank Melli had foreign exchange to supply to importers. And the black market which had seen dollars selling in July for as much as 132 *rials,* thirty-two above the highest official commercial rate, was immediately eliminated. With these achievements behind us we settled down to the hard work of making use of the time we had bought. Never have I worked more arduously than I did in the next three months. And never have I felt more heavily the weight of the responsibility of any assignment.

The Iranian officials were as green at their internal financing as I was. And we had time neither to assemble a staff nor to deal with any problem except as it cropped up. There were times when success seemed impossible. I almost felt that the patient was so sick that even the shock of applying medicine might kill him.

The exhaustion of the *rials* available in the Bank Melli presented a nightmarish problem. I was caught between the unassailably correct positions of each of two diametrically opposed agencies. The Iranians said that $10,000,000 of the aid should be deposited with the Currency Control Board as backing for an issue of additional *rials*. Washington felt, on the other hand, that this would sterilize the money and would not be constructive use. Mr. A. A. Nasser, governor of Bank Melli, said that the new government's precarious political position ruled out trying to solve the problem in any other way. The two governments finally worked out a compromise, barely in the nick of time, I felt, to forestall a complete collapse, for the bank was having difficulty cashing government checks.

The $10,000,000 was deposited with the Control Board, and

Rebuilding Iran

the Bank Melli was authorized to issue *rials* against it. The Iranian Government contracted to pay into its own aid account in monthly installments enough *rials* to replace the $10,000,000. At the time some thought this arrangement lacked realism. No one could tell then where the government was going to get the *rials* with which to pay itself back. But as the months wore on things worked themselves out. Increased revenues from reviving trade brought Iran enough money to fulfill its agreement. Thus this portion of our aid was not sterilized but put to vital use. Returning confidence in the government helped too. For one thing it stopped the hoarding that had helped to make the *rials* disappear from circulation in the first place. The situation was saved.

By the first of October I could report this cheering news:

Calm returned to Iran in the month of September so that it was possible for the regional directors, holding their regular meeting, to report the stopping of the organized badgering of our people. No more was being heard "Yankee Go Home."

This calm was not broken. We settled into a comfortable, unstrained situation. In the spring of 1955 our newer staff members had to search far and wide, cameras in hand, to find one faded anti-American slogan remaining on a wall. We saw no more street disturbances. No longer was riot incipient in every crowd, whether a handful gathered about two cars with locked fenders or a group of hikers headed for the snow line on Tchotchal. Tanks disappeared from the streets. We could walk on the sidewalks and meet, no patrols with submachine guns. Order prevailed.

But Iran still faced a financial emergency on October 1, 1953. Import trade had almost ceased. Even government factories were idle part of the time for want of spare parts that had to be imported with foreign exchange. Government employees had not been paid for two or, in some cases, three months. I shall never forget the shock that realization of the depth of the crisis swept around the table to both American and Iranian conferees at our first meeting to seek ways and means to make our aid effective. That conference lasted for more than six hours. It broke up late at night more because we were completely exhausted than because we had found clear solutions.

Another emergency, the shortage of sugar, which Mr. Radjy of the Plan Organization drew to the attention of a hastily organized group that became known as the Finance Committee, proved to be a godsend in disguise. By pumping 100,000 tons of sugar into the Iranian economy during the next several months we managed to obtain enough local currency to keep the government solvent.

The mass of the people in Iran have three staples in their diet, bread made from whole wheat flour, sugar and tea. Sugar, usually taken with tea, is the energy food. Most Iranians prefer a lump sugar they obtain by cracking up large sugar cones. The practice is to put two or three lumps into the mouth and sip tea through them. The people of Iran consume, when they can get it, almost 200,000 tons of sugar every year. The consumption during the twelve months just preceding autumn 1953 had been about 160,000 tons.

In Iran governments fall if there is any major crisis in the sugar market. Sugar has therefore been brought under a complete government monopoly. In order to free herself from utter dependence on a fickle world market Iran has been trying to stimulate local sugar production. This was the reason for the Plan Organization's whole program to encourage planting sugar beets and importing sugar mills.

For several years Iranian sugar production has been able to meet approximately one third of the nation's need. When the 1953 crop was just reaching the harvest period Mr. Radjy estimated that it would yield between 60,000 and 70,000 tons. Iran imports some sugar, perhaps 10,000 or even as much as 20,000 tons annually, from Russia, usually by bartering Iranian rice.

Rebuilding Iran

Obviously Iran needed to buy millions of dollars worth of sugar aboard.

Dr. Amini also had the Sugar Bongah under his direct supervision, since this agency was attached to the Ministry of Finance. The Bongah reported less than two months' supply of sugar in stock. Previous studies had indicated that whenever the stock fell below three months' supply grave dangers arose. The difficulty of transporting sugar or anything else over the Iranian roads into remote areas was serious. Only a pipeline about three months long could prevent shortages in some areas. It seemed to me very likely that some local sugar famines were already in progress.

Dr. Amini made a check and reported to the Finance Committee the next day that many of the more distant villages were out of sugar. Black markets were already operating in many sections. A poll of our regional directors indicated that in some places black-market sugar was selling for as much as twice the legal retail price of eighteen *rials* per kilogram (about eleven cents a pound at today's rate of exchange).

The Finance Committee soon saw that the fastest, surest way to turn dollars into *rials* would be to sell sugar bought with dollars to the people for their *rials*. (Sometimes Americans forget that dollars can only be used by people in the United States. Helping the people of another country requires turning dollars into something else. In Iran this something else was sugar at first. Later it was trucks and, eventually, many other items.) We wanted quick answers to new questions. How long would it take to get sugar from places like Formosa, Puerto Rico and Cuba? How should we buy it? Could the Sugar Bongah distribute large quantities of sugar rapidly? If not, were there storage places for whole shiploads? If an ample supply of sugar could be made available, how much would the monthly consumption in Iran rise? What price in *rials* should the Sugar Bongah pay to the Iranian Treasury for the sugar bought?

I contended it was safe to assume that sugar consumption would climb rapidly and would reach 200,000 tons in a year if we could get that much. The Finance Committee was in session. It was composed of Dr. Amini, who acted as chairman, Mr. Nasser, a representative of the Plan Organization and myself, with members of my staff and other Iranian officials sitting in as needed from time to time. A great deal of discussion went into fixing the amount of the first sugar purchases. It was decided that we would act on the assumption that 200,000 tons could be used a year.

The United States Department of Agriculture would act as our purchasing agent. That department thought it could buy as much as 100,000 tons at a reasonable price, but no one there could see any way to get the first of the sugar to Iran in less than ten weeks. And the new Iranian government was frantic to get sugar at once.

To appreciate what followed one must understand the Iranian penchant for bargaining. A prime minister, a minister of finance, or a minister of agriculture may chuckle over little stories of the absurd lengths to which his fellow countrymen will carry their efforts to bargain, but foreigners should never be misled by this good-humored levity. Any one of these gentlemen—like the bazaar merchant or street peddler—will bargain as though his life depended on it when he sits down to do business.

At the first meeting of the new Joint Commission, for example, the main item of business was the allocation of the annual allotment of United States technical assistance funds among the various programs for the 1954 fiscal year. A proposed allocation schedule was laid solemnly before the membership for discussion and approval. A furious controversy in Farsee swirled about the Iranian side of the table. Its center was a minister representing a department co-operating in fewer projects than most.

Finally Chairman Adl leaned across to me and said seriously, "He is not satisfied with the amount set down for his ministry."

I asked whether anyone could suggest any modifications. I said that certainly the suggested breakdown could be modified, but explained that any amount added to the projects of one ministry would have to be subtracted from some other.

"I think this will quiet down in a few minutes," Dr. Adl whispered when I had finished speaking.

I could see that none of the other members were giving the protesting minister much support. Finally that gentleman made some bright comment and sat back in his chair, apparently satisfied.

The chairman explained to me, "His Excellency has given up. He says that the amount is not even sufficient to give him a place from which to start bargaining."

In this solemn sugar contest I said I thought the Sugar Bongah ought to pay into the aid account of the Iranian Treasury about nine *rials* for each kilogram of sugar. Some of my staff advisors had determined that this figure would about equal the cost in American dollars to purchase and transport the sugar.

But when I suggested that amount the Iranian members said it would be impossible. They insisted that eight *rials* would be nearer the correct amount.

No one could explain how eight *rials* had been arrived at. It seemed to bear no relation either to cost estimates or to the fixed retail price. After more discussion the Iranian officials agreed that eight and a half *rials* would be satisfactory price.

Though I recognized the bargaining technique I was amazed to find it used in this instance.

Why?

Because actually the contestants were the Sugar Bongah and the general Treasury, both agencies of Dr. Amini's Ministry of Finance. This was robbing Peter to pay Paul with a vengeance!

Since there was no other way to arrive at a final figure I bargained it out with Dr. Amini to 8.75 *rials* per kilogram.

The price of later sugar shipments was raised a little. It mattered very little, because any profit the Sugar Bongah made was transferred into the general Treasury anyway.

The first sugar transaction involved 100,000 tons and more than $10,000,000. Once the details were agreed to we turned every effort toward getting the stuff delivered to Iranian Persian Gulf ports. The industry and energy with which busy men in the State Department, the Foreign Operations Administration and the Department of Agriculture turned to and got an emergency job done lifted my heart and gave me secret confidence. The first shipload of sugar arrived at Khorramshahr four whole weeks before anyone had dreamed possible. Just six weeks from the day of the agreement longshoremen unloaded sugar at the dock.

But almost as soon as we disposed of this first problem we ran into others. One of the most perplexing of these grew out of the fact that suddenly there was no more Iranian demand for imported goods. For many months dollars had bounced through the exchange ceiling. Point 4 had been swamped with every conceivable kind of request to supply dollars to meet foreign exchange requirements. But almost overnight the situation was reversed. All at once Bank Melli was buying more dollars than it was selling. Our aid dollars could generate no *rials* that way! As the month wore on a balance was restored. Foreign trade revived, and by the end of the month importers had begun again to bring essential goods into the Iranian economy.

To appraise this period for what it was, the most critical of all my months in Iran, one must realize the extreme tensions that had been generated when Iran sank deep into the valley of the shadow. Her people believed they had heard the sound of the iron curtain descending in their land. The fright was not to be dispelled quickly.

An air of gloomy expectancy at the outset of the Zahedi regime reminded me of some dreadful days I experienced as a child. When I was about eleven years old a very severe earthquake

Rebuilding Iran 267

struck the Imperial Valley. The earthquake was bad enough, but it was over in a few minutes, except for aftershocks that continued most of the night. Bad though the earthquake was the real subject for concern to my childish mind arose the next morning when I became aware of the sustained terror of some of our neighbors. My father was plowing in a field. Some of them came and leaned over the fence to talk with him.

"Why do you plow, Mr. Warne?" one of them asked. "That shake-up we had last night was the beginning of the end of the world. It was just how Brother Edwards predicted it would start."

"I think it was an earthquake," my father said. "But even if your friend Brother Edwards should happen to be right, I think that I should just as leave have the end of the world come while I was plowing."

It was several days before the clear evidence that the end of the world had not come sustained my confidence in my father's point of view.

So it was in Iran. But at the end of that trying month confidence began to flood back. It came to the new government. It came to the market. Thereafter import trade moved progressively forward from one peak in new ground to another.

The Zahedi government, as I pointed out, restored order immediately. Some critics complained of a heavy hand, but I could see no merit in this complaint. It is true that police and security forces showed a new spirit, and it is true that some of the apostles of disorder found this most annoying. The first time a fledgling mob began to organize in defiance of the law the police cracked a few heads and arrested the leaders. When rowdyism broke out at the university security forces forcibly restored order. Only the year before the school had been forced by rioting to suspend for more than half of its scheduled class days. Three students were killed when the new administration's police moved in. Many more students than that had managed to get themselves killed during the previous year in street fighting, but these three deaths were, regrettably, at the hands of organized law enforcement agents. I observed though that as soon as it became clear that the government intended to maintain order the number of occasions to use a firm hand rapidly diminished. In fact there was a gradual and progressive relaxation of the many extraordinary measures taken in earlier unsuccessful attempts to achieve the same results.

The curfew was moved back hour by hour and after a few months was relinquished altogether. Tanks and soldiers were gradually removed from the city. Soon only guards of honor remained about such places as the palace. The police force regained some of its self-respect and began trying to enforce such regulations as the one against riding the back bumpers of buses to avoid paying the modest fare. This and other such rowdy tactics had previously been symptoms of a major breakdown of orderly city life. The military were recalled from the university campus. I was even freed from my "private eye."

The Zahedi government went about the business of re-erecting a constitutional government just as methodically as it quelled lawlessness. The Shah had immediately resumed his position. Soon the general called new elections. In a short time a new Majlis was organized. A Senate was again established in accordance with the Iranian constitution. Some critics complained that the elections were rigged. It seemed improbable to me that any more justification was given in the election of the Eighteenth Majlis than in any previous election for assertions that democratic processes were not evenly applied. Co-operative programs such as ours will have to register a great deal of progress before a literate and informed electorate will exist in all areas of Iran. The Iranian constitution calls for a Majlis and gives it certain authority. Regardless of the manner in which these deputies are elected, no one can successfully contend that they are the tools of any prime minister. Prime Minister Razmara could not control

Rebuilding Iran 269

Dr. Mossadegh when the latter was in his Majlis. Nor could Dr. Mossadegh control General Zahedi in his Senate. And General Zahedi could not control the membership of the Eighteenth Majlis.

My most wonderful experience of this period was observing spirits revive in the people of Iran. Antiforeign feeling was thrown off as though it were a conquered disease. The hospitality that characterized the rural areas seemed suddenly to flow into the cities as well. The morose mood lifted. The radio programs may not have been any better—I don't know, since I couldn't understand them—but at least they no longer sounded like dirges. And the people were happier. Beggars all but disappeared from the streets. Goods flowed back into the shops, and more people had money to buy them. There was some difficulty in Tehran for a time with the management of meat and bread supplies. This was partly the result of some rather ill-planned attempts at price-fixing and partly of the fact that demands rose steadily as the economy began to revive.

It became safe for women to be on the streets again. There was a time when Iranian women who did not wear the *chadora* had their arms scratched in the bazaar. There were even a few cases of acid-throwing. No foreign women had been involved in these outbreaks for the simple reason that none dared to enter the bazaar. There had been a few occasions when some of them had suffered crude and contemptuous indignities on such broad, modern streets as Shah Reza or Naderi.

Long before the first year of the new regime was out all this had passed. Our wives and even our young daughters were safe to prowl about the old shops and to visit Tehran's wonderful bazaar. This, incidentally, is reputed to be the most colorful and, the Iranians say, the largest in the world.

The Joint Commission during the late months of 1953 and the beginning ones of 1954 ground away at reviewing technical assistance projects and allotting funds to them. The United States allocation of $23,000,000 was made early in September. The budget of the Government of Iran placed 100,000,000 *rials* at the disposal of the Joint Commission to augment the budgets of the co-operating ministries and to help support local projects.

Some projects added that year were radio production training, opening a laboratory on soils and industrial chemistry, providing technical assistance in the construction of the Karadj dam and making studies in the Ziandehrud basin. We also established an audio-visual training center and a Tehran municipal demonstration children's home. Another project sought to improve selection and placement of personnel. Improvement of the wood treatment plant at Shirgah, assistance in Caspian lumbering operations and establishment of a bonded warehouse were among new projects. We continued training co-operative specialists and our demonstrations in tea processing. We introduced automatic bottle-making and began the rehabilitation of wells in Yazd area. In the 1953-54 fiscal year we also provided professional services and established an institute of public administration at Tehran University. And of course we extended projects we'd started in earlier years.

Allotments for the technical co-operation program in the 1955 fiscal year were made early in this one. The initial United States appropriation was $19,500,000, to which $2,000,000 was added on March 31, 1955, as part of a loan to Iran. The Iranian contribution to our budget was estimated at 150,000,000 *rials*. One of the few new projects proposed to us during this year was one which would begin co-operatively to compile the basic data and to conduct planning studies which would eventually lead to a comprehensive program for the development of the Khuzistan Plain, using the waters of the Karun river system. This became the major project of our Point 4 program, which was by now well-rounded and functioning efficiently.

The second anniversary of the Joint Commission was noted at its sixty-second meeting, in February 1955. Neither this nor any

Rebuilding Iran

of its predecessor commissions had ever been forced to cancel a scheduled meeting for want of a quorum. The interest in its work held by the high Iranian officials who made up the majority of its membership needed no further documentation.

Though the economic emergency occupied most of my time during this period important things were happening on other fronts as well.

Prime Minister Zahedi set about restoring Iran, first by providing security for the people, then by reviving the economy and rebuilding the government institutions. This done, he took the bold political step of exchanging ambassadors with the Court of St. James's and resuming negotiations for a settlement of the festering oil problem. Though, as I said, this is not the story of the Persian petroleum controversy no one in Tehran could have been unaware of the gradual process by which the government made preparations and instituted the negotiations, which were brilliantly carried to their successful conclusion. Herbert Hoover, Jr., was invited to advise and was in and out of Tehran for a year. Though he and Ambassador Henderson were not among the negotiators their contributions were even more important. Times of high expectations alternated with periods of gloom, but to a complete outsider it all seemed to move inexorably forward to its resolution in mid-October 1954. President Eisenhower presented the State Department's highest award to Ambassador Henderson just before he ended his exceptional tour in Iran. In his presentation the President pointedly mentioned his work in connection with the oil settlement. When Mr. Hoover became Undersecretary of State his patient and unobtrusive work in Tehran was widely heralded in the press.

The long negotiations impinged very little on the work of Point 4. The Joint Commission yielded its conference room in the White Palace of the Ghulistan group to the negotiators. We did little more.

The Zahedi government was confronted with one additional

problem of explosive political significance locally. He had to determine what to do about Dr. Mossadegh and the wilful group that had defied the Shah and held the government for three days in contravention of the royal *firman*. Dr. Mossadegh and his chief military aide faced a long trial marked by histrionics and legal procedures that would seem somewhat bizarre to an American. A letter from the Shah was interpreted as a plea for clemency. An appeal from the verdict of the lower court caused the appellate court to lengthen the general's sentence by one year to make it equal Dr. Mossadegh's.

The public did not react as some had feared it would. Apparently the good doctor had been fooling himself with his oft-repeated asseverations that he alone held the popular affection. About nine months after his deposition the former prime minister began serving a three-year sentence in the comparative comfort of a suburban house of detention.

Dr. Fatemi, Mossadegh's foreign minister in the turbulent final days, alone of the cabinet members was not quickly taken. He was sought amid sound and fury, and was finally found after several months. The search reminded me of the earlier one for Ghavam, which had ended so differently. Dr. Fatemi had grown a beard and was living in his own house at the time of his arrest. Only he of all the civilian cabinet officers was tried or even formally charged. He was convicted of treason and executed.

As he faced these problems General Zahedi also tried to launch a constructive program to rebuild the country, to revive the Plan Organization as an affective agency and to meet some of the most pressing needs of the people.

Many important tasks of the Point 4 mission have barely been mentioned, if not omitted altogether. One additional phase, though, does deserve comment. This was the Impact or public works phase of the Special Assistance Program. The Special Assistance Program was begun in September 1953 with the allocation of $45,000,000. Later sums added to that amount brought the total to $82,800,000. The budgetary grants of this program ended when oil revenues resumed in January 1955. The Impact program was financed from these funds. We had earlier determined to undertake a forceful public works program of wide distribution as a part of this program. The Joint Commission approved forty-five projects, the largest of which was the construction of a relocated road in Karadj Canyon. The public works program completed two unfinished buildings at Tehran University and repaired three airports used by the Iranian Airways, the internal airline of Iran. Building schools and improving streets in a long list of places from Bandar Abbas to Tabriz were two more of the many other public works projects. The minister of finance allotted from the aid account *rials* equivalent to about $8,000,000 to help the program.

During the whole period to the end of the 1955 fiscal year, June 30, 1955, Iran received $258,000,000, only 1.2 per cent of the total United States foreign aid expenditure in the same period. This total receipt included $85,000,000 loaned in 1955, including $53,000,00 for economic development projects by the Export-Import Bank and $30,000,000 to help the government with its budget until the oil revenues could strengthen the economy. So from October 19, 1950, when the first Point 4 agreement was signed, until June 30, 1955, the technical co-operation program in Iran operated on approximately $90,000,000.

While the oil settlement was still pending Abolhassen Ebtehaj returned from Washington, where he had been in the International Bank, and became head of the Plan Organization. He immediately set about arraying projects to resuscitate Iran. His was a monumental task. With help from many sources, Mr. Ebtehaj in 1955 laid his plans for a large-scale, long-range development program based on plans laid out by the Overseas Consultants, Incorporated, an American group familiarly called OCI. It was to execute these plans that the Plan Organization had been created in the first place. The major part of my job in Iran was done. We had crossed our chasm of crisis.

But no matter our success the propaganda from the north never let up. Happily it now seemed to have little effect, where once it had been able to incite street riots in Tehran. Perhaps this was because there were now other, stronger voices on the air.

In the winter of 1954-55 the Shah and his Empress went to the United States to have physical examinations and to fulfill her lifelong ambition to see our country. They were hospitably received, and the news of their daily doings was carefully followed in Iran. In Washington, at a National Press Club luncheon on December 15, His Imperial Majesty said that "a gradual but deep social awakening" had followed the Second World War in Iran.

"Economic and political freedom became an integral part of the national aspiration," he continued. Apart from a "limited number of misguided fanatics and Tudeh adherents," he said, no one wanted to smash up the oil industry. But in August 1953 "Iran stood on the brink of catastrophe." At the "eleventh hour, by the grace of God and the patriotic exertion of her people and their loyalty to the crown, Iran was delivered." The Shah then reviewed his land distribution program. "In a vast country like Iran, where poverty is endemic, and where subversion tries to make the most of this ancient problem, such schemes . . . will steadily but surely improve general conditions." Then he went on to say, "I would like to record my heartfelt appreciation for the most valuable and effective financial, technical, and other assistance so generously given to Iran by the U.S.A. I can assure all our American friends who are working for mutual understanding between our two peoples that their efforts are bearing fruit."

At about the time the Shah was giving this report the Soviet Near Eastern Service from Moscow broadcast in Persian one of a series of weekly talks by a commentator named Alexandrov.

Rebuilding Iran

The title of his address was "The American Way of Life Means Fascism." Mr. Alexandrov said, among other things, that United States "advisors stifle Iranian freedom." Part of this broadcast, as reported in the USSR International Service on December 27, 1954, follows:

When I read reports in Iranian newspapers regarding U. S. attempts to impose the American way of life on the Iranians and to represent it as an example of freedom and democracy, I cannot help recalling the words of an Indonesian youth. In his letter addressed to the office of the American periodical *Progressive* this young man stated:
"When you talk of freedom and equality, we shudder with indignation. No one in the world likes freedom *à l'American.* Freedom *à l'American* indeed! When I recall that 115,000,000 American citizens—that is, almost the entire adult population of that country—have been summoned to police stations to have their fingerprints taken like criminals, I realize that what you understand by freedom is exactly the opposite of what we mean by the word.

"I could not possibly call a country free where records are kept in its police stations for 131,000,000 of its citizens and where tapping of telephone wires is permitted by law; where, according to a statement made by President Eisenhower some time ago, people are afraid of amateur investigators and of crises. Such a freedom, which in reality is fascism, disgusts one. My indignation reaches its height when I see that the uncultured of Wall Street strive to spread their culture in countries such as Iran, which possesses an ancient civilization."

Iranian newspapers reported some time ago, that under the leadership of U. S. advisors and by means of special equipment imported from the United States, fingerprints of the entire population of Tehran would be taken after December 1.

The head of the special mission for the propagation of the American way of life in Iran, Warne, is resolved to subject all Iranians to highly humiliating regulations.

U. S. ruling circles like to represent themselves as [the kind Uncle Sam], but a wolf in lamb's clothes is still a wolf. At the beginning of last month, the United States announced that it intended to give some machines to Iran as a gift. These machines were not the tractors sorely needed by Iran's agriculture, neither were they the [machines] required by Iranian industries. They were special police cars used in the United States for the transport of criminals.

When delivering these police cars to the Iranian authorities, Warne referred in his speech to the need for preserving freedom. In reality, he made a mockery of freedom. Such a method of preserving freedom in reality deprives people of it.

Alexandrov had at least followed some of the news in Tehran. A few days earlier I had delivered to the chief of police in Tehran nineteen police cars equipped to train police in traffic control. This was done under the law enforcement training phase of the public administration project. None of the other facts reported were facts at all.

In April 1955, a month after I left Iran, General Zahedi resigned because of ill health. The Shah expressed his "appreciation for the brilliant services rendered" by the general as prime minister.

Hossein Ala succeeded as prime minister. He had been ambassador to Washington during the Azerbaijan crisis, prime minister for a brief time in 1951 and minister of court during the Mossadegh and Zahedi regimes. Prime Minister Ala carried forward his predecessor's program. Point 4 carried on.

Khiaban Asle Chahar

Mr. G. H. Ebtehaj, mayor of Tehran, stood waiting in the bright sun while Hossein swerved my car to the curb. The chief of police stood with him in the group on the sidewalk. I was puzzled. I had been going over in my mind the mayor's rather peremptory summons. It still nettled me a bit.

Shortly before, as I sat working in my office, the telephone had rung. Elsie Hartman told me that the mayor was on the line.

Mayor Ebtehaj was enigmatic. "I want you to meet me at once at the corner of Shah Reza Avenue next to your technicians' building."

I paused a moment to give the mayor a chance to explain further. "Hello!" he said. "Hello! Are you there, Mr. Warne? Are you there?"

"Yes, Mr. Mayor, I am still on the line," I reassured him. "I was just seeing what appointments I had."

"I want you to meet me there at that corner right away," he insisted. "There is an urgent matter. Can you be there in exactly ten minutes?"

My calendar was blank for the hour beginning at 11:00 A.M. I agreed to meet him, not hiding too well a little irritation I felt with him. "Yes, Mr. Mayor, I can make it since you feel it is so urgent."

"I'll explain why I want to see you when you get here," the mayor said and abruptly hung up.

In the car, with Dr. Moghadam beside me, I had even toyed with the idea of turning back.

But Dr. Moghadam said, "Mayor Ebtehaj is a very polite man. This is not like him. It must be a most important matter."

Dignity! I thought, with just a touch of chagrin. Why should I feel ruffled because the mayor sounded curt? In any event curiosity was beginning to come to my rescue. What on earth did the mayor want? I hoped it was not serious trouble—not after all we had been through—not now when things seemed to be going so smoothly.

When I reached Shah Reza Avenue I quickly saw that despite the place our meeting was to be rather formal. The men with the mayor were the heads of all of the departments of the city government. When my car drew up they seemed almost unconsciously to array themselves as for a groundbreaking. The police chief came forward, smiling broadly, to open my door.

"I am sorry this isn't a more important street," Mayor Ebtehaj said, without other introduction, "but it is the one beside your most important building."

Pulling a paper from the pocket of his light summer jacket, the mayor read loudly:

In appreciation and gratitude for the Mission's valuable contributions to the Municipality of Tehran, that is asphalting the streets, building of inexpensive housing units, completion of the slaughterhouse, and so forth, this municipality has decided to name one of the streets adjacent to the Point 4 Shah Reza Building after Point 4. This morning this street was re-christened and a sign was put up on the corner of this street. It is hoped that the city will continue benefitting from additional constructive aids.

I hadn't seen the new street sign until just then. There it was, fifteen feet up on the wall, spanking new in blue and white. Written in Persian calligraphy, the name was repeated in Roman letters, *"Khiaban Asle Chahar"*—"The street of Point 4."

Here in the capital of Iran, with its Roosevelt, Churchill, and Stalin avenues named to commemorate the wartime Big Three

Khiaban Asle Chahar

meeting held there, a new street name had appeared. There was handclapping and much good-natured laughter over my bewilderment.

"You did not know anything about it, Mr. Warne?" The mayor asked more than once. "Dr. Moghadam did not tell you?"

"No," I said wryly, "no one told me." But now I understood that the fact that my calendar was clear at 11:00 A.M., June 10, 1954, had been contrived in advance. Several of my closest associates had entered an elaborate little conspiracy with the entire city government.

It was pleasant to know that so many people would take such pains just to lift a small ceremony above the ordinary. It lent sincerity to the tribute of the naming of the street.

As I walked to the car after the ceremony the chief of police said, "We appreciate the help of your traffic experts too. It was their idea to put up street signs. Most of our streets never had any before. How do you like them?"

"They look fine," I assured him. "This one especially."

We shook hands and I left.

Only a short while before this touching tribute I had taken a trip into the Kurdish country beyond Kermanshah. There was no doubt that even down the byroads the name Point 4 had a special meaning. We had driven rapidly to Sahneh, where we met General Ali-Gholi Golpira, commandant of the Imperial gendarmerie mission, and other officials. Colonel E. M. Sleeker of the United States gendarmerie mission to Iran and Mr. Mathieson, Point 4 regional director at Kermanshah, were with me. We met in this out-of-the-way village that day to dedicate the twenty-first of the demonstration housing units constructed under project number fifty-five. This project's purpose was to show what could be done with local materials to improve housing in widely scattered rural areas, and also to show how a little better design could provide decent, sanitary living quarters.

Each of the new compounds built under the project contained, in addition to quarters for companies of gendarmes and their families, office, garage and stable space, a public room, a first aid station, a jail and a schoolroom, as well as a sanitary community bath, a well, a sanitary laundering room, *mostaras* (privies) and other health facilities. Twenty men and their families were assigned to the compound at Sahneh.

Miss Bowles of our staff and the Ministry of Education were conducting a pilot project in adult education in co-operation with the gendarmerie. Gendarmes all over Iran suddenly began carrying around with them their specially prepared primers.

It had not been unusual in other days for gendarmes to stop a passing car and ask if any of its occupants could read. "I have a new instruction from Tehran," the gendarme would explain, "and have not been able to find out what it says."

Hardly had any of our projects met with such hearty enthusiasm on the part of the participants. The individual gendarme felt highly complimented that he had been selected to receive adult instruction ahead of the rest of the population. We had brought in instructors, given them courses in methods and an armload of the new books and fanned them out through all Iran.

Here at Sahneh General Golpira picked a gendarme at random from the company. He asked the young man to step into the schoolroom and up to the blackboard. The popularity of this instruction among the men had greatly impressed the gendarmerie's entire chain of command. I hoped that General Golpira's enthusiasm wouldn't lead him to put the project to too severe a test.

The gendarme selected stood stiffly at attention. Obviously his uniform had been made to look its best. His hair was combed and his mustache too. A good man, I thought. Maybe he had been able to learn to read and write in five months after all.

General Golpira proceeded. "Write on the board," he ordered the gendarme, who had not moved a muscle, *"Zindeh-bad Shah-in-Shah Iran* (Long live the Shah of Iran)."

The gendarme reached nervously for the chalk, then turned to the board. To my great relief he laboriously traced out the Farsee characters. I do not know whether the young policeman or I felt more pleased when the general told him that he had done well.

General Golpira said he had received reports from all over the country indicating that his men were becoming literate. He thought they would soon need new books. They were outgrowing their primers.

"When these men learn to read and write they will be of greater service to the nation," the general explained to me. "Often they are the only representatives of the government in their areas. And often too no one else can read or write in their communities. So if all my men learn we will be able to get information to the villages much more rapidly and accurately."

Another time I visited a class when it took its final examination. I thought the test was very stiff. The examiner called on men at random to read any paragraph he selected in the textbook. As one man read his paragraph the others were required to write it on their examination papers. Each of the forty or fifty men taking the test was busily writing. I could not tell as I went about the room whether they were accurately setting down what was read but I learned later that most of them had.

Miss Bowles reported a great demand for literacy classes among the women in the villages. She was already working out a project. The Near East Foundation also organized classes of the same sort among the men and the women meeting separately, in many of the villages of the Veramin Plain. These two experiments, the one in Veramin and the other with the gendarmerie had showed Miss Bowles that it would be possible to carry out a widespread program.

Before a little formal ceremony at the gate of the gendarme compound at Sahneh General Golpira and I inspected the rest of the installation. We saw the women, wrapped in *chadoras*, timidly standing inside the doors of their one-room apartments.

One lady, apparently designated spokeswoman by the others, did not duck into her doorway but stood forth to speak.

She indicated her one bare room, a rug laid neatly on the floor and a samovar standing in the corner. "Now," she said, "my family can live decently. May God bless us every one."

Several hundred visitors from Sahneh and the surrounding villages came to see the station that day. Some were landlords and some were khadkhodas, but most were peasants from the fields.

General Golpira explained to them that this post had cost 620,000 *rials*. This amounted to about $372 for each family. The office, company room, jail, first aid station, stable and garage were, so to speak, thrown in free. He told the people that the gendarmerie was glad to call to public attention certain specially designed new features of the compound. He asked them to note particularly the cheaply made windows, the well and the *mostaras*. These things all might easily be duplicated in the neighboring villages.

I, in turn, told the crowd that we from America hoped through such Point 4 projects as this to assist them to resolve some of their own problems. I too urged them to try to duplicate some of the new construction features.

Many prowled through the station examining every detail.

We were at this time also making significant demonstrations in housing for the poor people in the cities. Low-cost units for industrial workers were under construction in three widely separated areas, Chaluce, Isfahan and Tehran. Each project involved 100, 200 or 300 units. The most important Point 4 contributions in these were a sanitary water system, a sewage system, and a community and shopping center for each. These innovations were widely heralded.

On the return trip from Sahneh to Kermanshah, Mr. Mathieson took me by Darius' Behistun inscription high above the road that once led to Babylon. This ancient road is still in use. Here

Khiaban Asle Chahar

the great king memorialized his victories over nine separate pretenders. He had told his story in three cuneiform languages, Old Persian, his own tongue, Elamite, the language of Old Susa, and the language of Babylon. The triple inscription has enabled scholars to decipher all. I was always interested in the old monuments. They seemed to lend depth to an understanding of Iran and her people.

A short distance off the road a number of ancient mounds caught my eye. Archaeological sites are so numerous in Iran that most of them go unnoticed. Often a modern village stands at the base of such a mound. The mound provides a handy source of adobe, which is screened out with no eye to study and no thought of its origin. Amateurs "go digging," and some have large collections of clay pots and other artifacts. Strange little objects are forever turning up in the shops in Tehran. Some undoubtedly are counterfeited in a rear-room work shop, but others must date back centuries to unlettered civilizations. Many places still bear their Old Testament names, though they may be changed slightly. Susa, for example, has over the centuries become Shush. Unmistakable signs of the glory of old Persia abound—of Cyrus, Darius and Xerxes, who lived 2,500 years ago. The Sassanian Kings, Ardishir II, Shapour III and Khosru Parviz, who came along almost a thousand years later than the Persians, left their marks. The many monuments left by Shah Abbas the Great nearly 400 years ago attest to the grandeur of his court and the scope of his reign.

Graves of important cities destroyed by invaders, ruined strongholds of lesser men, holy places, early Zoroastrian places of silence, tombs of slain Mongol princess, monumental burial places of poets, all add their bits of evidence to the chain of history. Such engineering works of great age but modern appearance as the Valerian Dam at Shuster, the Bandeh Amir Dam near Shiraz and several in Khorrassan especially impressed me.

The great stone faces that Gutzam Borglum carved in the

Black Hills of South Dakota testify to our youth as a nation; any schoolboy can recognize the features of Washington, Jefferson, Lincoln, and Theodore Roosevelt. But the likenesses in the stone of the mountains of Iran bespeak to the people there the age of their culture, for no one recognizes a face and the names have been supplied only after painstaking labor by advanced students of antiquity. Only an utter clod could stand unmoved in the presence of this unmistakable evidence left by the men who hewed history!

Legend has it that Daniel was buried at Shush—a story disputed by some scholars. Here the French Archaeological Mission, under a concession from the Iranian Government, excavated for decades, peeling off layer on layer of civilizations. Great kings brought skilled labor and stone from Egypt and artisans and wood from India to build the immense Apadana. Its seventy-two heroic pillars furnished for centuries a rock quarry for the rude generations that followed. Now only bits and fragments on the ground trace its majestic outline. Canals once irrigated the plains and created a land so attractive as to make Alexander desert for it his capital in Macedonia. These too are gone.

The Valerian Dam at Shustar takes its name from the captured Roman emperor said to have been put to work to improve the Karun River. The base of the dam is a natural rock formation. Instead of raising a barrier Valerian lowered the river by digging out a channel across a wide loop made by the river as it issued from its canyon onto the Khuzistan Plain. This canal forms the island on which Shustar stands.

The dam has an intricate system of river controls and a series of penstocks that serve ancient flour mills. One very new 500 kilowatt generator was recently put in service. The slick and shiny little powerhouse, oddly out of place on the toe of the antique dam, is the source of great pride for the Shustari. Mr. H. Farzad, resident manager of the Shustar Irrigation Company, would hardly let us leave it to inspect the old works. Mr. Y. Soleimanipour, senior engineer of the Irrigation Bongah in Khuzistan Province, pointed out an ancient *ghanat* built through stone. This well once tapped the Karun River for water to irrigate lands near Susa, at the bend immediately below the Gotwan damsite. Someday this dam may again unlock the riches of the plain.

In a deserted, hard-scrabble plain north of Persepolis stood the tomb of Cyrus the Great, founder of an empire. The tomb had been pitted and scarred by the millennia. Old pillars that once must have formed gates in a wall around the monument now lean askew. No highway led to this ancient memorial. Only an earthen path rutted by donkey hoofs showed the way. From the high door of the tomb we could see a few shepherds with their flocks passing near by. In the distance was a wandering farmhand. Inside the stone sepulchre visitors had tied shreds of cloth, both to show respect and to fulfill a folk tradition that had grown up since the days of Cyrus. The conqueror and his grave should never be naked. I noticed as I ripped apart a handkerchief to pay my own homage that even these sad little remembrances were nearly all faded and decaying.

I thought of the Roman Forum, of the Parthenon, of ruined Byblos, of the junk left on three continents by the Roman Empire. I thought of Machu-Pichu in the Inca Altoplano of Peru. When I mentioned these thoughts to Khalil Taleghani he confided that he had been thinking of monuments he had seen.

He spoke of the Lincoln Memorial in Washington. "As an American you might not understand it," he said, "but until I read the Gettysburg address from the south wall there, I had no acquaintance with Lincoln. I went out and bought a book of his speeches."

Khalil's linking of the ruins of past civilization with the living temples of our own gave me a turn. "Our monuments are not ruins yet!"

"Oh, Bill," Khalil pressed my arm in his fervor, "may they never be!"

Persepolis, in Fars, was built by Darius, Xerxes and Artaxerxes.

It is somewhat better preserved than other of Achaemenian cities. The Iranians believe Alexander the Great responsible for destroying the ancient Persian capital. They are unforgiving of the Greeks' deliberately misconstruing its Persian name and calling it Persepolis, "the destroyer of cities." But despite the unabated animosity the name Persepolis is in common use in Iran today.

A magnificent platform about 1,500 feet long and 1,000 feet wide was leveled out of the mountainside. It looks over the valley toward the modern city of Shiraz. Here Professor Olmstead of the Oriental Institute in Chicago in 1937 recorded the following dedication of Darius, inscribed in three languages:

> Great Auramazda, greatest of Gods, who established Darius as king, has delivered to him the lordship.
> This land Parsa, which Auramazda gave me, this is beautiful, possessing good horses and good men. By Auramazda's will, it fears not an enemy. Against this land may there come neither enemy host nor bad harvest nor the lie. This favor I pray Auramazda with all the Gods.
> By Auramazda's will these are the lands of which I took possession with the Persian army—Persia, Media, and the other lands of other tongues, mountains and lowlands, this side the sea and that side the desert.

At another gate, built by Darius' son Xerxes, the professor translated:

> Xerxes, great king, king of kings, king of the lands of many races, king of this great earth far and wide, who by Auramazda's aid made this gate "All Lands." Much else that was beautiful was done in this Parsa that I accomplished and that my father did. What now has been built and seems beautiful, all that we did by the will of Auramazda.

The West has often accepted the views of Greek historians without looking behind them to Persia herself. Dr. Moghadam once shocked me out of that attitude by declaring that it was doubtful whether that "Macedonian Princeling Alexander" ever reached Persepolis.

"You are carrying your nationalistic enthusiasm too far," I protested.

"I do not say that Alexander didn't get there," Dr. Moghadam explained. "I simply observe that we have found no contemporary record of it. The first account of the conquering of Persia didn't appear in Greek historical writings until more than two centuries later. So I think there is room to doubt."

Not so very much room I contended silently, remembering old Greek coins found in Iran. Nevertheless I wished more windows opened onto the ancient past.

Iran's pride in Isfahan grows out of the city's many reminders of the renowed court of Shah Abbas the Great. The Maidan, or city square, was originally a polo field. The King could watch the games from the balcony of his stately palace facing the square. The Blue Mosque, widely believed the finest in all Persia, stands near by. The Chehelsatoon dominates the Shah's garden. This is an exquisite building canopied by a great porch supported by twenty exceedingly tall and beautifully fashioned wooden pillars. In this unique structure the Shah held his audiences. Before it a great pool reflects the palace. The Chehelsatoon, which means "forty pillars," was named for the effect of the view across this pool. The forty pillars are the twenty supporting the high canopy of the great house and the twenty reflected in the limpid waters.

The Chehelsatoon today is a museum. In its back rooms repose fine old relics from the Shah Abbas regime and tokens of Isfahan's history. The decoration of its walls and ceilings, above mirrored panels, is among the best of Persian mural art.

On one occasion I attended a dinner given for me in the Chehelsatoon by the officials of Isfahan. The great table was set in the area from which the king used to look out upon his garden. After dinner we gathered under the stately portico on chairs, hassocks and rugs. Here we enjoyed the beauty of a warm summer night, starlit and peaceful. On occasions like this one I felt now and again full participation in the life and history of this wonderful land. I understood that night why Iranians say, "There is Isfahan, and then there is the other half of the world."

The great Shah who held his splendid court here built the caravan route to China. To Isfahan he brought the Chinese artisans whose influence on the design of the best of Persian rugs, tile and silver is strong even today. In Isfahan he received emissaries of the great nations of Europe. Here he planned the many works that bear his name. His was the unmistable imprint of a great man. Many cities in Iran have at one time or another served as the seat of government. But the mark of Shah Abbas in Isfahan is more nearly indelible than the signs other dynasties have left in other capitals.

Isfahan dominates the valley of the Ziandehrud, the richest agriculture area of the country. The law which governs diversion of the river for irrigation was laid down by Shah Abbas.

Northward from Bandar Abbas, the port built by the Shah on the Gulf of Oman, the ruler laid out a system of caravanserais that made of Persia for hundreds of years the corridor through which the trade of central Asia passed. A romantic chapter in history developed around them. The caravanserais are in ruin now, except a few adapted to serve as military posts. The one near Khupayeh is among the best preserved. On a road roughly following the old camel route to Yazd it stands, a gigantic pile of brick with walls as thick as a fortress's. A heavy gate guards its entrance. From its tower its keepers once watched the approach and departure of the desert trains.

Seeing the ancient caravanserai I could imagine piles of silks and tea in its vast courtyard at night. I could almost see scores of camels in its stables and hear the noise of the escorts in their wardroom. It was easy to picture the travelers relaxing in their quarters and to envision the smoke of cooking fires rising in thin ribbons against the evening sky. Only the booted feet of thousands could have worn the cuplike depressions in the steps up to the major-domo's office as they climbed to pay their tolls, to pass along news of the world beyond or, perhaps, to report the repulse of a gang of bandits in the hills. Gone from the world—along with the pony-express stations of the American West and the roadhouses along the dog-sled trails of the Yukon and Alaska—are these old ports of call on the inland routes. They have been replaced by the railroad stations and airports of what seems to me a less colorful day.

A reminder of Shah Abbas, more amazing than this web of caravanserais, even more remarkable than the Chehelsatoon is on the Mountain of the Workers between the Kuhrang River, which joins the Karun and flows into the Persian Gulf, and the Ziandehrud, which flows into the Great Salt Desert. Shah Abbas saw that if the waters of the Khurang could be diverted to the Ziandehrud the farms and gardens surrounding Isfahan could be greatly extended and improved. He determined to dig a ditch through this Mountain of the Workers. Several thousands of men picked out the rock and carried it to spoil piles. After nearly ten years they had excavated more than a million cubic meters. It would have taken another twenty years to finish the ditch, but the work stopped when the Shah died. The mountain was named for the workers who made the cut. With Khalil Taleghani I climbed the mountain to see the old diggings, remnants of which are still plainly discernible. In some places the cut was hundreds of feet deep. The plan that fired Shah Abbas had never been lost. It has continued to inspire engineers for nearly four centuries.

The new Khurang tunnel served the same purpose Shah Abbas had planned for his great ditch. But like the ditch, the tunnel came very close to being abandoned. This time the bottleneck was grave financial difficulty. In 1951 the Iranian government had no foreign exchange to buy cement and steel to line the tunnel. One of Point 4's first projects was to help complete this great work. With this assistance Shah Mohammed Reza Pahlavi was able at last to realize his predecessor's dream. In a ceremony in October 1953 he cut the ribbon which signaled workmen to divert the first waters into the tunnel carrying the life-giving flood to the Ziandehrud basin.

At the time of this dedication I was deeply involved in the financial emergency following the overthrow of the Mossadegh government. When I received my invitation to the ceremony I called Clark Gregory. Clark, then my assistant and legal counsellor, was later country director in Jordan and is now my successor in Iran.

"You must go to the opening of the Khurang Tunnel," I told him. "I simply can't get away."

"But," Clark protested, "where am I going to get a suit of tails and a sleeping bag?"

"Wearing a white tie and tails up on that mountaintop will be a good experience for you," I answered callously.

The full dress suit is the uniform of American diplomatic representatives abroad. Some nations dress up their diplomats like admirals from *Pinafore,* but the United States sticks to more conservative costume.

"It won't be so bad," I assured Clark.

"Sleep in a tent!" he lamented. "And wear a silk hat at noon!"

"I'll loan you my suit," I told him. "And I know where you can borrow the hat. You can draw the sleeping bag from supplies. The committee will furnish tents."

My suit, by the way, fit Clark very well.

There was every reason, of course, for the Iranians to be proud of their work. The Mountain of the Workers was at last penetrated. The new tunnel was 2,830 meters (almost 9,300 feet) long and eleven meters (just over thirty-six feet) in radius.

Clark told me later that His Majesty was especially gracious to him at the reception following the dedication. Now mollified, he even confessed that he hadn't felt conspicuous. "Everyone else was all decked out," he admitted. "But you'll have to tell the cleaner to be careful with those dress pants of yours. I picked up burrs clear up to my knees."

The labor of these busy days was interrupted only briefly by such formal ceremonies as the Khurang dedication and by visits from people interested in our work. Mr. Thorpe D. Isaacson, chairman of the board of trustees of Utah State Agricultural College, and Dean R. H. Walker of that school visited Tehran. We were then negotiating for a renewal and expansion of the Point 4 contract with the USAC, which had been working with the mission from the outset of the program.

After he had seen some of our work Mr. Isaacson told our staff, "Some people must change their philosophy. This work is not 'wasting public money,' and our government and others must understand that. You could give people money and not help them, but you can't give them education and training, as you are doing, and not help them. The things you are giving will pass from generation to generation and will last forever."

In the past 150 years Iran has been visited by a plethora of foreign assistance missions. If even a few of them had been successful in introducing permanent reforms today's problem would probably be much less difficult. Between the Point 4 mission and previous missions is one basic difference. Point 4 works co-operatively to develop in Iranian institutions strength to conduct their own improved programs. The missions that went before for the most part operated their own various institutions and programs.

Mr. Zia-ebdin Chaffari, an Iranian member of our staff, advanced a compelling argument to our group in a review of the Millspaugh missions. Mr. Chaffari contended that the first Millspaugh mission had lost public acceptance and support and that the second had never received it because the Iranian people believed that these missions attempted to influence the country's internal policies—that is, that they had a political objective. Germany, Austria, France, Belgium, Russia and Sweden had at other times introduced missions to perform certain functions in

Iran. These too failed, if we judge them by the permanence of their influence.

"Iranians have a remarkably high opinion of the Americans," Mr. Chaffari reported. "They esteem the United States more than other nations. They regard Americans as more benevolent than those others to Iran. They do not believe that America is seeking concessions or commercial advantages. They hope that a more perfect understanding to benefit the amicable relations of both nations continues to exist between them."

It seemed to me then as it does now that it is even more difficult for Iranians to understand fully the United States than it is for Americans to comprehend the psychology of Iran. And this understanding is vital to programs of technical co-operation. I feel that as the bigger, stronger, richer nation, with more responsibility for the future of the world, the United States must expand rather than diminish its efforts to generate international understanding and good will. We must be flexible in our attitudes in order to avoid affront. And we must be exceedingly slow to anger and generous of the reactions of our friends.

Of course, the money that Point 4 has spent for technical assistance in Iran would have paid for some monumental structure. But it would have been very un-American to use it in that way. The whole American way of life is based on education for all and on free access to basic knowledge and training. We have found in our country that monumental structures are results of a better life and not its cause. Lacking our background of educational freedom, some Iranians had difficulty seeing that Persepolis 2500 years ago did not make Persia great. The fact that Persia was great made Persepolis. But not understanding the fundamental difference in background, some Americans grow angry when people who have not yet learned this truth request large sums of money for spectacular construction projects.

I am proud to think that *Khiaban Asle Charar* leads toward reciprocal understanding.

Mission/20

Co-operation with Other Missions

OBSERVERS often presume conflicts between what are called bilateral and multilateral technical assistance programs. The bilateral program is one arranged between two nations. Point 4 is bilateral. The United States enters into a separate technical assistance agreement with the government of each host country. Such programs as those conducted by United Nations specialized agencies are multilateral. The UN agencies draw their funds and experts from many nations.

Because Point 4 and the various UN technical assistance programs are similar and often operate simultaneously in the same countries many assume that they cannot get along. Since the aim of both Point 4 and UN is identical—to stimulate social and economic development—many taxpayers think we may duplicate our efforts. Because the United States contributes a liberal share of all the United Nations aid funds and also finances Point 4 those who suspect duplication fear that the government may be wasting some of their money.

Some of these people feel that all technical assistance should be extended through the multilateral agencies. Others insist that we are foolish to finance, even in part, the United Nations technical agencies. They think we should put all our eggs in the Point 4 basket. Still others simply regret the duplication and waste of energies that they imagine must exist because multilateral programs are extended into the same areas.

While I was in Iran there was neither duplication nor competition between Point 4 and the UN agencies. The two programs supported and complemented each other.

Dr. Marcel deBaer, a Belgian with an English wife, was the resident representative of the United Nations secretary-general in Tehran during the same time I was there. His job was to help co-ordinate the various separate missions and to represent them with both the Iranian government and the United States Operations Mission. Many of the UN specialized agencies had either continuous or part-time programs in Iran. These included the WHO, the FAO, the ICAO, the UNESCO, the UNICEF and the ILO. Some of them, such as the World Health Organization and the Food and Agricultural Organization had several different missions operating there at the same time. At peak times the combined UN agencies had more than eighty technicians in Iran.

We worked closely with these missions. Early in 1955 Dr. deBaer, who now lives with his family in Switzerland, prepared to leave Iran. His mission there was completed. On February 8 he and the heads of several of the UN missions attended the meeting of my principal Point 4 staff. We reviewed our common relationships.

More than three years had passed since the morning at breakfast in the Darband Hotel when I had found I had a companion for the first time in weeks. Seated in a lonely corner I had seen Dr. deBaer. Over the breakfast table that day we formed a union of technical co-operation for Iran. That union had persisted.

The officer on our staff responsible for maintaining liaison with the United Nations group was James J. Goulden, assistant director. Jim recalled that on February 6, 1952, we had organized a technical club among the technicians gathered from all over the world under Point 4 and United Nations banners. The technical club had remained active. It drew its membership from the

Co-operation with Other Missions 295

staffs of UN agencies, Point 4 and the technical ministries of the Iranian government.

Dr. deBaer suggested soon after we first met that we bring together the principal technicians of all staffs to discuss collaboration. The first of these meetings was held on March 27, 1952. One result was that UN technicians participated in more than one third of all the Point 4 projects.

Dr. M. S. Adiseshaih, director general of UNESCO, visited Tehran in May 1953. I had called on this talented Indian at the UNESCO offices in Paris on my way to Iran in 1951. Dr. Adiseshaih found us in the process of establishing vocational training schools for agriculture and industrial arts. Iran had previously had no schools of this sort. Point 4 and UNESCO were working together on the project. Dr. Adiseshaih reviewed the co-ordination we had achieved so far and noted that Dr. Herbert Heilig, chief of the UNESCO mission, regularly attended the Point 4 staff meetings. The director general paid a glowing tribute to his staff and ours. He said that in all of the world Iran "provided the best example of co-operation and collaboration."

That same week Hans Ehrenstrale and some associates from the UNICEF regional headquarters office had been in to discuss collaboration to complete a milk pasteurization plant. Many agencies were playing their parts to bring the project to near-completion in 1955.

Before the pasteurization plant was built Tehran had no safe milk. The emergency children's fund appropriately decided that this plant should have highest priority among its activities. UNICEF made the plans and purchased the machinery. Iran built the buildings. Point 4 dug a deep well. With the Ministry of Agriculture we also planned ways to increase milk production and set up a system of dairy inspection. With the Ministry of Health we worked out a scheme to insure sanitary distribution of the milk after it had been pasteurized. Ice-cream production will help the plant become self-supporting. UNICEF obtained an agreement stating that a sizable fraction of the whole milk would be distributed to underprivileged children in a school-lunch program.

On September 7, 1953, F. T. Wahlen, director of the agricultural division of the Food and Agriculture Organization, wrote from his headquarters at Rome:

As the technical assistance program progresses through vicissitudes and produces failures and successes, one begins at headquarters to look upon the different countries in which we work more or less as one's own children. You could understand that Iran, having been so much in the spotlight and public attention during the last two or three years, has absorbed more than its proportionate share of interest among the countries for which we feel, even though in a very small degree, somewhat responsible. I can hardly tell you how pleased I am that, in spite of political tension and temporary economic impotence, our team in Iran seems to have developed in the past year a fruitful program. In fact, the reports of our experts and of our mission chief have contrasted so greatly with the newspaper reports that I often felt quite puzzled how such an amount of useful work could be accomplished. In this whole picture, the excellent cooperation between TCA—or shall I say FOA?—and FAO has been a particularly bright spot. There is hardly a report reaching headquarters where reference is not made to good cooperation and to help by you good people in technical projects, in the matter of transportation, or in the financing of such worthwhile and essential things as the soils laboratory or the pilot tea plant. Since my division is responsible for the lion's share of FAO's technical assistance program in Iran, I should like to express to you my warm appreciation for this state of affairs. When you visited Rome, briefly, before taking your assignment in Iran, I felt that such cooperation was within the bounds of possibility. Let me tell you that my expectations have been exceeded and let me again thank you.

Before Dr. deBaer left we gave a dinner party for him. At the party I glanced around the table at each of our principal officers. Pat Regan, chief of the agricultural division, reviewed a great

Co-operation with Other Missions 297

deal of our work with the UN agencies. He spoke of Dr. J. R. Pelletier, a Canadian who had headed the Food and Agriculture Organization Mission in Iran until October 1953. Hearing his name, I recalled Dr. Pelletier's remarks at another dinner, given by the Plan Organization and the Ministry of Agriculture for some thirty-five of his associates and friends. Good neighbor Pelletier had said that peoples all over the world had learned from experience that the United States could always be counted on to help, whether in a forest fire in Canada, an earthquake in Iran or a typhoon in Japan and whether in a disaster or a less dramatic situation, one that called for help to correct underdevelopment. He went on to say that Iran should not forget that the United States was extending its help at a time when to do so required that it increase its own national debt.

When I had heard Dr. Pelletier's praise I had not been able to avoid comparing the friendliness and trust along the border between our two countries with the deep fear and distrust on the northern frontier of Iran. An unguarded line thousands of miles long separates the United States and Canada. But watchtowers and patrols form the demarcation between Iran and her powerful northern neighbor. The only communication between the two countries is the radio, which beams propaganda southward to incite unrest.

When Pat Regan finished speaking, Mr. Stickney, the chief of our industry division, reviewed the joint projects that came under his jurisdiction. One of these was the Point 4 sawmill built as part of the lumber project on the Caspian Sea frontier. One of the UN technicians had drawn the specifications for the mill. The whole project's aim was to demonstrate other uses for hardwoods besides charcoal.

The technical direction for the tea-processing demonstration project, also reviewed by Mr. Stickney, was all handled by the United Nations. A Point 4 project mechanizing the bottle-making industry supported the joint milk pasteurization project. On the Persian Gulf a project of great potential importance was under way. The crew of the FAO research boat was collaborating with Point 4 and Plan Organization technicians in fishery research. We hoped this work would help us to establish a modern fish-canning industry, both to furnish employment in that devastated area and to provide a source of food for many people.

Tom Kilcrease, chief of the engineering and construction division, reported, "Our efforts have been combined under ventures relating to water resources, railroads, civil aviation and telecommunications." He enumerated a long list of engineering projects in which the United Nations technical experts had worked shoulder to shoulder with ours. One of Tom's joint projects was a school at Mehrabad airport with courses in radio mechanics, radio operations, meteorological forecasting and observation, air traffic control and radio-teletype communication. More than a hundred young Iranians were trained in this last skill.

Dr. Cherry, public health division chief, enumerated in addition to malaria control joint projects in dietary education, in venereal-disease control and in tuberculosis control. Point 4 and UN had together built a tuberculosis center at Sangalaj Park and had also labored with the Iranians to compile sound medical records and statistics. Through our joint efforts maternal and child health clinics were set up in the provinces and public health nursing was incorporated in the basic curriculum of the Princess Ashraf School of Nursing. We collaborated to train personnel to help form the Iranian nurses' association and to help draft constitutions for a proposed school of public health and a national institution of hygiene.

"Looking back on these three years that I have spent with you," Dr. deBaer said after our staff members' reports, "we must confess that they have been extremely difficult years from every angle. We have had political difficulties and economic difficulties. We have had shooting in the streets. When our experts

Co-operation with Other Missions

made recommendations we were told by the Iranian Government there was no money to carry them out. Fortunately in some instances we had Point 4. Successes have come where we have co-operated together. It is satisfying that I have had one very small part in creating something here which I hope is permanent. This is the feeling of friendliness and co-operation between our two missions, without which I maintain it is quite impossible to work here."

Many, many opportunities for co-operation and collaboration presented themselves to us, the UN agencies and Point 4. Some UN technicians' assignments, because of the specialized nature of the Iranian Government's requests, did not relate to our work. And some Point 4 projects were not in their field of expertise.

And in these differences in scope, of course, lies the justification for both the UN and the Point 4 approach. The main difference between them is that the UN agencies for the most part send into the countries in which they work teams of experts in unrelated fields. Once in a country these men go to work to find ways to apply their special abilities. Point 4, on the other hand, first works out projects in areas of immediate need, then sends for only such technicians as are required to complete those projects and to train local technicians to duplicate the project activities on their own. Iran, at least, needed both types of help, intelligently applied.

Other influences besides Point 4 were at work in Iran weaving a reassuring web of friendship with the United States. The American embassy under Ambassador Henderson and his fine professional staff was a constant beacon. I worked particularly closely with the officers in the economic section, led by Robert M. Carr and, later, William Bray, the economic counsellors. This section served as integral staff members to the Technical and Special Assistance programs. The contributions these men made were of utmost importance to the success of our mission.

The United States Army mission and the Military Assistance Group under generals William Zimmerman and, later, Robert A. McClure played vital parts in training and equipping the Iranian Army, which was the country's only effective internal security force. Colonel Leslie A. McClellan's small but effective training mission with the Imperial Gendarmerie made major contributions, some in co-operation with Point 4, toward building up this important agency, the civil police force for all non-urban Iran. Lest it appear that Point 4 was the only operation in Iran I hasten to point out that it was simply the most pervasive.

Quite beyond the collateral official efforts were activities and institutions that preceded us and helped create an atmosphere receptive to United States aid. Two among these deserve special mention.

The unostentatious and devoted service of the missions, hospitals, and schools of the Presbyterian Foreign Missions Board had built up Iranian confidence in the honest altruistic purpose of America. The late Dr. Jordan's American school, in which many of today's Iranian leaders were once students, has also left an indelible mark. Many people have expressed regret that the government, which took over this institution after its thirty years under Dr. Jordan, has not maintained his standards. Iranians mourned when they learned that this fine old gentleman had died at his home in Ohio.

Malek Mansour Ghashghai, one of the brothers who led that great tribe, told me of his experience in the American school.

"I was a wild boy," he said, "living in the hills with the nomadic bands when my father, the khan, called me to him.

"'You will soon be thirteen,' he said. 'I have entered you in Dr. Jordan's school. We shall leave for Tehran tomorrow.'

"I felt rebellious, but no one questioned the authority of my father. To leave the hills! To leave my horses! To leave off hunting! To leave the people! I thought my heart would break. I could see no reason to go to school."

Co-operation with Other Missions 301

When after several days they reached Tehran the khan took Malek Mansour directly to Dr. Jordan's office.

"He looked like Moses to me," Malek Mansour recalled. "'You will obey Dr. Jordan,' my father said. Dr. and Mrs. Jordan would have us in to tea. We had to dress neatly and behave just so. If it was our turn we had to pass the cakes and we had to wash the dishes. It was the beginning of the civilization of Malek Mansour!"

This cultured gentleman is now equally at home in Paris drawing rooms or astride a stallion in the chase in Fars. It is difficult to picture him as the wild boy from the hills he remembers himself to have been. But I never doubted Malek Mansour's story.

"If we should fracture some rule, and I am afraid at first I did so frequently," my friend continued, "Dr. Jordan would come right out into the yard after us. He was a kindly man, this we quickly learned, but he was implacable. He would take us by the ear and march us right into his office.

"'Now, young man,' he would say, 'your father left you here so that I could help make a man of you. Our rules are made for all, and they apply to you too. They are laid down to treat you young people fairly and to protect the rights of others. See that you obey them the next time.' Then, his eyes less stern, he would add, 'Mrs. Jordan and I would like to have you come to tea today.' We respected him and we loved him and Mrs. Jordan."

I met dozens of Iranians who spoke as fondly of the "old American school" as had Malek Mansour.

"How does it happen," I once asked Khalil Taleghani, "that you speak English like an American when you took your engineering degree in England?"

"I went to Dr. Jordan's school," he explained. "A great many of us learned our English there."

"How long have you been a teacher?" I asked Dr. Moghadam

one day. He had been on the staff at Columbia University for six years and was when I knew him professor of linguistics at the University of Tehran.

"At eighteen I was a teacher in Dr. Jordan's school," he replied. "You have met many older men who have said that they were once my pupils. I taught them twenty years ago at the old American school."

Though the work of missionaries to Iran has changed from time to time, it has been continuous for several decades. Kindly and devoted people have grown old in mission service. Iranians with whom I talked repeatedly referred gratefully to their work.

The old Near East Relief agency was converted twenty-five years ago to the modern Near East Foundation, which made several important contributions to the work of Point 4. Dr. Stephanides, the livestock specialist, was a war orphan who had been cared for and educated by the Near East Relief. Charles White and Frank Appelbee, comptroller and assistant comptroller of our mission, were both old Near East hands. Thirty years before, they had spent two years together in the Caucasus working for the Near East Relief. The interest this work kindled drew them back to us.

The Near East Foundation preceded Point 4 by several years with a rural improvement project in the Veramin Plain. Its men freely shared with us the lessons they had learned at Mamazon and helped us to avoid many mistakes. Point 4 contracted to assist the Veramin project in enlarging its work, and NEF served Point 4 as field liaison among the 350 villages of the Veramin Plain. Even more valuable to us were the many intensive experimental programs that NEF under Curtis Spalding undertook for the Ministry of Agriculture, the Ministry of Education, the Ministry of Health, Amlock and Point 4. NEF's field laboratory work proved, for one thing, that it was efficacious to give rural teachers brief special training and use them as village super-

Co-operation with Other Missions 303

visors. The field-trial program also demonstrated the value of training village boys with modest education to be efficient sanitary aids and tractor mechanics and drivers. We relied on NEF to test the effect of such projects as our home extension services among village women, and of our own adult education classes in the villages. Reports from the trials indicated to us which programs we could expand without risking colossal failure.

NEF representatives participated in all our staff meetings. At one of these meetings Curtis Spalding filled us in on the history of his organization. Near East Foundation began its work in Iran in 1946 on invitation from the Iranian Government. Its work covered three broad fields—agriculture, health and education. NEF operates the farmlands of Mamazon Village in partnership with twenty-four village farmers. Here it tests farm machinery and experiments with various methods to increase production. Those that prove useful are extended to surrounding villages through village-worker programs. Each worker serves from five to seven villages within bicycle range of one another. These men help the village people to mobilize their efforts and resources so they can help themselves. The village workers are supported by technicians in agriculture, education, health and sanitation and home economics.

Other NEF agriculture programs in Veramin include technical support of the first twelve land-reform villages distributed by the Shah among his peasants, work with co-operatives, formation of rural credit societies and village councils and home-welfare work with women.

In its education program NEF works closely with the Ministry of Education. In 1946 Veramin had few rural schools. Now NEF supervises seventy-eight with a total enrollment of approximately 7,000 boys and girls. In addition it sponsors a vocational training school for teachers and village workers and a teacher-training school for girls. Literacy classes offered by the Foundation serve about 2,500 adults each year. In co-operation with the PHCO the Near East Foundation directs and supervises a school for sanitarian aides. Upon graduation these young men are sent to work in villages throughout Iran. In health and sanitation NEF works with the Ministry of Health and the PHCO. Largely through its efforts malaria in Veramin has been stamped out. And it is making progress in improving domestic water supplies, waste disposal and fly control.

The NEF has received major financial and technical support from the Ford Foundation as well as from Point 4. That support has allowed it to expand and at the same time intensify its activities. Many practices and procedures developed on the NEF projects have been adopted nation-wide.

Besides helping the NEF to build its teacher training center and to establish a rural credit program the Ford Foundation, through Paul Maris, worked with Point 4 and the Ministry of Agriculture on plans for a block-development program. The first example of this kind of program will probably be the Khuzistan Plain project, which will use waters impounded by Kharkeh Dam on newly reclaimed lands. The Ford Foundation also helped the Iran Foundation to establish a vocational school in Shiraz.

The Rockefeller Foundation for several years conducted a village nursing school in the Shariar area. Young women trained there became the nucleus of Point 4's rural nursing staff.

The Iran Foundation is largely financed by Mr. Mohammed Nemazee, but it has a staff of advisors in both New York and Tehran. This foundation has a monumental project in Shiraz—a sanitary water-supply system and a hospital. The former has operated for several years, and the latter opened on October 14, 1955. Point 4 staffed the hospital's nursing school and gave it some financial assistance.

All of the several agencies I have mentioned have contributed very much to improving relations between the United States and Iran.

A Country Director Goes Home

"YOU CAN'T BUY FRIENDSHIP," one of my friends once blazed at me indignantly. "These nations will just take our help, all they can get, and demand more, Bill Warne, but they won't like us for it!"

Oh, old friend of mine, what you say is like so many catchwords. They may reduce arguments to a simplicity that wins elections but they have no bearing on the issues at stake. Nations are not individual men as we seated here in your study are. They are instead whole peoples. They differ from one another even more than do individual men. They live in lonely isolation.

If both were men, the United States would be forty-four feet tall and Iran only five feet, six. Iran would be 880 years old and the United States but seven. In economic and social development the differences between the two countries are even more marked than in size and age.

Like the big fish of the sea large nations have in the past attacked and swallowed whatever smaller ones happened to fall within the range of their darkling "known worlds." On our continent we have tried the experiment of living together in peace with Canada. It worked. So why should we not try the same experiment with other countries farther away? We are dedicated to individual freedom and national self-determination. We are not imperialists, yet we can nevermore live alone on this shrunken planet.

In Iran men were as curious about our motives for Point 4 as were many Americans like my friend. They were not afraid that Point 4 was an attempt to "buy friendship," but some did wonder if the United States might not really be just another big fish with a new way of swallowing a smaller one. This is what they repeatedly heard from outside propagandists.

At a medical conference called at Ramsar by the Empress Saroya I was pressed for an answer to the question, "Why Point 4?" This was my reply:

The United States of America feels that it has been blessed by God and that its people have inherited their culture, energy, ingenuity and their ability to live peacefully side by side from those who emigrated to America from all parts of the earth. America, therefore, in token of her gratitude, is giving some of herself to help others to help themselves, believing that when other peoples can witness that they, too, are going ahead to a better future, greater hopes will come to the common man, and peace will be buttressed within every village throughout the world. America is striving, therefore, to help the people of Iran to help themselves through improved agriculture, more education, and better health. These objectives are in line with the aspirations of men everywhere that their children may live, grow up in health to labor usefully and have a chance better than that of their fathers to find happiness.

The words are a little warmer than those of the 1950 Act for International Development, in which the Congress declared the policy of the United States to be "to aid the efforts of the peoples of economically underdeveloped areas to develop their resources and improve their working and living conditions by encouraging the exchange of technical knowledge and skills and the flow of investment capital...."

The Congress in the amended Mutual Security Act of 1954, said this over again in these words (Title III, Section 301):

It is the policy of the United States ... to aid the efforts of the peoples of economically underdeveloped areas to develop their resources and improve working and living conditions by en-

A Country Director Goes Home

couraging the exchange of technical knowledge and skills and the flow of investment capital to countries which provide conditions under which such technical assistance and capital can effectively and constructively contribute to raising standards of living, creating new sources of wealth, increasing productivity and expanding purchasing power.

One day in 1952 Dr. Mossadegh insisted to me that Iran needed $30,000,000 at once. "It would be much cheaper," he said, "to give $30,000,000 now than for you Americans to have to fight your way back to Tehran."

I replied that his statement indicated that he thought this program politically motivated. I told him I thought he understood that the Technical Cooperation Program was designed to help people in underdeveloped areas to help themselves.

"Oh but, Mr. Warne," he said, "if it weren't for our neighbors at the north you would not be here."

This I denied, pointing out that my country had missions similar to this one in other countries that did not have common frontiers with the Soviet Union. The Point 4 program, I reminded him, was almost world-wide in its application.

Under goading I finally burst out, "I don't wake up each morning, Mr. Prime Minister, wondering what I can do this day to fight Communism. No, I wake up wondering how I can better help the Iranian people fight ignorance, disease and starvation. If carrying the fight against these ancient enemies of mankind attacks the roots of Communism, then it must be a despicable plant indeed to grow only in such soils. If by cleaning out these backyards of the world we eliminate a noxious weed it will still be but one incident in the work of improving the lot of mankind."

I recalled this conversation when I was preparing to leave Iran. When I reviewed all that had occurred during my stay I felt that we had answered any lingering question of the effectiveness of this type of program. We had held the friendship of the people even during times of great stress, not by purchase but by giving hope. Our work was not finished in 1955. It seemed that it had only just begun in earnest. But no matter what might happen in the future we had already given full justification for our efforts and the expenditures. Iran remained free and independent. She stood strongly in her traditional grounds and supported in all the councils of the world the philosophies of free and united nations.

Our program had ridden its roller coaster to the bitter end. When the final throe had come the Iranian people had turned away from the statue defacers with their red flags and had smiled on us with approval for our work done in friendship.

Some of the things that occurred at and immediately after this moment of climax erased from my mind some of the irritation and the anxiety caused by "Yankee Go Home."

In the midst of the general disorder crowds stormed past the TCI regional office in Kerman shouting, "We are with you!"

Mr. Mathiesen, our regional director in Kermanshah, had one of the ugliest "Yankee Go Home" signs painted on his door with tar. And I had been paid the personal compliment of having painted on the wall of the near-by regional compound another sign which said, "Dirty Warne Go Home."

The first night after Mossadegh's fall the guard at the compound telephoned Mr. Mathiesen to report that someone was painting the door again. Mr. Mathiesen said tiredly, "Let them go ahead."

In the morning he saw a new legend. "We want you to stay here."

All of us felt confident of the real effect of our technical field work. Yields of wheat were greater. Malaria had been brought to bay. Thousands of teachers had passed through our training schools. A modern textile mill was under construction. Pure water ran in the pipes along the streets of Tehran. We could point to a thousand tangible achievements.

A Country Director Goes Home 309

A cleverly conceived and ardently promoted propaganda campaign had challenged the program's fundamental concept and had threatened its whole effect. But if Iran can be considered typical of underdeveloped countries, as I believe it can, we demonstrated that if our program and the propaganda against it are laid down side by side the people will pick up our shovels and hoes, our health advice, our better seeds and our baby chicks and will reject the vicious rumors and nebulous promises.

As I understood Toynbee's definition of the growing civilization, it is the one being sought after, respected and emulated by the alien people of the world, whom he called "the external proletariate." By this measure our western civilization continues as the world leader. A cult has grown up in America, which though it doesn't doubt the power of our way of life at home erroneously concedes to another philosophy and economic system the place in the very vanguard of world revolution. Doesn't this cult realize that the American revolution still rings around the world, that our idea appeals? The dignity of man, the decent self-discipline of democracy, the practical struggle for a better life and the honest, generous interest in human welfare everywhere are the ideas and the ideals of America. These will appeal to the world.

Many invaders have used force to impose their systems on Iran for a time. None of them seems to have changed the country's basic ways of living very much. I have seen peasant women gathered with their distinctively modeled water jars about a village well and thought it must have been the same when Mary went to the watering place. The boy David might be among a group of lads taking their flocks to the hills. They go now exactly as he did then. Or Ruth might be among a row of gleaners in the wheat stubble. Time has stood still in Iran. No matter how rigorously it is applied force will not change these ways.

But Point 4 has changed some of them. The people want new methods. Villagers at Khonsar, Khupayeh, Zarghan, Marvdasht and every other community we have entered have sought us out to show us their pitiful needs and to voice their hope for guidance and help.

One "how-to-do-it" film, one demonstration planting of cotton or sugar beets, one summer course for rural teachers will not help these people.

Here where the people are weighted down by 6,000 years of traditionalism even the adventurous in spirit need to be sustained in their revolts against old usages. But when the village women learn that deep-well water will keep their babies from dying they will come and will send their children to the prosaically squirting spigots at the corners of their *kuchehs*. The men will lead their cows to the artificial insemination center when they see that their neighbors have that way obtained astonishingly fine calves. The herdsmen will bring their sheep by the millions to the mobile veterinary teams for innoculation and treatment when they hear that those who have done so have lost no sheep from anthrax. When they see the heavier fleeces and the fat on the sheep freed from parasitical worms, the shepherds will step forward and ask, "When will you come to our village with those pills?"

I never heard of a single instance of a Communist propagandist's being besought by a village. I have heard of several villages that have forcibly driven them out. Rare indeed is the village that has rejected Point 4 and none has ejected us. But we have received in numbers too great to count humble petitions to come to villages the program has not yet reached.

In Iran we fought the war of ideas and words, and the victory has certainly been ours. Our idea has been action and our word is hope.

The voice of America in the villages of Iran is, as Lucy Adams once said, the voice of an American talking with his Iranian co-worker at village council meeting to plan a village school. The voice is heard when an American nurse and her Iranian

A Country Director Goes Home 311

counterpart teach a village midwife how to wash a newborn baby or train bashful girls to work in a village health center. It is heard when a malaria team sprays every house in a mosquito-infested village and when they paint the Point 4 emblem on a mud-walled enclosure.

A veterinarian team with Point 4 insignia on its saddlebags spreads our message by treating sheep and cattle and by explaining how the tribesmen may keep their animals healthy.

A mobile health unit drawn up under the trees beside a canal speaks by treating the thronging villagers.

A Point 4 truck going from village to village with sacks of improved seed wheat to exchange for poor speaks loudly. The voice grows even louder when the same truck returns two weeks later with cardboard boxes of fine baby chicks to exchange for the stunted poultry scratching around the village compounds.

An American nurse working with an Iranian doctor and nurse to examine and treat the children in a village school . . . an American county agent and his Iranian co-workers demonstrating irrigation methods and water conservation to a water-hungry village . . . an American instructor teaching a class of Iranian rural teachers how to prepare a school garden . . . an American sanitary engineer and his Iranian staff seated cross-legged on the floor of a village mayor's house to discuss digging a shallow well for safe drinking water . . . an American agronomist with Iranian help showing groups of farmers how to spray their fruit trees, how to start nurseries, how to plant cotton in rows, how to hoe out weeds, how to operate a cheap steel plow—all these bespeak our way of life in strongest accents.

Every Iranian who sees a Point 4 film made in his own country, or watches an American cameraman patiently instruct Iranian boys in motion-picture techniques, or observes Americans and Iranians working together to help a group of village weavers form a co-operative for a better product and better marketing walks away with the voice of America ringing in his ears. We strengthen our message a little each time we drain a foul swamp, build a new bathhouse or dig a *mostara*.

Iranians pore over each new issue of the Point 4 magazine *Land and People* written in Farsee. They discuss it at the village teahouses and plaster pictures torn from its pages on their whitewashed walls.

Every day in village communities throughout Iran Point 4 was in the field with agricultural teams, educational teams, health teams, engineers, agronomists, nurses, doctors, teachers. Americans work with American machines and supplies. They work in their own ways, ways they learned in their own government departments and colleges. They talk in villages, talk with Khadkhodas, with village councils, peasant cultivators, peasant proprietors, village craftsmen. They go to these people because they have been invited by letters, by petitions, by government officials. Of every twenty villages that beg them to come they can visit only two or three. In a given year they may meet only two of a hundred requests for help with schools, baths, wells, chickens or seed. From among all the villages that offer land, labor, materials, buildings, and sometimes money they have to select those that will serve best as demonstration examples.

In its operation in Iranian villages, through the Iranian agencies Point 4 has made history. It has helped to build or equip hundreds of village schools. It has distributed hundreds of thousands of chickens and many hundreds of tons of improved wheat, barley and cottonseed. It has opened health centers, drilled wells, treated millions of animals, sprayed 16,000 villages in every province, built bathouses, located safe water supplies, trained thousands of rural teachers. It has finished roads, dams, power plants, a cement mill and a sugar factory. These, in turn, open up new land and new markets. Point 4 has helped to establish an agricultural extension service, a rural public health service, a central statistical service, a public adminstration institute, an educational film production center and a bonded warehouse.

A Country Director Goes Home 313

Response to our efforts is not always unmixed thanks. Gratitude sometimes turns to complaints. Eggs do not hatch, chickens die, the pump for the deep well costs money to run, patients want pills, not health education. It is easier to promise a thousand mud bricks for a village clinic than it is to make them. The pipeline should be longer; the bathhouse should be bigger; the school's roof leaks. Why do you help Mohammadabad and not us? Where are the benches and desks that you promised us? What is the use of showing us how to feed our children when we are so poor? What you are showing is against our religion. It would make the women bold. What do *you* want?

But when agitation against our program was greatest and noisiest, when agitators came by the busloads from the larger cities to warn the villagers of the dangerous Americans who wanted to exploit Iran, who were tools of the hated British—even during that period rural support never languished. The political and economic unrest that racked the country obscured some contributions. But Point 4 was saying something to the villagers that they could see and weigh and test for themselves.

It was speaking with a voice that everyone could understand. It was promising the villager nothing he couldn't see and touch and help to make for himself in his own village—a healthier sheep, a bigger ear of wheat, a tree where none grew before, water where the land was dry, a school building partly built by the men of the village, a bathhouse of homemade mud bricks, medical and health services with a doctor who had time for each patient and drugs and remedies for his ills.

The voice is answered by action. The weavers of Khupayeh answer it by meeting week after week in the evenings and slowly form their co-operative.

The village of Tiran answers by deciding that even girls should have a chance to go to school and by offering to build a school for them.

The teacher of Dastgerd-I-Piaz (Dastgerd-of-the-Onion) answers by getting some of the richer peasants to whitewash the schoolroom and knock out a window in the wall so the children can see the new books that he has brought back.

An old Mullah answers by asking for someone to teach the midwives at Riz.

Amanullah answers by exhibiting his beautiful Point 4 chickens, which have the run of his best room when his guest comes, and by jealously saving the eggs to set.

The village girl who has been away to the city for six months to train with Point 4 answers by working daily at the village clinic, going out to the homes when women and children are sick.

The village youth who trained at the Point 4 school and became a sanitarian aid answers by helping to keep his village's water supply clean.

The Point 4-trained district extension worker answers by going out to help the peasant to irrigate his land, to exchange his seed, to plant cotton.

Thus the voice of America is translated into the lives of people in another land. And thus the voice is answered by the people's learning new ways, by their strengthening hope.

Now I had been asked to take a month off, then to go to another part of the world. I found when I packed to go home that more articulate voices were speaking for Iran too.

One newspaper said, "'It has been the assistance of our friends that has enabled us, despite all sorts of intrigues, to save our country from economic bankruptcy and utter ruin."

And another, "Nowhere in Iran can you find a place that has not enjoyed directly or indirectly the good results of the Point 4 programs."

In Hossein iAla's words, "This has been creative work of a new and a high order, namely, the raising of the standards of life of the Iranian people, thereby contributing to the peace and security of the world."

And that is the story of Point 4 in Iran, 1951-55.

# Index

Abayaz Palace, 18, 36
Act for International Development (1950), 18, 306
Adams, Dr. Lucy W., 55, 172, 174-175, 200-201, 310
Adiseshaih, Dr. M. S., 295
Adl, Dr. Ahmad Hossein, 156, 201, 223, 224, 225, 233-234, 240, 258, 264-265
Adl, Madjid, 51
agricultural program, 56, 75, 76; extension service, 228-231
Ahwaz, 31, 120
Akhoosh, Ali, 191
Ala, Hossein, 190, 192, 276, 314
Aldridge, Fred, 144
Alexandrov, ———, 274-276
Amanullah, 314
Amini, Dr. Ali, 259-260, 263, 264, 265
Amlock, 37, 190, 192, 193, 302. See also land distribution program
Amuzegar, Dr. Jamshid (Jim), 157-158, 159, 160, 161
Anglo-Iranian Oil Company, 20, 21
Ansari, Reza, 5, 64, 159, 220, 221, 222
Appelbee, Frank, 302
Ardalon, Dr. A. H., 104
Associated Press, 51, 52
Atai, Dr. Mansour, 224, 225, 226, 227
Attai, Dean M., 63
Avonek, 80, 83, 85, 174, 175
Azar, Dr. Mehdi, 92
Azerbaijan, 38, 86, 87

Baba Adam, 117
Babolsar, 31
Bahmanbegi, Mansour, 130
Bakhtiar, Mrs. Helen, 143, 172
Bakhtiari Mountains, 13
Bakhtiari tribe, 100, 101, 102, 103, 108, 109, 112

Bandar Abbas, 158-159
Bank Melli crisis, 239, 260-262, 266
Bayan, Azizz, 187-188, 189
Behnia, Dr. Abol Hassan, 160
Bennett, Dr. Henry Garland, 18, 20, 31, 38-39, 40, 41, 224
Bernhart, Richard (Dick), 195, 199
Besuye Ayandeh, 96
Bingham, Jonathan and June, 98, 99
Bowles, Luana, 172, 173, 280, 281
Bray, William, 299
Bryant, E. C., 127, 128, 129, 130, 131 132
Bunnel, LeRoy, 230
Busheri, Javaud, 44, 45, 63
Byrne, Horace, 38

Cabinet Committee, 46-47, 55, 56, 61, 62-63, 92, 118, 190, 192, 205
Carr, Robert M., 38, 299
Caspian, 120
Chadegan, 215
Chaffari, Zia-ebdin, 291, 292
Chapman, Oscar, 24
Cherry, Dr. R. Leslie, 140, 298
chick project, 75-79, 85-86
Communists, 48, 49, 51, 52, 96, 120, 131. See also Tudeh
cotton-classing project, 183, 184-186, 186-189
Country Agreement, 45, 160
Cressy, Dr. George B., 167
Crilley, Albert Cyril, 41

Daliri, Amir Moazemi, 215
Dara, M., 161-162
da Silva, Silvino, 186
David, K., 98
Davudabad, 190-192
Dawson, James R., 48

315

deBaer, Dr. Marcel, 133, 294, 295, 296, 298-299
deep-well program, 159-162, 169
Demavand, 33
Demavandi, Motamed, 96-97
Destgerd-of-the-Grapes, 214-215
Development Bank, 192, 193
Djaffari, Reza, 5, 173, 182
Douglas, William O., 91
Dryer, E., 156
Dulles, John Foster, 222

Ebtehaj, Abolhassen, 273
Ebtehaj, G. H., 277, 278
Ecbatana, *see* Hamadan
education program, 173, 177-178, 180-181, 182; audio-visual aids, 217-218; students sent to U. S., 177, 187-188; technical training program, 178-180
Ehrenstrale, Hans, 295
Eisenhower, Dwight D., 258-259, 271
Elburz Mountains, 39, 40, 79, 214
Emami, M., 195, 198-199
Empress, the, 172-173
Emron Bongah, 202, 204. See also village council program.
Etheridge, Charles H., 187, 188
Etteld'at, 97
Evans, John, 21, 31, 33, 38, 172

Falarbarjan Village, 98-99
Fallahi, Ahmad, 123
Faraman Orphanage, 77
Fardad, Abolhassan, 230, 231
Fariman, 195, 198-199
Farman, 199
Farmanfarmayan, Dr. Saber, 92, 141, 150
farm mechanization, 232-233
Fars Province, 90, 126, 127, 170
Farzard, H., 284
Fatemi, Dr. ———, 125, 126, 242, 272
Finance Committee, 262, 263, 264
Ford Foundation, 193, 304
Foreign Operations Administration (FOA), 12, 57, 206. *See also* Point 4
Frederiksen, Dr. Harald S., 139-140
Freyman, Dr. Moye, 162
Fried, Jerome, 55

Fryer, E. Reeseman (Si), 19-20, 21, 24, 30, 31-32, 60

Gagan, Dr. Glen, 102
Ghamsar, 167, 188, 201-202
ghanats, see Iran: water and well system
Ghashghai, Malek Mansour, 300-301
Ghashghai tribe, 50, 101, 102-103, 128, 129, 130-131
Ghavam-Es-Sultaneh, Ahmad, 87, 88, 92-93
Ghavami, G. H., 63
ghazd, 36
Ghazvin, 228-231
Giaquinta, Dr. ———, 144
Gibbs, Sir Alexander, 152-153
giveh telegraph, 14
Grady, Ambassador Henry F., 18, 258
Gramicia, Dr. ———, 144
Gregory, Clark S., 64, 290-291
Golpira, General Ali-Gholi, 279, 280-281, 282
Goulden, James J., 245, 294

Halbrook, Dr. E. J., 75, 86
Hamadan, 218-222
Hardy, Benjamin Hill, 40-41
Harnish, Mrs. Jerene Appleby, 52
Harris, Dr. Franklin, 21, 38, 41
Hartman, Elsie, 251, 252, 277
Hassan, Ali, 80
Hayden, Dr. Lyle, 193
Heilig, Dr. Herbert, 295
Henderson, Ambassador Loy W., 34-35, 39, 43, 92, 119, 127, 160, 172, 246, 247, 258, 271
Hessabi, Dr. Mahmoud, 46, 63-64, 92
Hollister, John, 57
Hoover, Herbert, Jr., 271
Hossein, 14, 34, 208, 247, 277
Hunnerwadel, Mrs. Helen, 172
Hyderabad Livestock Station, 51, 86

Industry Program, 60
International Cooperation Administration, 12, 57. *See also* Point 4
Iran: Air Force, 53; Army, 50, 53, 63, 87, 88, 93, 211, 244, 300; culture, 94-95; description, 59-60, 79-80; education, 170-171; farming, 226-227, 234; future of, 234-237, 239-

Index   317

Iran—Cont.
240; government participation, 195-196; health, 140-141, 142, 143-144; history, 60, 80, 168-169, 282-289; landlord system, 113-115, 200-201; language, 5, 6, 43, 45, 61, 68, 86, 94, 120, 121, 146, 209; living conditions, 217; marketing problems, 238-239; nomad tribes, 101-102; potentialities, 235-236; races, 94; religion, 71-72, 94; river system, 68-69; sanitation, 158-159; social customs, 90-91, 171-172, 173-174, 175-176; village life, 89-90; water and well system, 163-168, 169
Iran-e-ma, 117
Iran Foundation, 304
Iranian Ministries of: Agriculture, 119, 180, 186, 188, 189, 201, 224, 225, 227-228, 229, 231, 295, 302, 304; Education, 173, 181, 182, 280, 302, 303; Health, 136, 137, 138, 144, 145, 295, 302, 304; National Economy, 186, 187, 189
Iranian-United States Joint Commission for Rural Improvement, 18, 31-32, 45-46, 47, 55, 118, 136. *See also* Razmara agreement
Iran-United States Joint Commission for Social and Economic Development, 47, 117-118, 132, 136, 175, 205, 248, 254, 255, 258, 269-270, 273
Irrigation Bongah, 163, 167
Isaacson, Thorpe D., 291
Isfahan, 31, 98, 120
Isfahanek, 38
Iverson, Kenneth, 193

jackass project, 48-51, 53-54
Jehengari, Brigadier General Mir, 128, 131
Johnson, Melvin, 254
Jones, Charles M., 153, 154, 156, 160-161
Jordan, Dr. ———, 300-302

Karadj Agricultural College, 63, 224-225, 226, 227-228
Kashani, Seyed Abdol (Ayatollah), 65, 66-68, 69-71, 72, 73-74, 88, 91

Kazemi, Mansour, 186
Kerman, 31, 120
Kermanshah, 31, 77-78, 132
Keyhan, 126, 206-207
Khazai, ———, 162
Khonsar, 13, 15-16
Khorramshahr, 184
Khoshkrood, 215-217, 218
Khupayeh, 211-213
Khurang Tunnel, 13, 100, 101-102, 289-290
Khuzistan, 100, 126
Kilcrease, Tom, 298
King, Mrs. Bernice, 172
Kurds, 101

land distribution program, 37, 190, 192-195, 198-199, 234. *See also* Amlock
Lane, Leslie, 186, 187, 188
Larsen, Harald, 193
Lavison Valley, 214
Lazarus, Dr. A. S., 128
Life, 52
Livestock Bongah, 48, 51, 53, 75, 104
locust-control project, 119, 125-127, 132
locusts, 118-119, 125-127, 132

Mabee, William, 118
McAnlis, Alan, 77-79
McCauley, John, 193, 195
McClure, Major General Robert A., 53, 300
McInnes, Eugene, 187, 188
Mahallat, 123
Mahkaday, ———, 153, 156
Majlis, 64, 66, 74, 87, 93, 96-97, 200, 242, 268
malaria, 149
malaria control project, 136-137, 138, 145-146, 147, 148-149, 150
Maleki, Dr. Mahammed Ali, 46, 92, 141, 145, 150
Maris, Paul, 190, 192, 193, 194, 304
Mathieson, Homer A., 97-98, 132, 279, 308
Maykadeh, Cholam Ali, 63
Mehra, Dr. Torab, 150
Mehrabad Airport, 30, 39-40, 52, 53, 77, 209, 298
Meshed, 31, 120

Middleton, George, 116
Military Assistance Group, 300
Miller, Orris, 162
Millspaugh missions, 291
Minges, Robert, 193
Mirurand, A., 128
Mitchell, James Thomas, 41
Moazzemi, Dr. Siafollah, 125-126, 132, 224
Moffagham, Dr. A. F., 183, 184-186, 187, 188
Moghadam, Dr. Mahmoud, 5, 13-14, 16, 216, 277-278, 286-287, 301-302
Moinaddini, Seyed Yadollah, 204
Mossadegh, Dr. Gholam (son of Mossadegh, Dr. Mohammed), 217, 252, 253
Mossadegh, Dr. Mohammed, 5, 35-36, 114, 127, 201, 209, 245, 250, 268-269, 272; government disturbances, 63-64, 65, 87, 88, 92, 93, 112, 123-125, 130-132, 222, 241-244; and oil controversy, 20-21, 116-117; and Point 4, 24-29, 32, 43-44, 45-47, 97, 117-118, 132, 133-134, 193, 206, 258, 307
Motamedi, His Excellency Ali, 195
Mutual Security Act of 1954, 306-307

Nakhjevan, Governor General ———, 128-129
Nasser, ———, 264
Navab, Sadegh, 229, 231
Near East Foundation (NEF), 142, 193, 281, 302-304
Near East Relief agency, *see* Near East Foundation
Nemazee, Mohammed, 304
Newsweek, 51, 52
New York Times, 52
Nixon, Mr. and Mrs. Richard, 52

oil controversy, 20, 21, 24, 29, 46, 65-66, 68, 93, 116, 119-120, 123-124, 135, 137, 153, 161, 176, 177, 183-184, 199, 206, 222, 242, 271, 273, 274
Overseas Consultants Incorporated (OCI), 273

Pahlavi, His Majesty Mohammed Reza (the Shah), 36, 37-38, 63, 88, 89,

Pahlavi—Cont.
93, 124, 125, 127, 192-193, 194-195, 196, 199, 219, 242, 243, 253, 268, 272, 274, 276, 289-290
Pahlavi dynasty, 60. *See also* Reza Shah
Palmquist, Dr. Emil, 144, 145, 154, 156
Pampana, Dr. ———, 144
Panahy, Abolghassem, 219
Panahy, Mrs. A., 219-221, 222
Paxton, Hall, 167
Pegg, Dr. Charles E., 53-54
Pelletier, Dr. J. R., 297
pistachio project, 228-231
Plan Organization, 138, 186, 219, 249, 262, 272, 273-274
Point 4: agreements with Iran, 58-59; and American embassy, 299; created, 16-20; definition, 12; effects of, 308-314; effects of agricultural program, 223-225, 226-228, 231-232; effects of health program, 139-140, 141-143; effects of housing program, 281-282; effects of literacy program, 280-281; and Ford Foundation, 304; Livestock Division, 48; methods, 27-28, 49, 61-62, 233, 291, 299; motives, 305-308; names of, 56-57; and Near East Foundation, 302-303; object of attack, 89, 121-122, 207, 275-276; program, 57; project pattern, 57-58; projects, 205-206, 270; purpose, 22-23; and Rockefeller Foundation, 304; technical assistance program, 134; and United Nations, 293-299
political crisis, *see* Tehran: riots of 1953
Pollard, Comdr. Eric, 244
Presbyterian Foreign Missions Board, 300
Princess Ashraf School of Nursing, 298
public domain villages, 201-202
Public Health Cooperative (PHCO), 136, 137-140, 141-143, 146, 150, 161, 304

Radjy, Abolghassem, 127, 128, 262
Ram, His Excellency Mostafa Gholi, 63, 195, 198
Rassi, Jafar, 230
Razmara, General Ali, 18, 20, 268-269

Index

Razmara agreement, 32, 254, 258
Regan, Pat, 188, 223, 296-297
Report (Ontario, California), 52
Resht, 31
Rezaieh, 120
Reza Shah (father of Pahlavi, Mohammed Reza), 60, 65, 87, 151-152
Richards, Jack, 160
Rockefeller Foundation, 304
Roskelley, Dr. R. W., 185, 186, 188

Saba, ———, 128
Sadeghi, Dr. ———, 248
Sadighi, G. H., 63
Saleh, Dr. Alayar, 222
Saleh, Dr. Ali Pasha, 35
Saleh, Dr. Jahanshah, 136-137, 141, 150
Samii, Abolghassam, 14-16
Samsan, Jamshid, 106, 107, 110, 111
Shahbaz, 133-134
Shahpassand wheat, 225, 227-228
Shalamzar, 105-109
Shariar, 38, 149
Shi'a sect, 65, 71, 72
Shimron summer palace, 37
Shiraz, 31, 50, 120, 126, 127, 128, 129, 130-131
Silver, Warren, 85-86
Sleeker, Col. E. M., 279
Soleimanipour, Y., 284-285
Spalding, Curtis, 193, 302, 303
Spalding, Mrs. Curtis, 173
Special Assistance Program, 272-273
Stassen, Harold E., 57, 206
Stephanides, Dr. C. S. (Steve), 48, 302
Stewart, Dr. George, 185, 186, 226
Stickney, Ray, 188, 297
Sugar Bongah, 263, 265, 266
sugar crisis, 262-266
Syracuse University, 217

Tabriz, 31, 120, 139, 140
Taleghani, Khalil, 13-14, 16, 46, 56, 80-81, 85, 125, 175, 224, 225, 285, 301
Taleghani, Mrs. K., 174, 175, 176
Taleghan River, 81, 82
Taleghan Valley, 79-85
Tchotchal, 33

Technical Cooperation Administration (TCA), 12, 18, 19, 25-27, 56, 58, 98, 206, 296, 307. *See also* Point 4
Technical Cooperation for Iran (TCI), 57, 133
Technical and Special Assistance programs, 299
Tehran, 30, 31, 32-34, 120; description, 33; riots of 1953, 241-253, 267-268; sanitation, 151-152, 154-156; water-piping project, 152-154, 156-157
Time, 21, 52
Truman, Harry S., 16-17, 41
Truman-Churchill note (Aug. 30, 1952), 116, 119
Tudeh, 49, 88, 91, 97, 117, 127, 128, 145, 207, 221-222, 243, 247, 251
Turkomen, 101
Turner, Prof. Hoyt, 120, 182

United Nations, 30, 43, 87, 118, 150; Food and Agriculture Organization (FAO), 296, 298; World Health Organization (WHO), 137, 138, 148. *See also* Point 4
United States Army mission, 300
United States Operations Mission in Iran (USOM/I or OM/I), 5-6, 57. *See also* Technical Cooperation Administration *and* Point 4
United States Public Health Service, 143
University of Tehran, 157, 170, 177, 189, 267-268; Agricultural College, 177; Audio-Visual Institute, 178; Institute of Public Administration, 178, 270; Malariology Institute, 133, 138, 148, 178; Medical School, 136

Verselus, Dr. Hendrik, 103
Veterinary Bongah, 104
veterinary service, 103-104
village-council program, 202-204
Vosough, Major General ———, 63

Wahlen, F. T., 296
Walker, R. H., 291
Warne, Jane, 24, 59
Warne, Margaret, 24, 36, 59, 89, 208, 245, 246

Warne, Rob, 24, 59, 107, 111
Warne, Mrs. William E. (Edith), 23-24, 59, 87, 89
Warne, William R. (father of Warne, William E.), 197, 267
Washington Post, 18
Wheeler, William E., 167
White, Charles, 302
Willson, Clifford, 20
women's activities, 172-173
Workinger, Ralph, 55, 229-230

Yantabad Village, 97
Yekzeban, Capt. ———, 130
Yellow Mountain, 13, 100

Yussefy, M., 212-213

Zagros range, 13, 79, 100
Zahedi, Ardeshir, 5, 39-40, 41-42, 66-67, 68, 70, 106, 112, 116-117, 124, 256
Zahedi, General Fazlollah, 5, 41-42, 47, 74, 80, 93, 116, 117, 125, 243, 244, 253, 255, 256-258, 259, 268, 269, 271, 272, 276
Zahedi, Mostafa, 186, 188, 224, 229-230, 231
Zanganeh, Dr. Ahmad, 46, 206, 249
Zarghan, 161-162
Ziandehrud basin, 167-168
Zimmerman, William, 300